KOBATO. ❷

CLAMP

Translation: William Flanagan • Lettering: Alexis Eckerman

KOBATO. Volume 2 © 2008 CLAMP. First published in Japan in 2008 by KADOKAWA SHOTEN Publishing Co., Ltd., Tokyo. English translation rights arranged with KADOKAWA SHOTEN Publishing Co., Ltd., Tokyo through TUTTLE-MORI AGENCY, INC., Tokyo.

Translation © 2010 by Hachette Book Group, Inc.

Yen Press
Hachette Book Group
237 Park Avenue, New York, NY 10017

www.HachetteBookGroup.com
www.YenPress.com

Yen Press is an imprint of Hachette Book Group, Inc. The Yen Press name and logo are trademarks of Hachette Book Group, Inc.

First Yen Press Edition: May 2010

ISBN: 978-0-316-08540-3

10 9 8 7 6 5 4 3 2

BVG

Printed in the United States of America

Kobato.

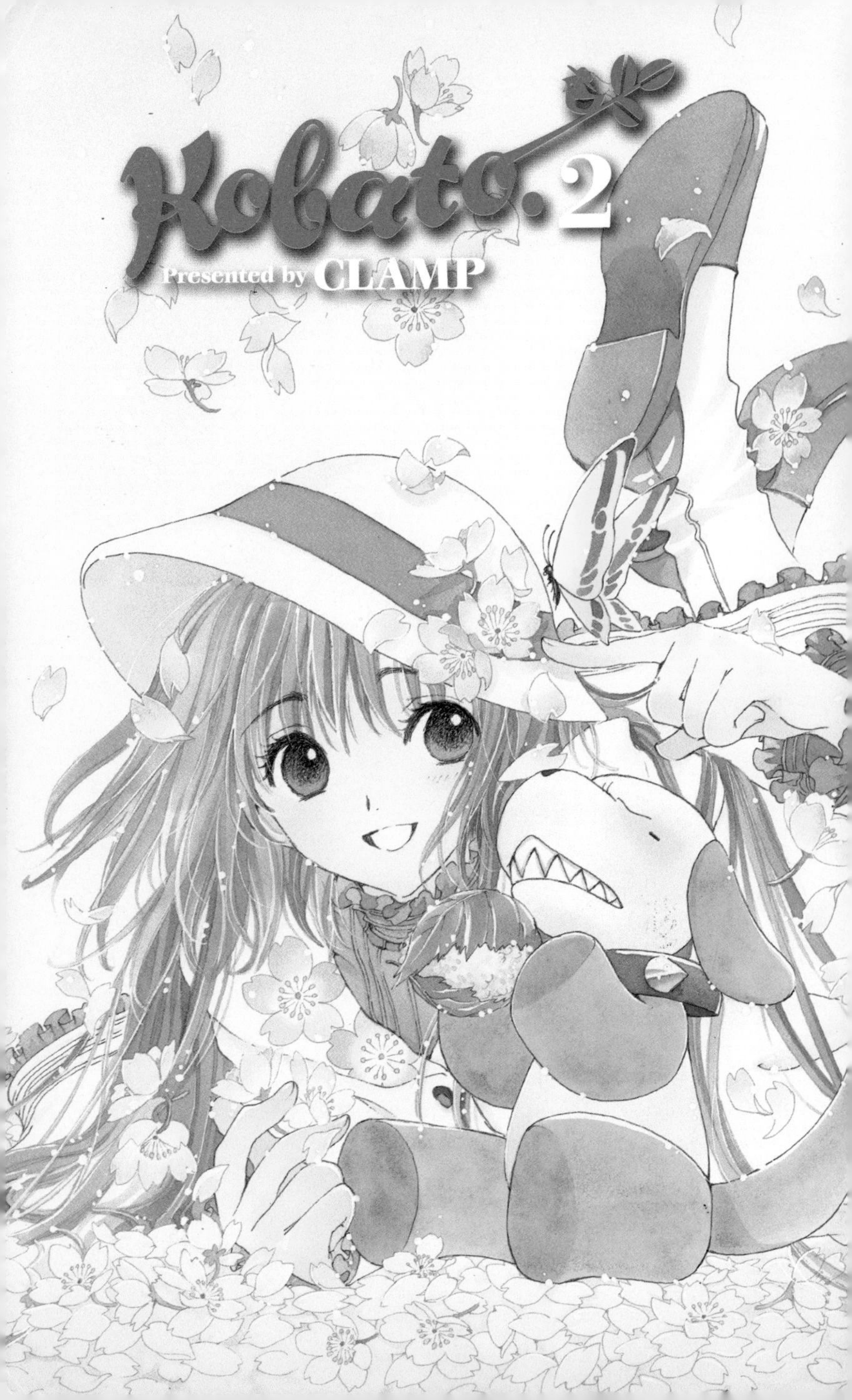
Kobato. 2
Presented by CLAMP

KOBATO.

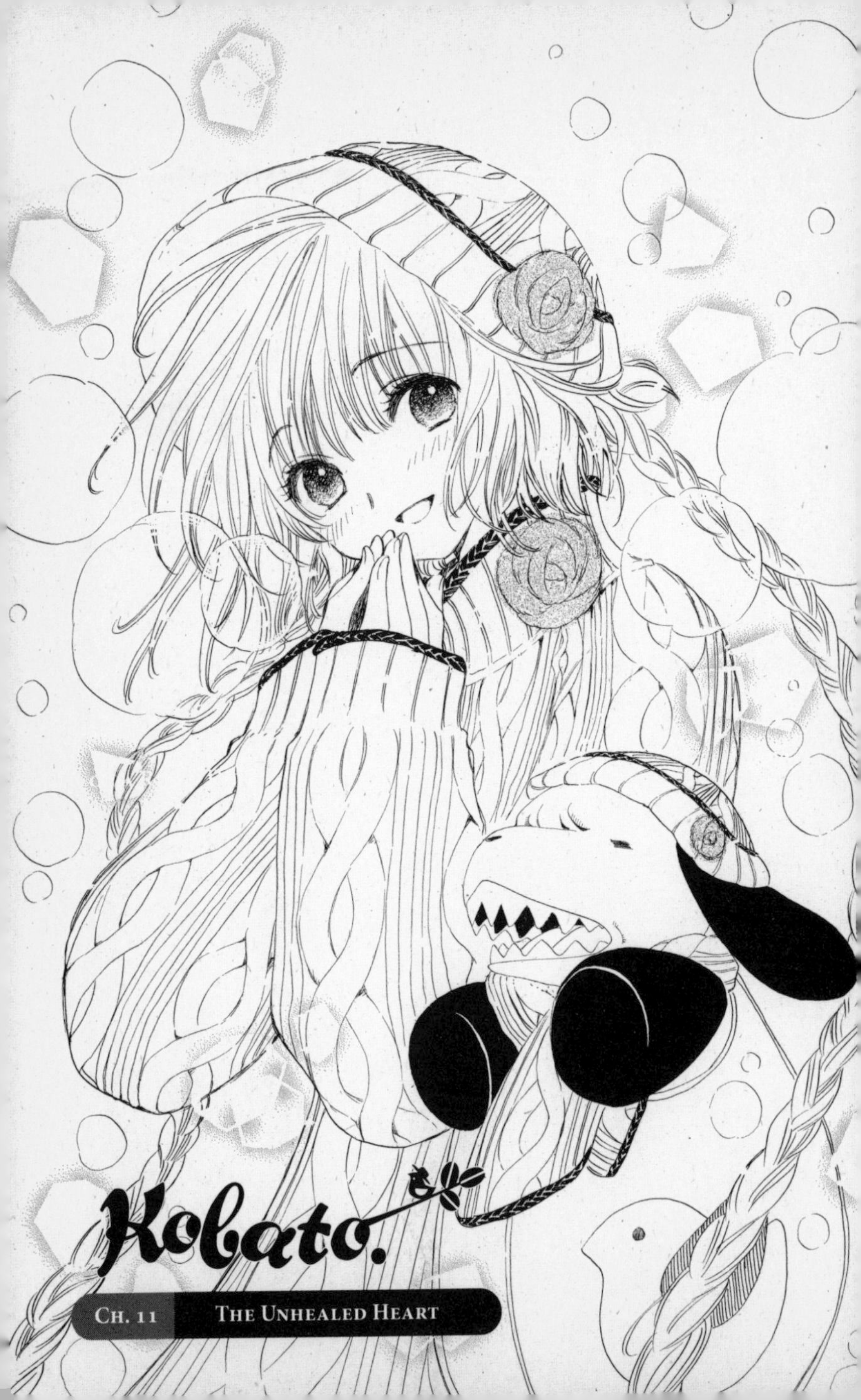
Kobato.
Ch. 11
The Unhealed Heart

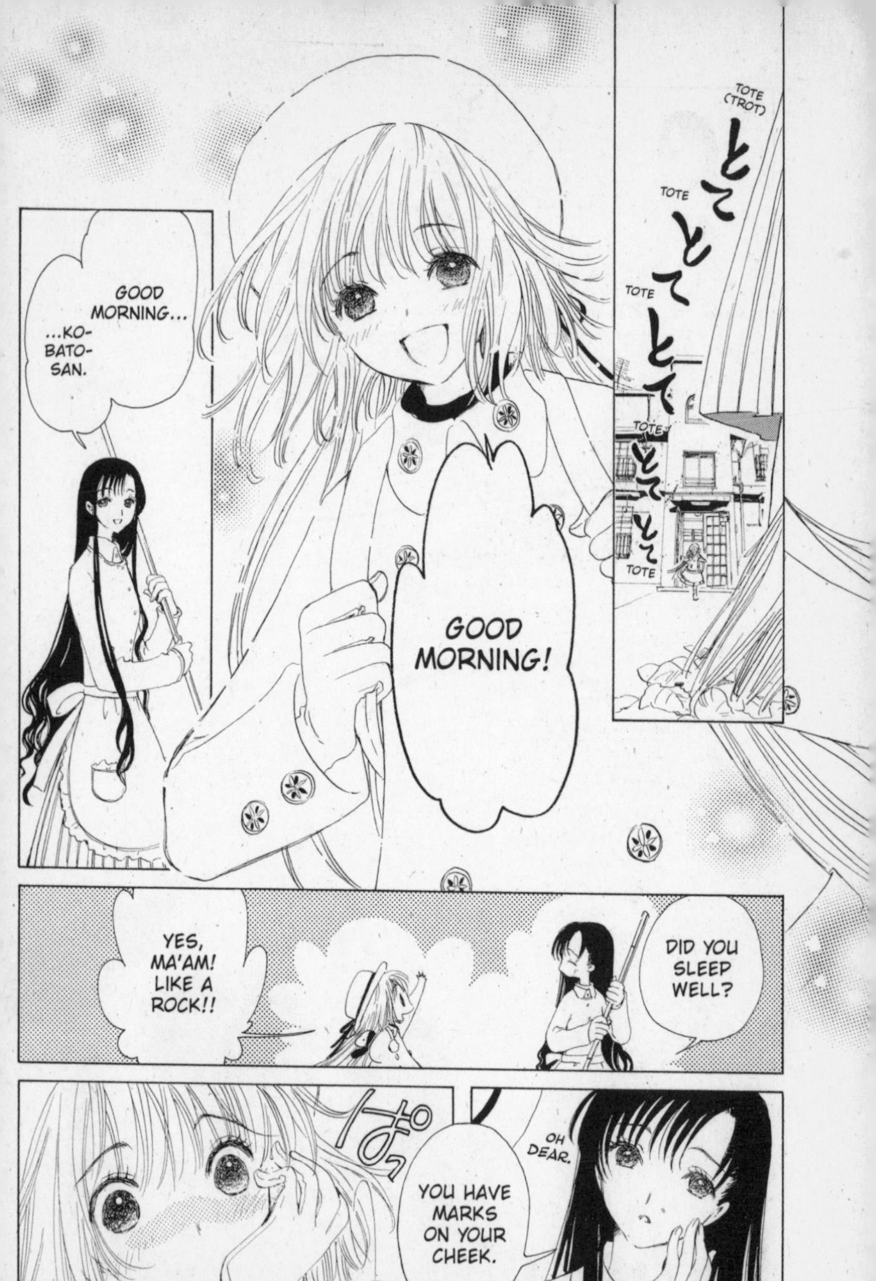
TOTE (TROT)
とてとてとてとてとて
TOTE
TOTE
TOTE
TOTE
GOOD MORNING!
GOOD MORNING...
...KO-BATO-SAN.
DID YOU SLEEP WELL?
YES, MA'AM! LIKE A ROCK!!
OH DEAR.
YOU HAVE MARKS ON YOUR CHEEK.
ぱっ
SFX: PA (BLUSH)

SFX: Go

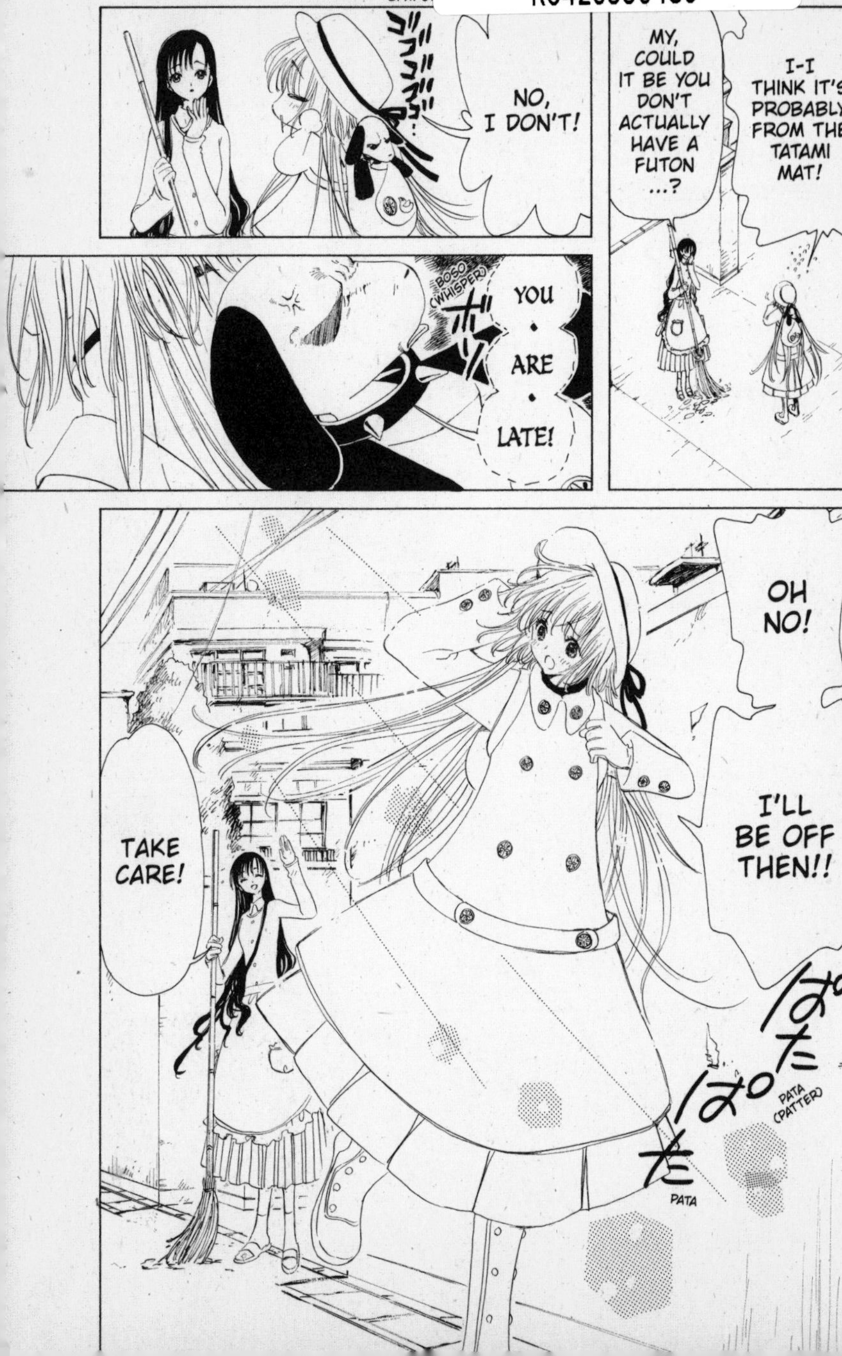
I-I THINK IT'S PROBABLY FROM THE TATAMI MAT!
MY, COULD IT BE YOU DON'T ACTUALLY HAVE A FUTON ...?
NO, I DON'T!
ゴゴゴゴゴ…
BOSO (WHISPER)
ボソ
YOU · ARE · LATE!
OH NO!
I'LL BE OFF THEN!!
ぱたぱた
PATA (PATTER)
PATA
TAKE CARE!

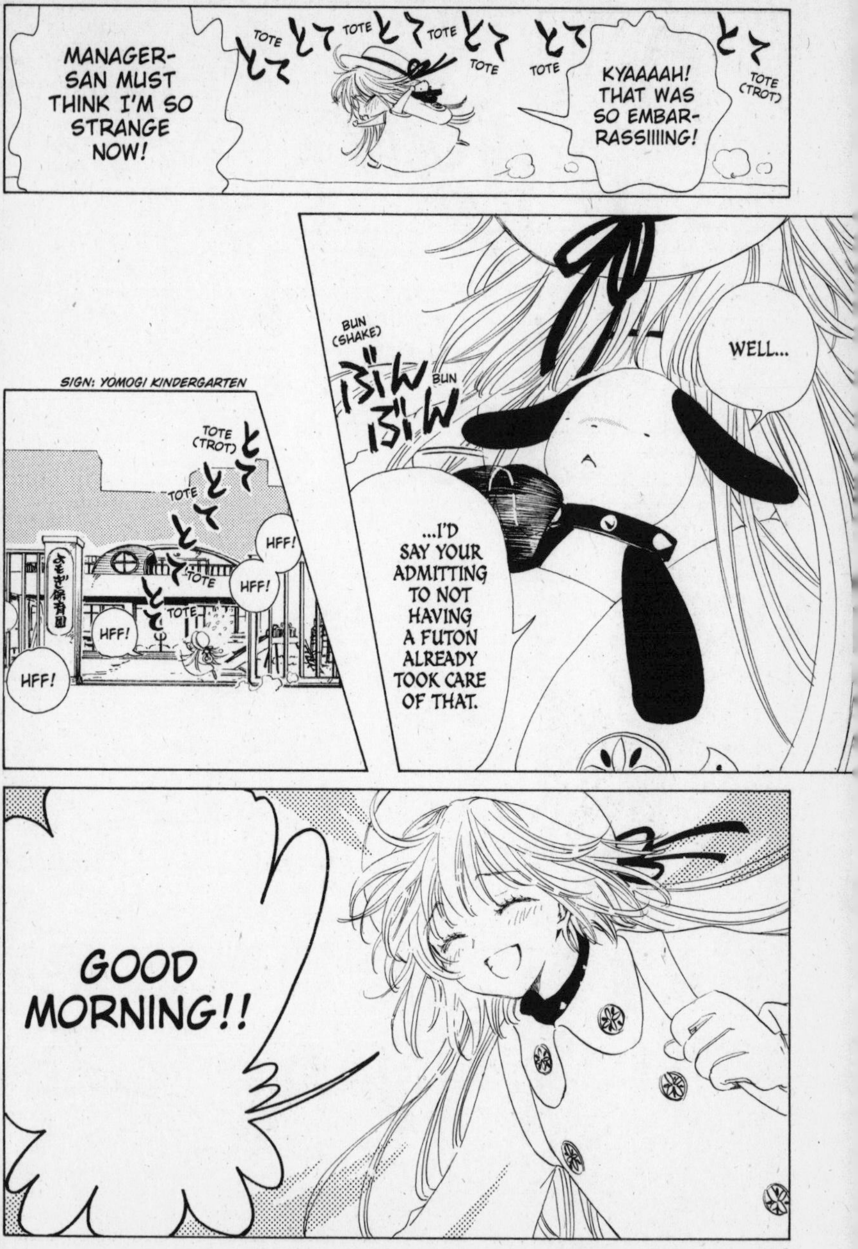
とて
TOTE (TROT)
KYAAAAH! THAT WAS SO EMBARRASSIIIING!
とて
TOTE
とて
TOTE
とて
TOTE
とて
TOTE
とて
TOTE
MANAGER-SAN MUST THINK I'M SO STRANGE NOW!
WELL...
BUN (SHAKE)
ぶん
BUN
ぶん
...I'D SAY YOUR ADMITTING TO NOT HAVING A FUTON ALREADY TOOK CARE OF THAT.
SIGN: YOMOGI KINDERGARTEN
TOTE (TROT)
とて
TOTE
とて
TOTE
とて
TOTE
とて
HFF!
HFF!
HFF!
HFF!
GOOD MORNING!!

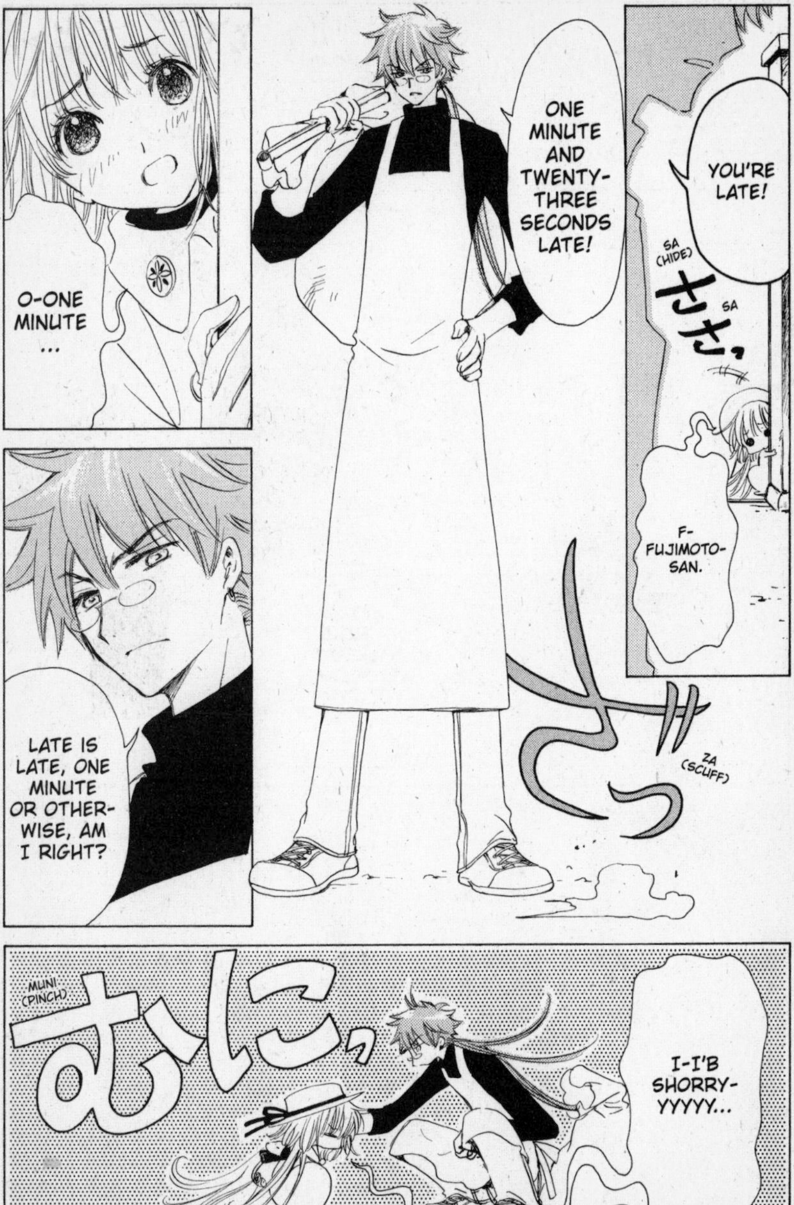

YOU'RE LATE!
SA (HIDE)
SA
F-FUJIMOTO-SAN.
ONE MINUTE AND TWENTY-THREE SECONDS LATE!
ZA (SCUFF)
O-ONE MINUTE ...
LATE IS LATE, ONE MINUTE OR OTHER-WISE, AM I RIGHT?
I-I'B SHORRY-YYYYY...
MUNI (PINCH)

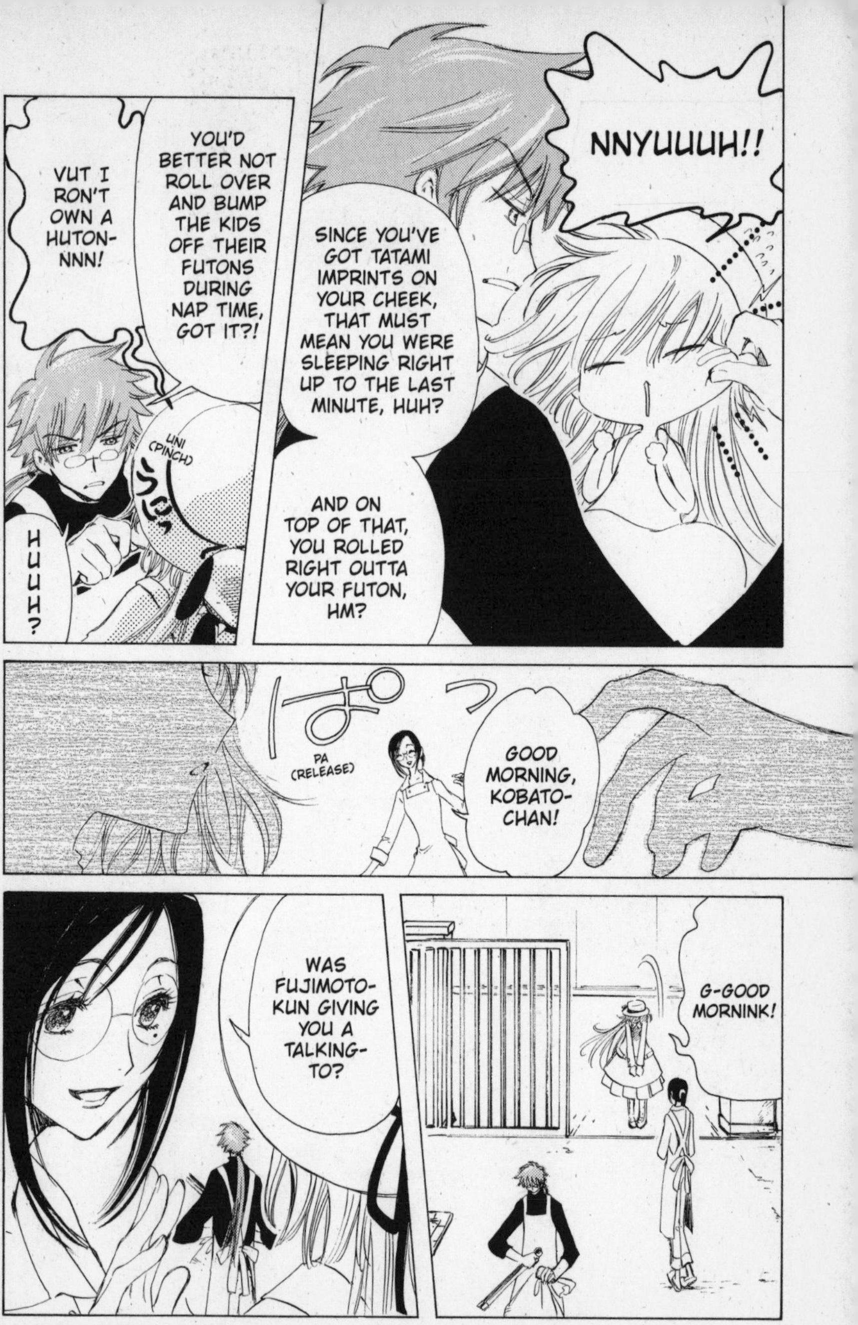
NNYUUUH!!
SINCE YOU'VE GOT TATAMI IMPRINTS ON YOUR CHEEK, THAT MUST MEAN YOU WERE SLEEPING RIGHT UP TO THE LAST MINUTE, HUH?
AND ON TOP OF THAT, YOU ROLLED RIGHT OUTTA YOUR FUTON, HM?
YOU'D BETTER NOT ROLL OVER AND BUMP THE KIDS OFF THEIR FUTONS DURING NAP TIME, GOT IT?!
VUT I RON'T OWN A HUTON-NNN!
UNI (PINCH)
HUUUH?
PA (RELEASE)
GOOD MORNING, KOBATO-CHAN!
G-GOOD MORNINK!
WAS FUJIMOTO-KUN GIVING YOU A TALKING-TO?

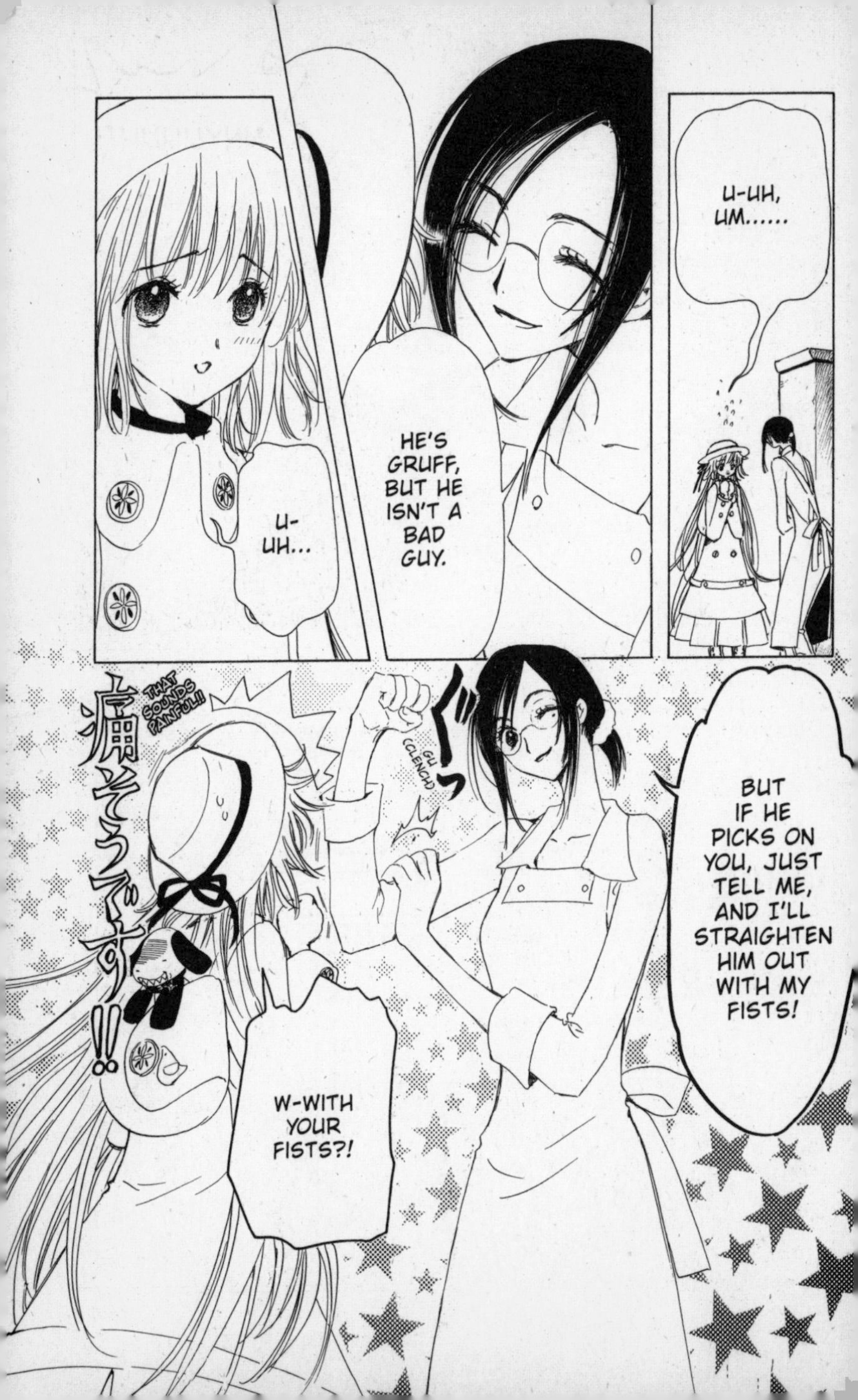
U-UH, UM......
HE'S GRUFF, BUT HE ISN'T A BAD GUY.
U-UH...
BUT IF HE PICKS ON YOU, JUST TELL ME, AND I'LL STRAIGHTEN HIM OUT WITH MY FISTS!
GU (CLENCH)
W-WITH YOUR FISTS?!
痛そうです!!
THAT SOUNDS PAINFUL!!

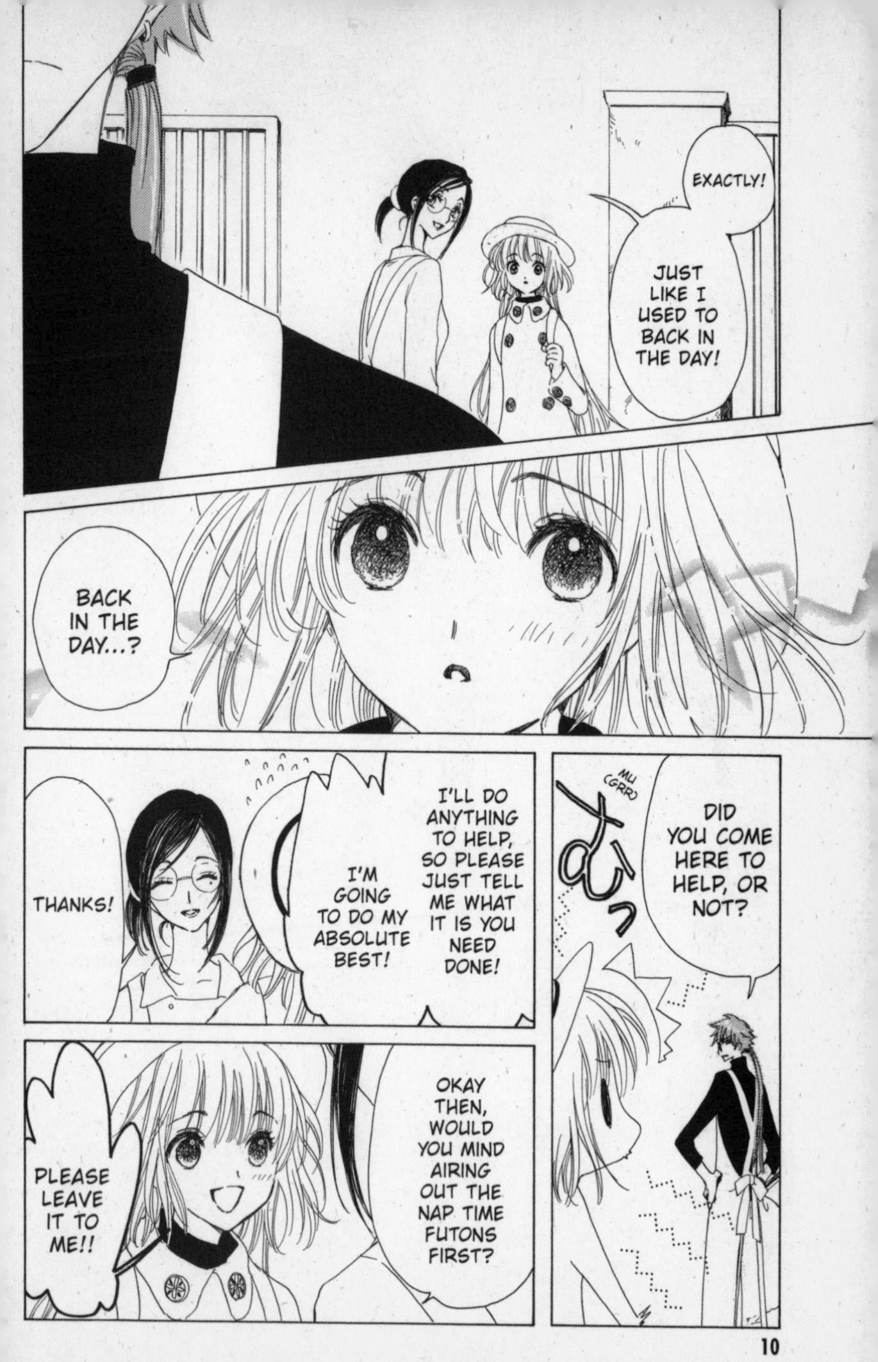
EXACTLY!
JUST LIKE I USED TO BACK IN THE DAY!
BACK IN THE DAY...?
MU (GRR)
DID YOU COME HERE TO HELP, OR NOT?
I'LL DO ANYTHING TO HELP, SO PLEASE JUST TELL ME WHAT IT IS YOU NEED DONE!
I'M GOING TO DO MY ABSOLUTE BEST!
THANKS!
OKAY THEN, WOULD YOU MIND AIRING OUT THE NAP TIME FUTONS FIRST?
PLEASE LEAVE IT TO ME!!

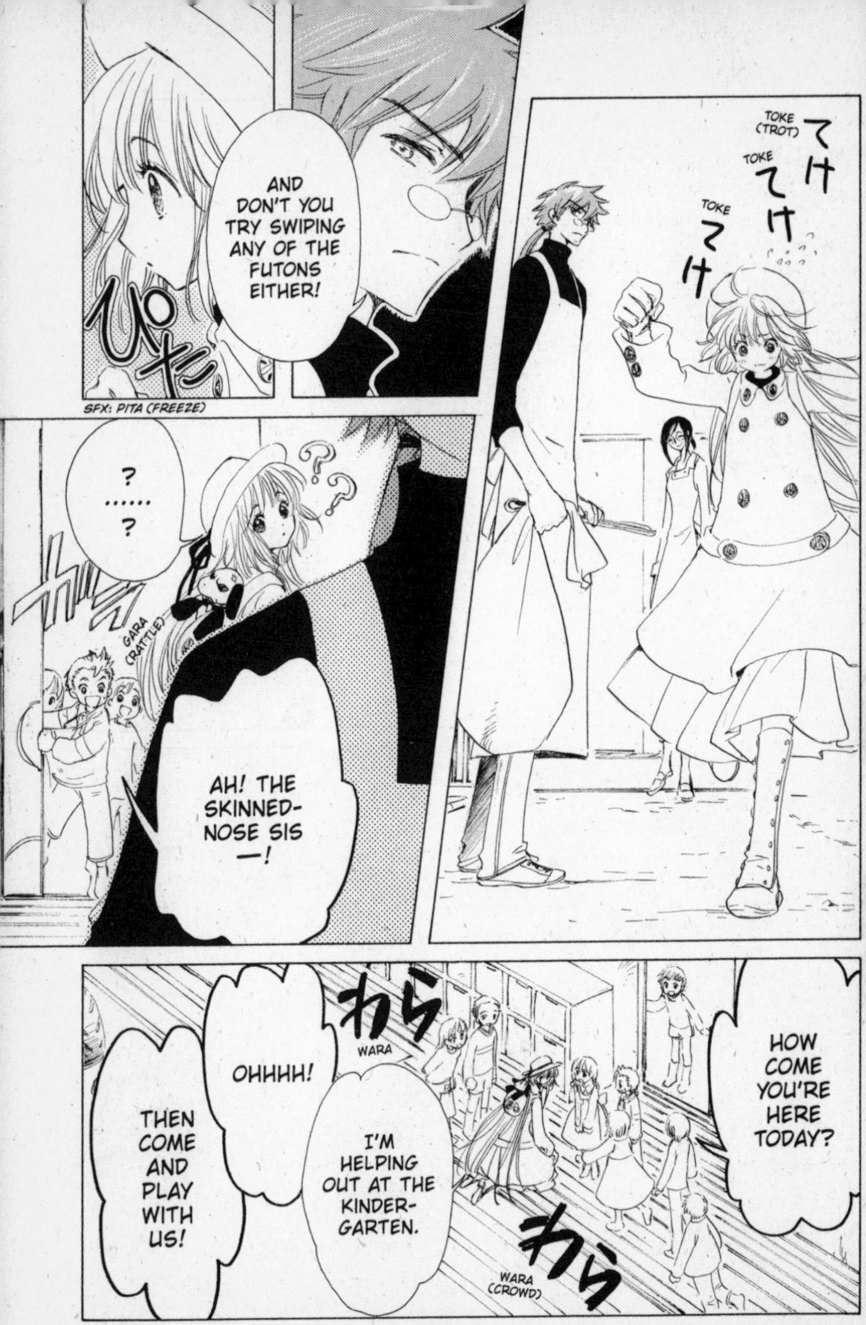
TOKE (TROT)
てけ
TOKE
てけ
TOKE
てけ
AND DON'T YOU TRY SWIPING ANY OF THE FUTONS EITHER!
SFX: PITA (FREEZE)
?
......
?
GARA (RATTLE)
AH! THE SKINNED-NOSE SIS—!
HOW COME YOU'RE HERE TODAY?
わら
WARA
I'M HELPING OUT AT THE KINDER-GARTEN.
OHHHH!
THEN COME AND PLAY WITH US!
わら
WARA (CROWD)

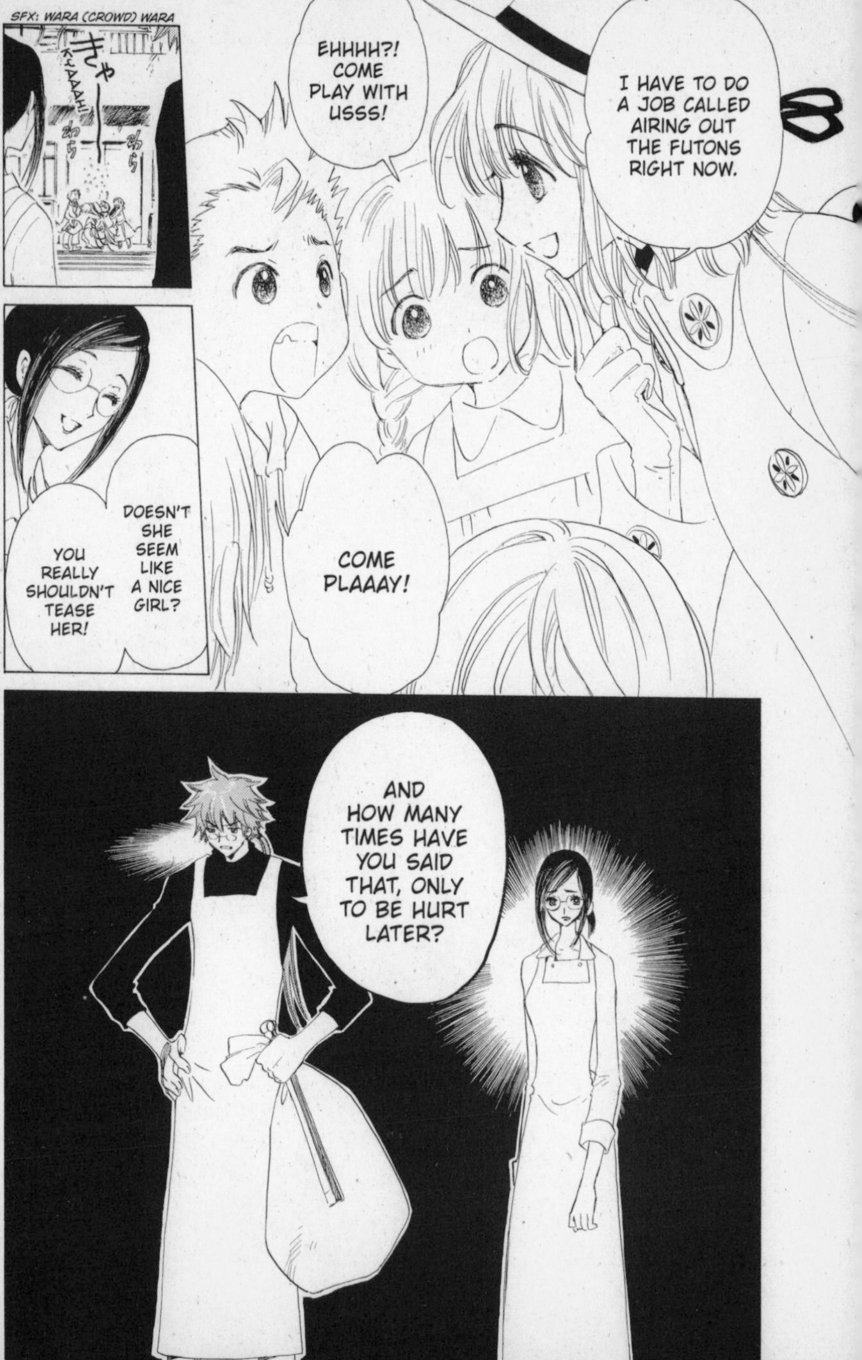
I HAVE TO DO A JOB CALLED AIRING OUT THE FUTONS RIGHT NOW.
EHHHH?! COME PLAY WITH USSS!
COME PLAAAY!
SFX: WARA (CROWD) WARA
きゃー
KYAAAH!
わら
わら
DOESN'T SHE SEEM LIKE A NICE GIRL?
YOU REALLY SHOULDN'T TEASE HER!
AND HOW MANY TIMES HAVE YOU SAID THAT, ONLY TO BE HURT LATER?

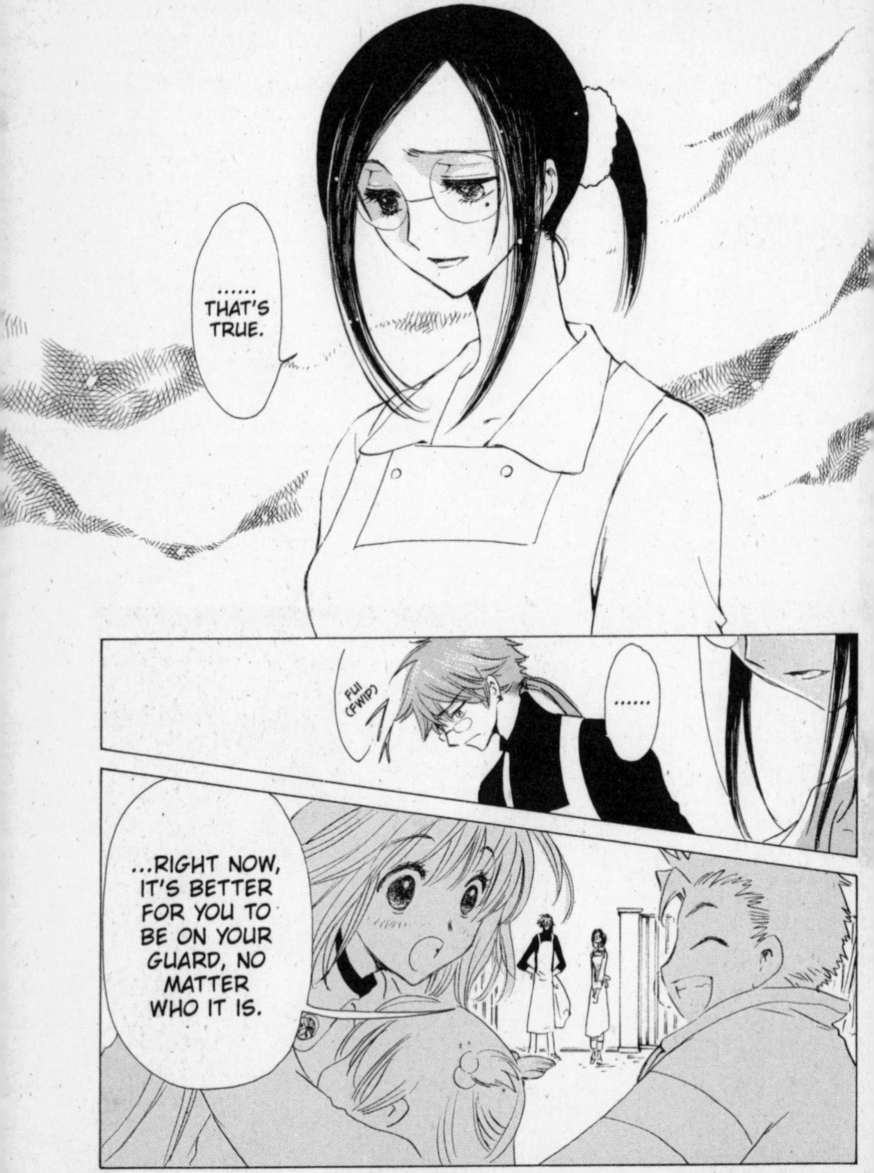

...... THAT'S TRUE.
......
FUI (FWIP)
...RIGHT NOW, IT'S BETTER FOR YOU TO BE ON YOUR GUARD, NO MATTER WHO IT IS.

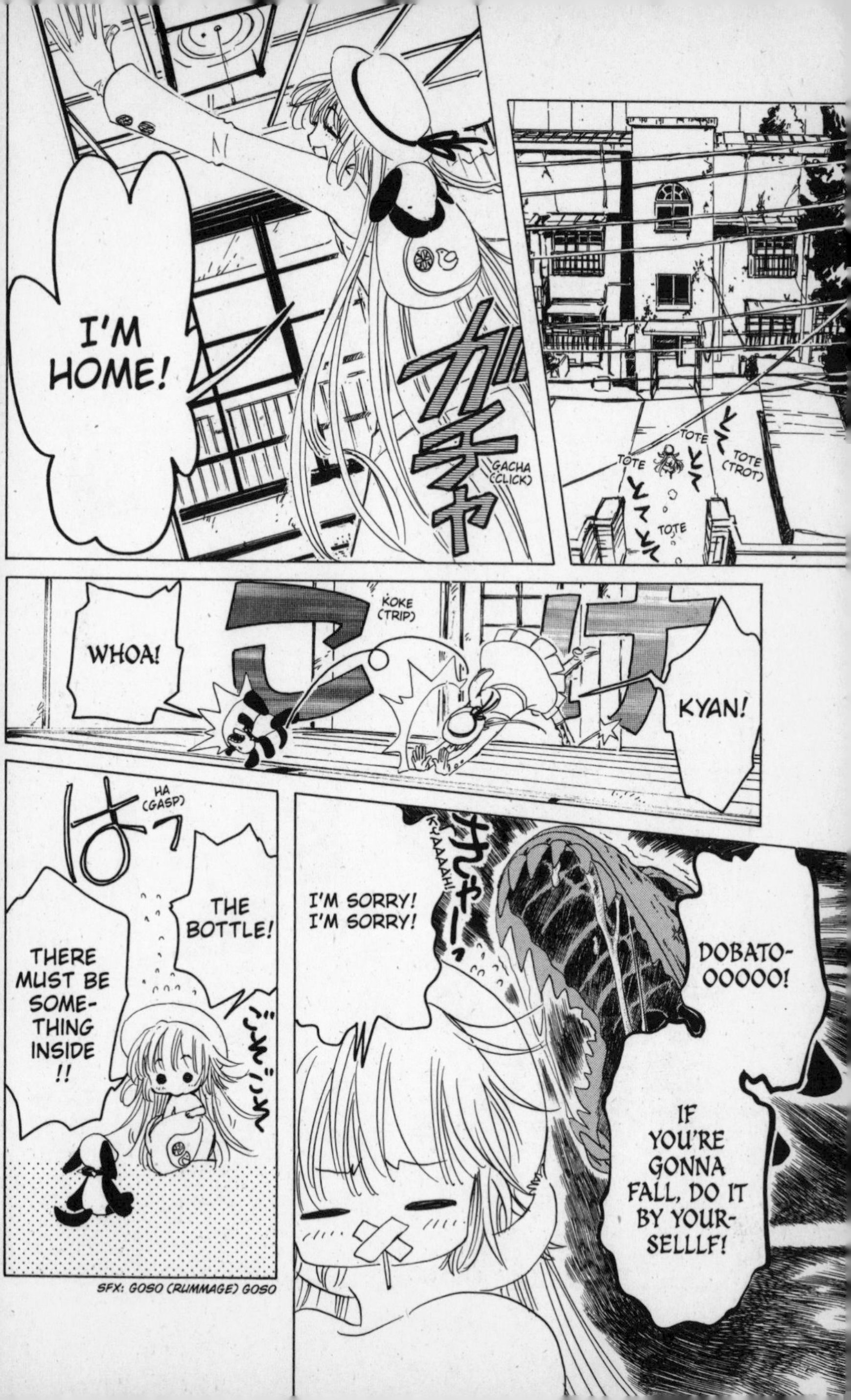
TOTE (TROT)
TOTE
TOTE
TOTE
GACHA (CLICK)
I'M HOME!
KYAN!
KOKE (TRIP)
WHOA!
DOBATO-OOOOO!
IF YOU'RE GONNA FALL, DO IT BY YOUR-SELLLF!
KYAAAAH!
I'M SORRY! I'M SORRY!
HA (GASP)
THE BOTTLE!
THERE MUST BE SOME-THING INSIDE !!
SFX: GOSO (RUMMAGE) GOSO

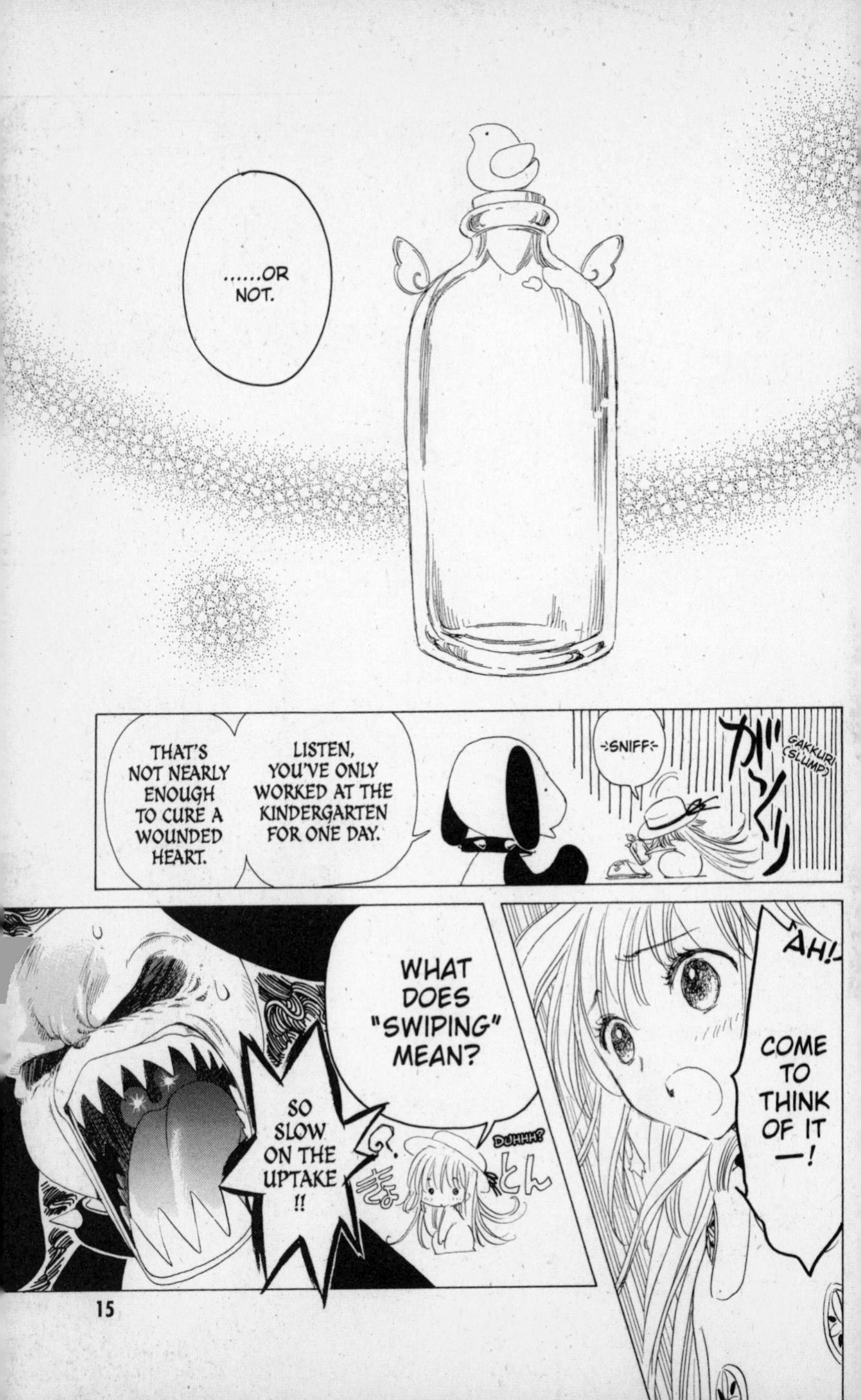
......OR NOT.
GAKKURI (SLUMP)
-SNIFF-
LISTEN, YOU'VE ONLY WORKED AT THE KINDERGARTEN FOR ONE DAY.
THAT'S NOT NEARLY ENOUGH TO CURE A WOUNDED HEART.
AH!
COME TO THINK OF IT—!
WHAT DOES "SWIPING" MEAN?
DUHHH?
SO SLOW ON THE UPTAKE!!

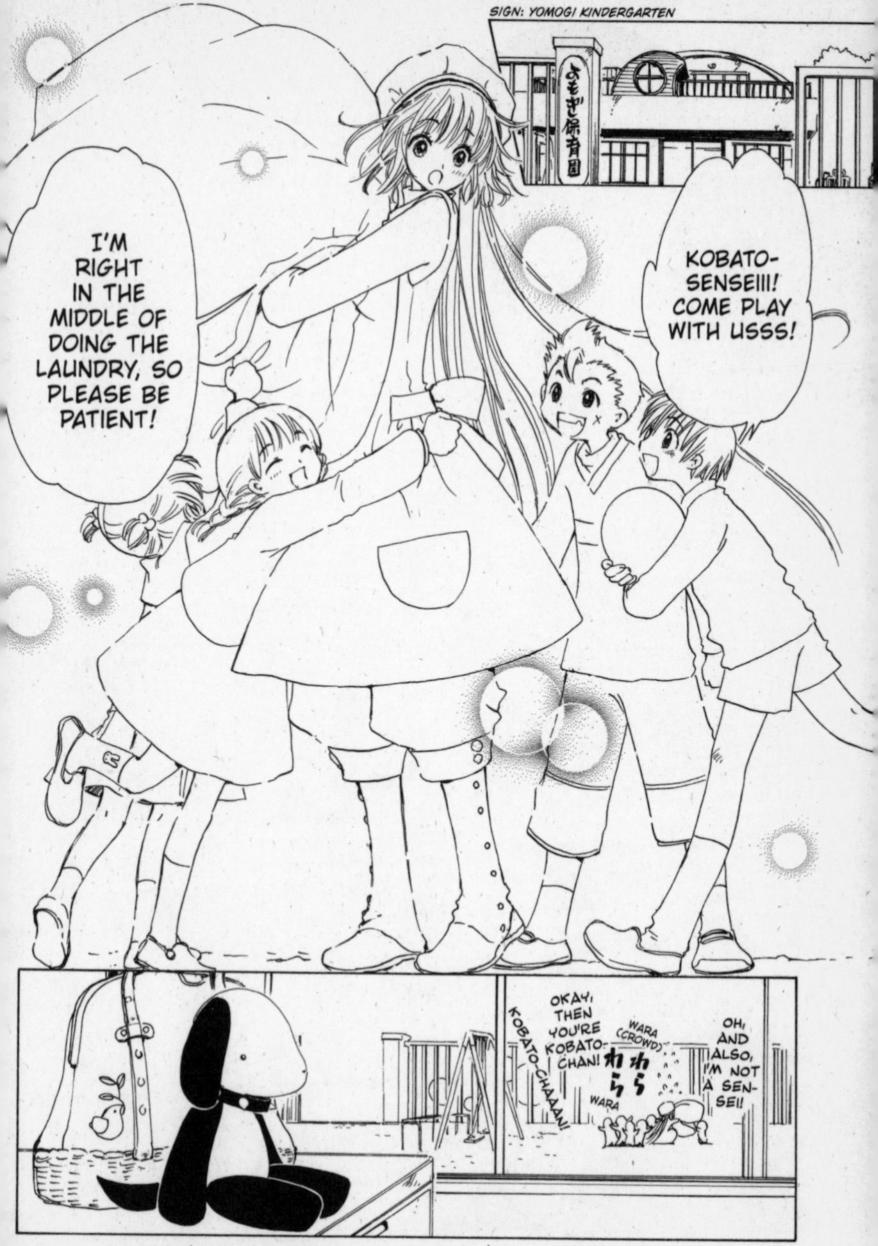
SIGN: YOMOGI KINDERGARTEN
よもぎ保育園
KOBATO-SENSEIII! COME PLAY WITH USSS!
I'M RIGHT IN THE MIDDLE OF DOING THE LAUNDRY, SO PLEASE BE PATIENT!
OH, AND ALSO, I'M NOT A SENSEI!
WARA (CROWD)
わら
わら
WARA
OKAY, THEN YOU'RE KOBATO-CHAN!
KOBATO-CHAAAN!

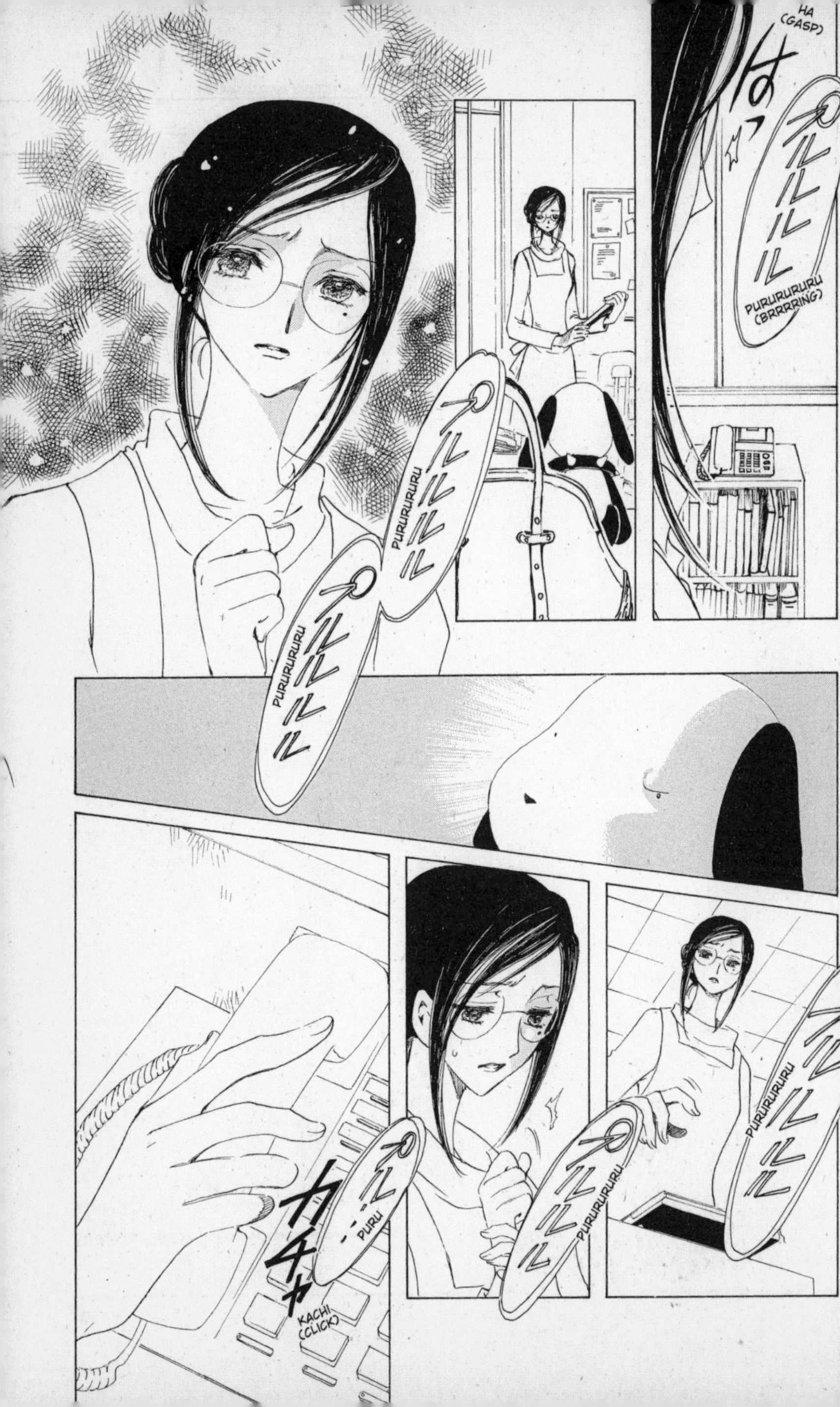
HA (GASP)
PURURURURU (BRRRRING)
PURURURURU
PURURURURU
PURURURURU
PURURURURU
PURU
KACHI (CLICK)

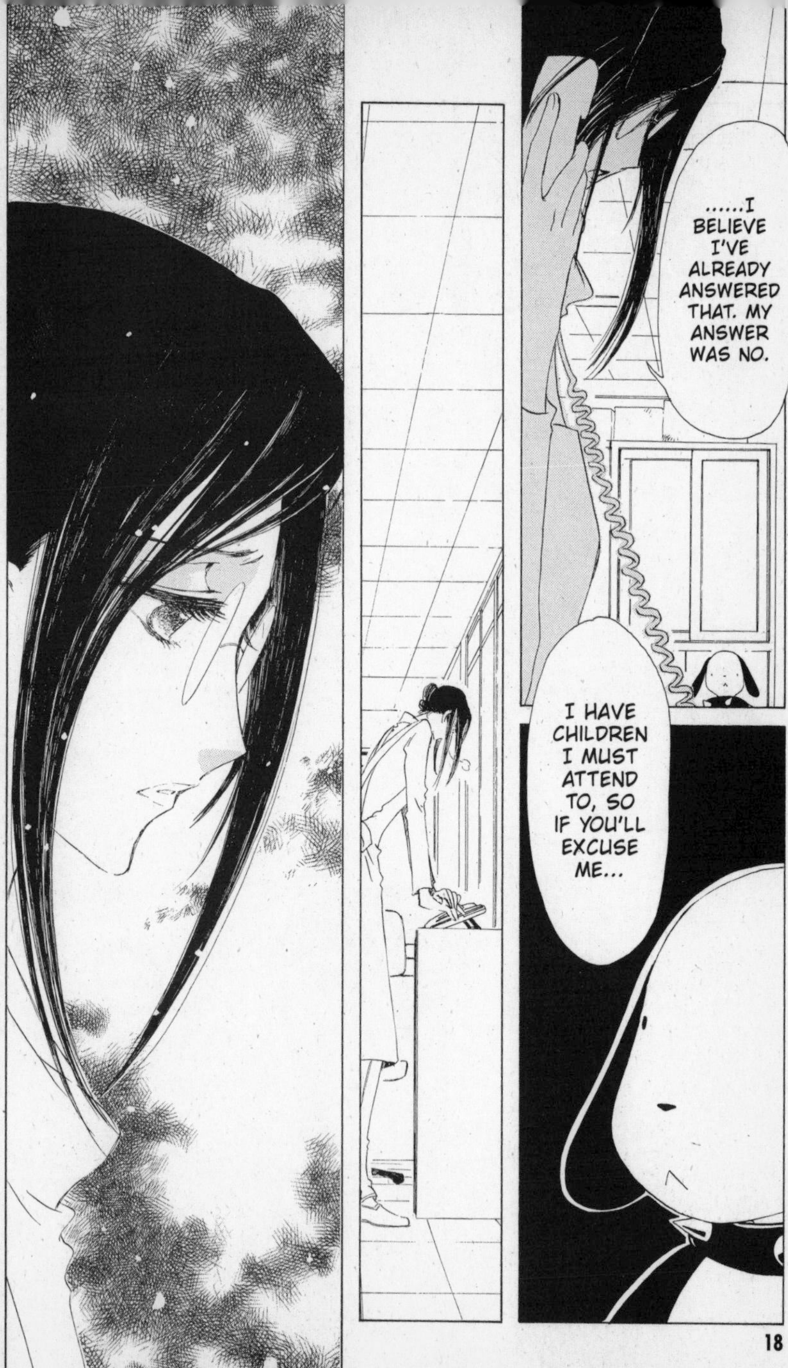
......I BELIEVE I'VE ALREADY ANSWERED THAT. MY ANSWER WAS NO.
I HAVE CHILDREN I MUST ATTEND TO, SO IF YOU'LL EXCUSE ME...

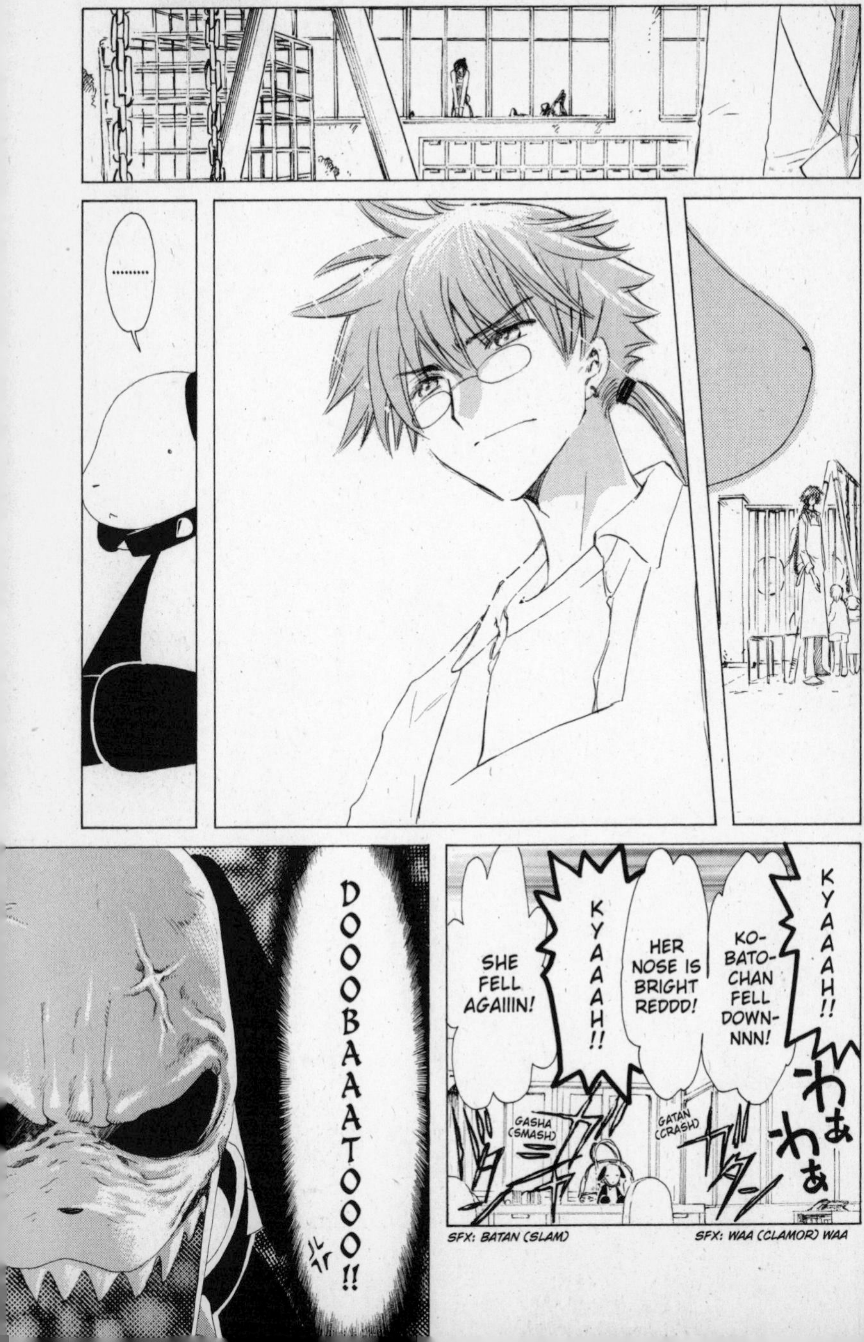
......
KYAAAAH!!
KO-BATO-CHAN FELL DOWN-NNN!
HER NOSE IS BRIGHT REDDD!
KYAAAAH!!
SHE FELL AGAIIIN!
GATAN (CRASH)
GASHA (SMASH)
SFX: WAA (CLAMOR) WAA
SFX: BATAN (SLAM)
DOOOBAAAATOOOO!!

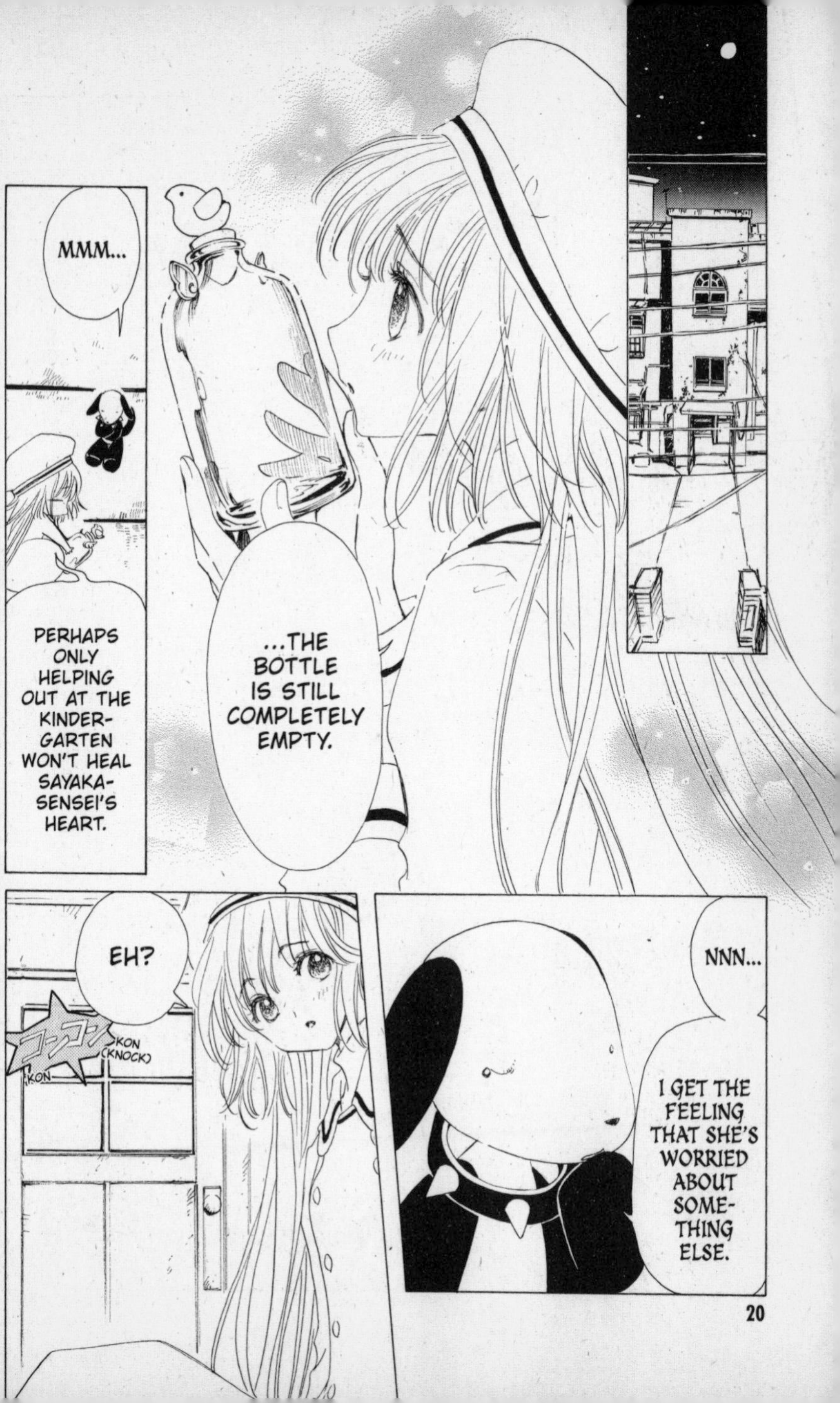
MMM...
PERHAPS ONLY HELPING OUT AT THE KINDER-GARTEN WON'T HEAL SAYAKA-SENSEI'S HEART.
...THE BOTTLE IS STILL COMPLETELY EMPTY.
NNN...
I GET THE FEELING THAT SHE'S WORRIED ABOUT SOME-THING ELSE.
EH?
KON KON (KNOCK)

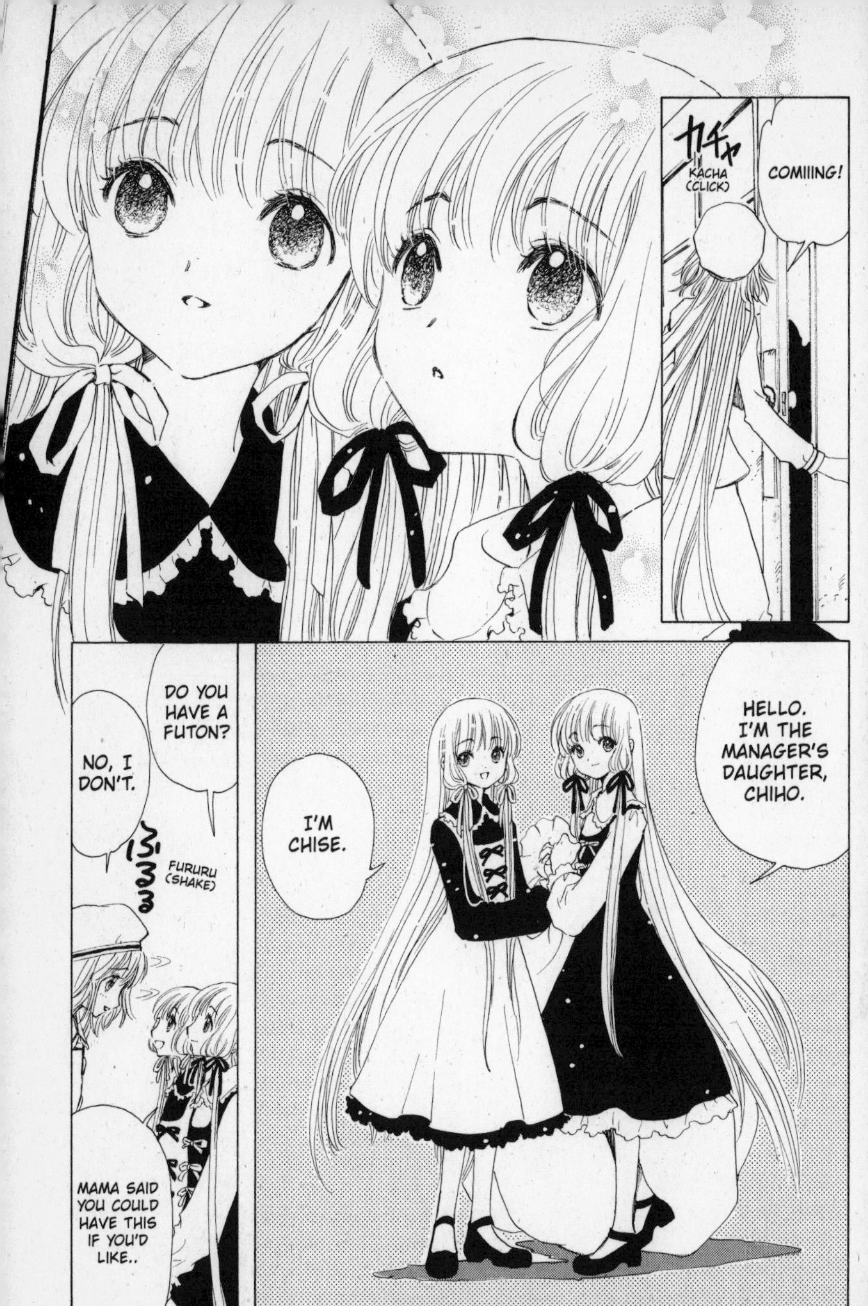
カチャ
KACHA (CLICK)
COMIIING!
HELLO. I'M THE MANAGER'S DAUGHTER, CHIHO.
I'M CHISE.
DO YOU HAVE A FUTON?
NO, I DON'T.
ふるる
FURURU (SHAKE)
MAMA SAID YOU COULD HAVE THIS IF YOU'D LIKE..

SFX: PEKO (BOW) PEKO

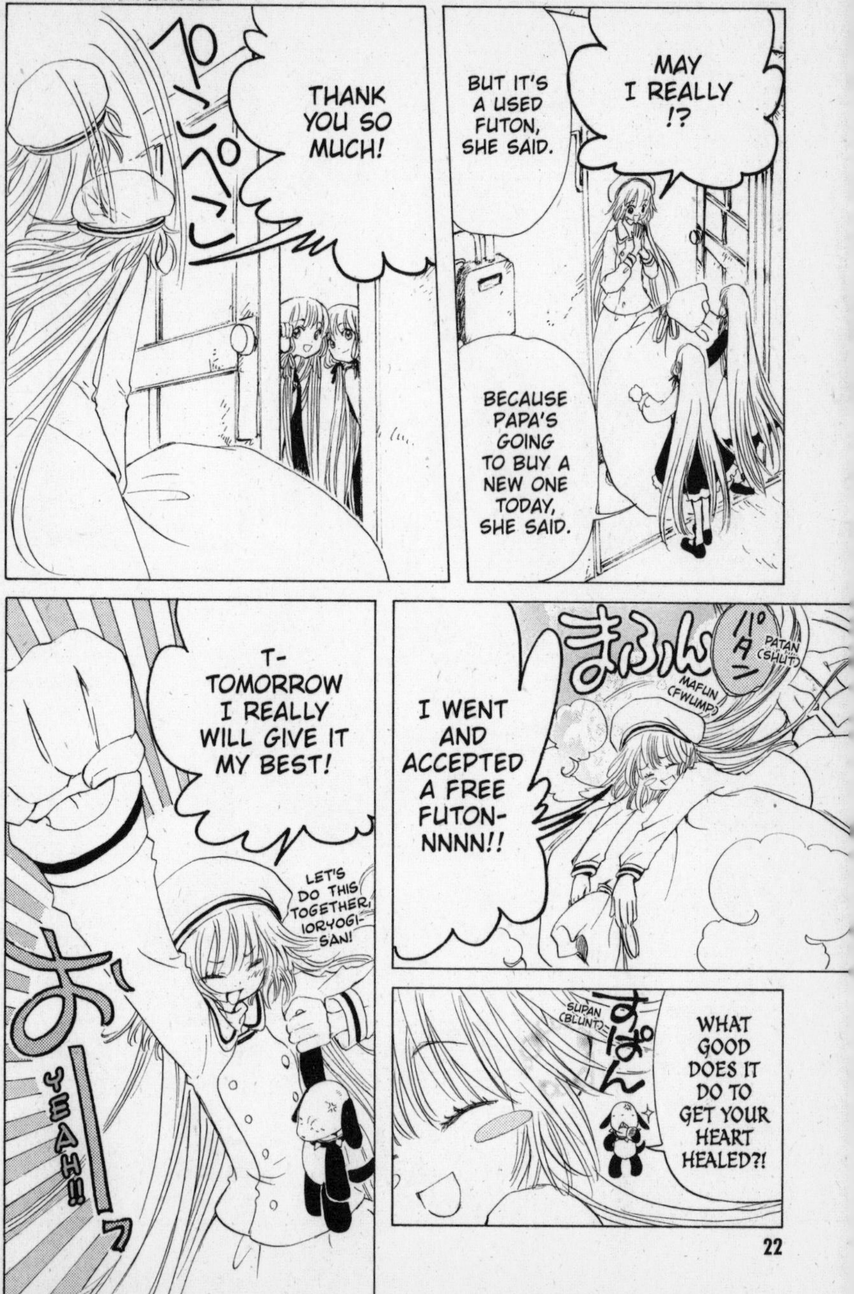
MAY I REALLY !?
BUT IT'S A USED FUTON, SHE SAID.
BECAUSE PAPA'S GOING TO BUY A NEW ONE TODAY, SHE SAID.
THANK YOU SO MUCH!
PATAN (SHUT)
MAFUN (FWUMP)
I WENT AND ACCEPTED A FREE FUTON-NNNN!!
SUPAN (BLUNT)
WHAT GOOD DOES IT DO TO GET YOUR HEART HEALED?!
T-TOMORROW I REALLY WILL GIVE IT MY BEST!
LET'S DO THIS TOGETHER, IORYOGI-SAN!
YEAH!!

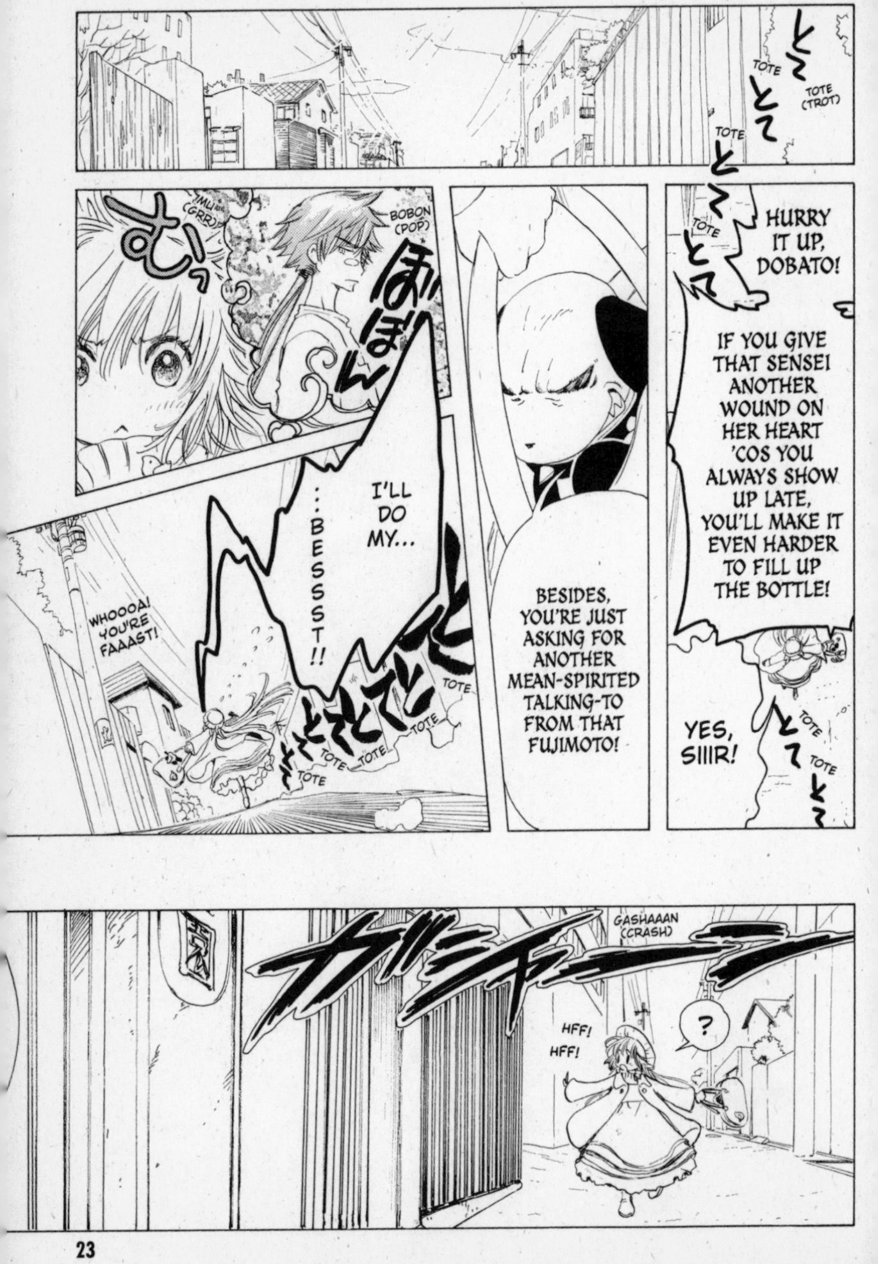
TOTE
TOTE (TROT)
TOTE
TOTE
HURRY IT UP, DOBATO!
IF YOU GIVE THAT SENSEI ANOTHER WOUND ON HER HEART 'COS YOU ALWAYS SHOW UP LATE, YOU'LL MAKE IT EVEN HARDER TO FILL UP THE BOTTLE!
YES, SIIIR!
TOTE
TOTE
BESIDES, YOU'RE JUST ASKING FOR ANOTHER MEAN-SPIRITED TALKING-TO FROM THAT FUJIMOTO!
MU (GRR)
BOBON (POP)
I'LL DO MY...
...BESSST!!
WHOOOA! YOU'RE FAAAST!
TOTE
TOTE
TOTE
TOTE
TOTE
GASHAAAN (CRASH)
?
HFF! HFF!

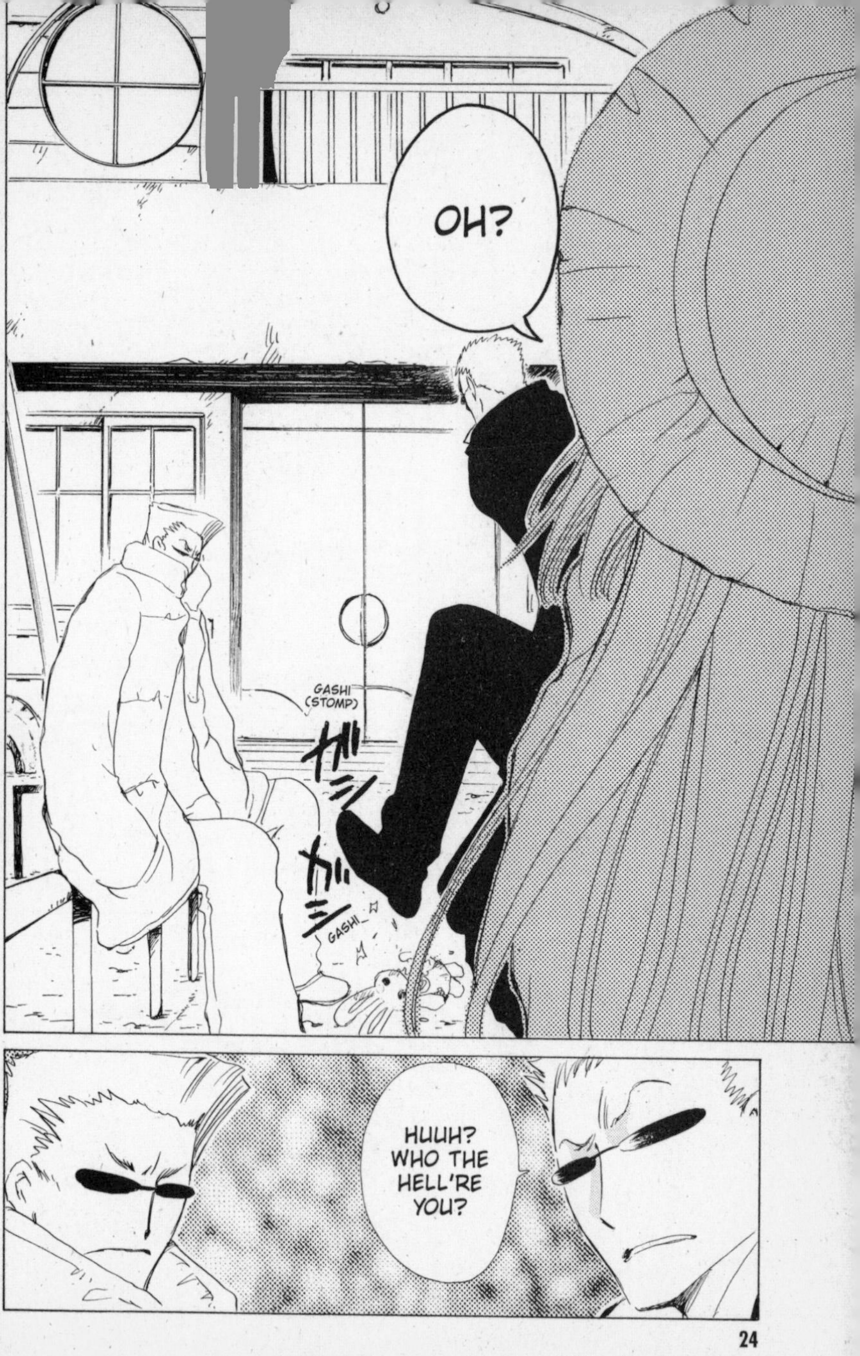
OH?
GASHI (STOMP)
ガシ
ガシ
GASHI
HUUH? WHO THE HELL'RE YOU?

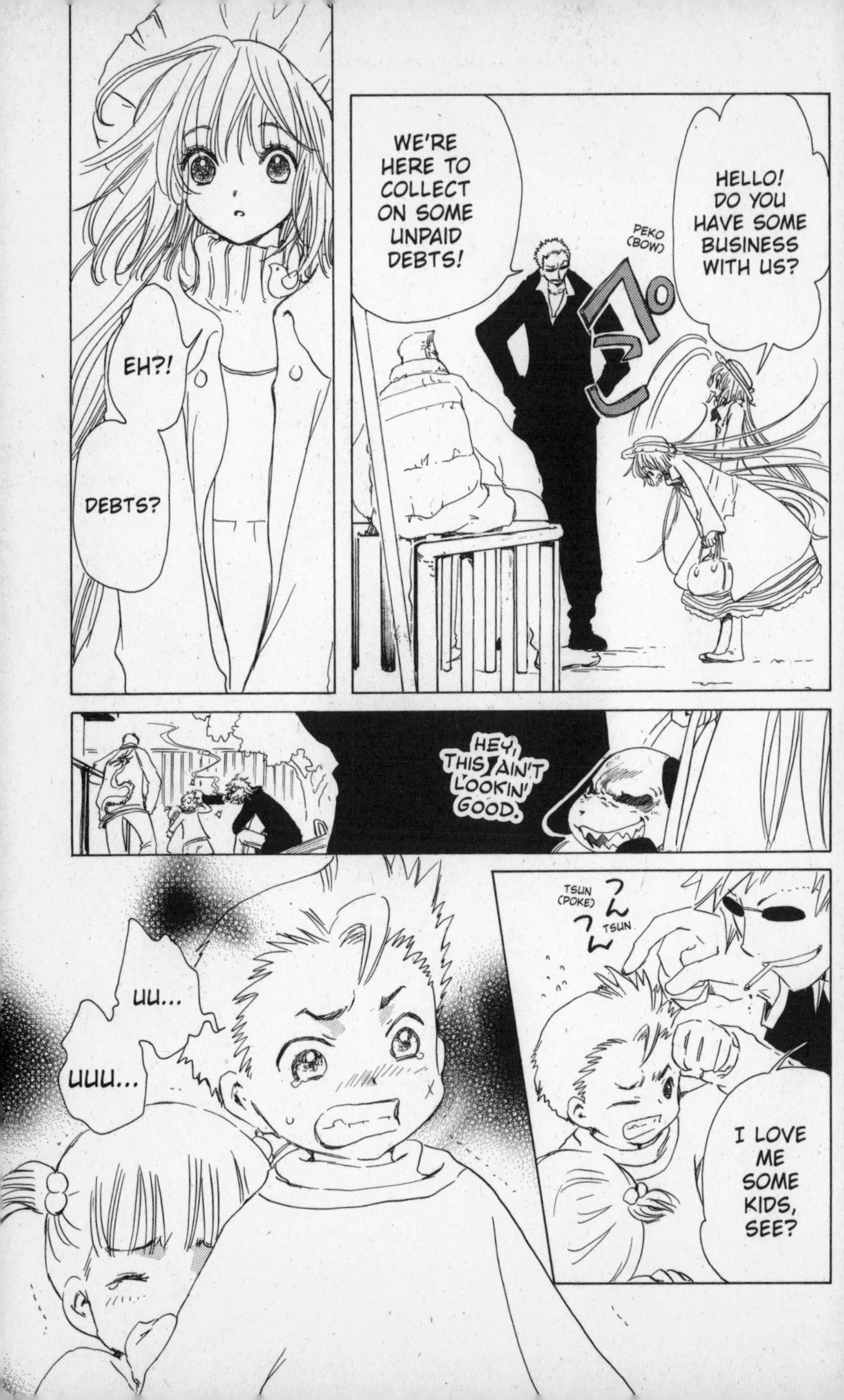
HELLO! DO YOU HAVE SOME BUSINESS WITH US?
PEKO (BOW)
WE'RE HERE TO COLLECT ON SOME UNPAID DEBTS!
EH?!
DEBTS?
HEY, THIS AIN'T LOOKIN' GOOD.
TSUN (POKE)
TSUN
I LOVE ME SOME KIDS, SEE?
UU...
UUU...

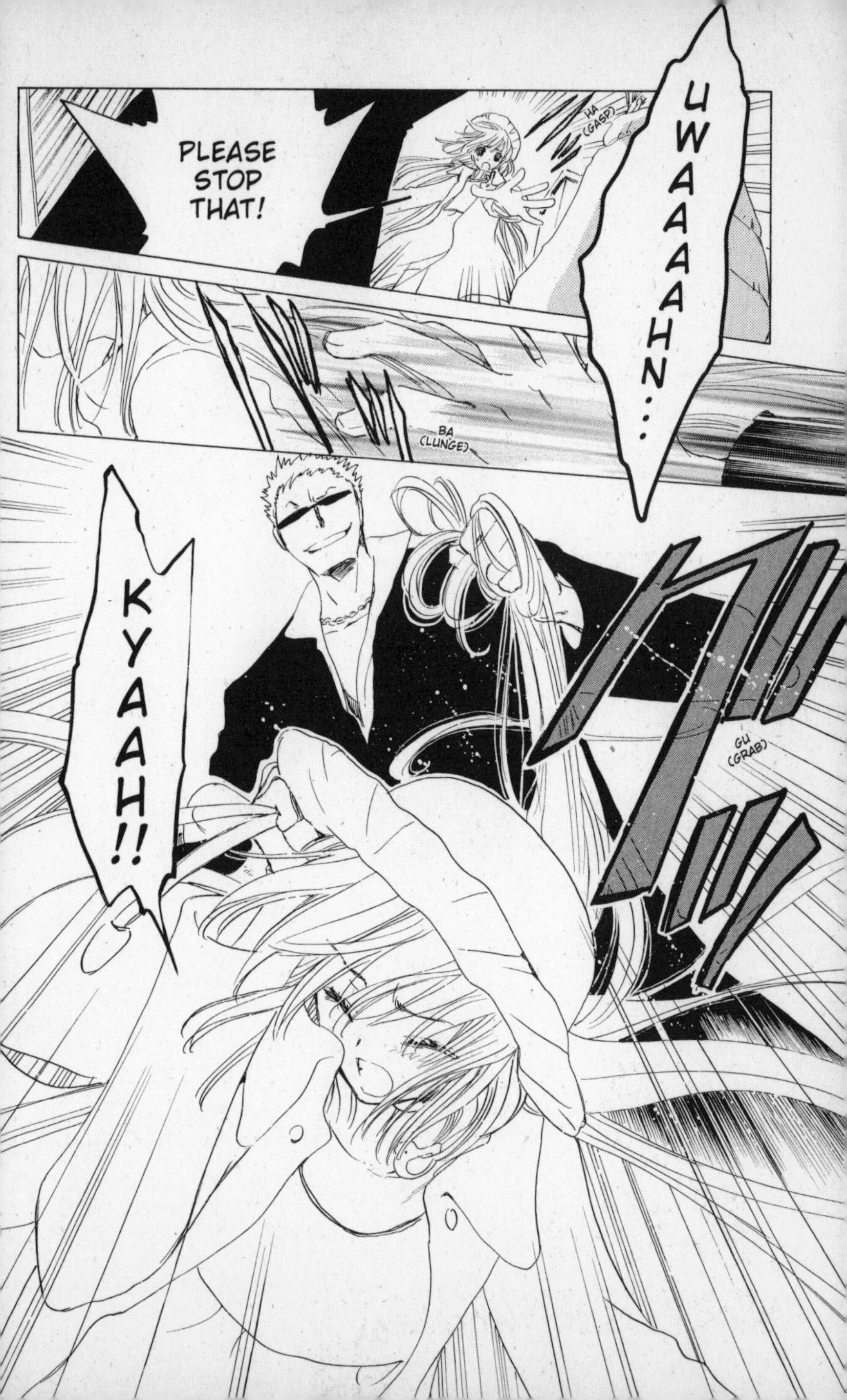
UWAAAAAHN...
HA (GASP)
PLEASE STOP THAT!
BA (LUNGE)
GU (GRAB)
KYAAAH!!

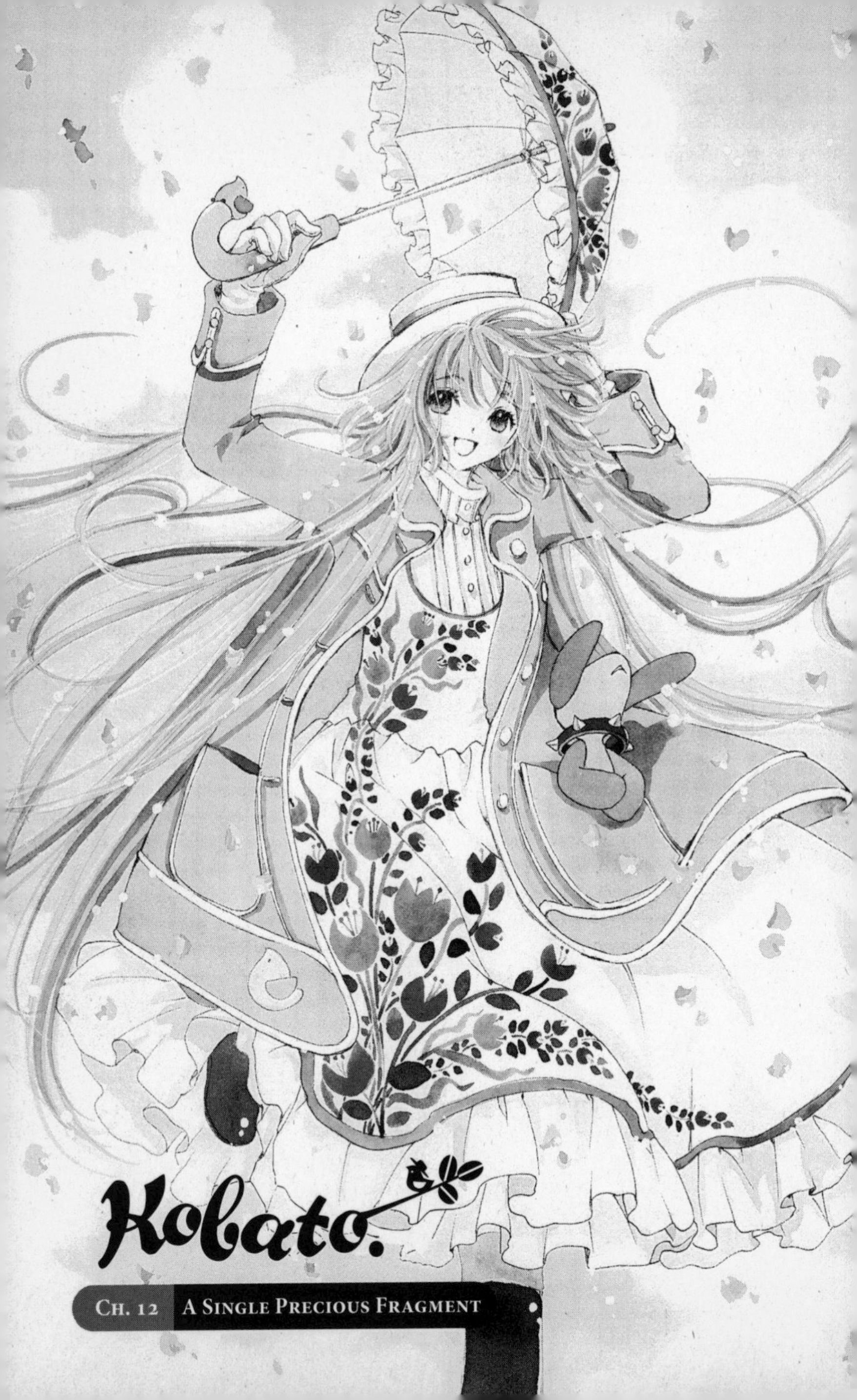
Kobato.
Ch. 12 A Single Precious Fragment

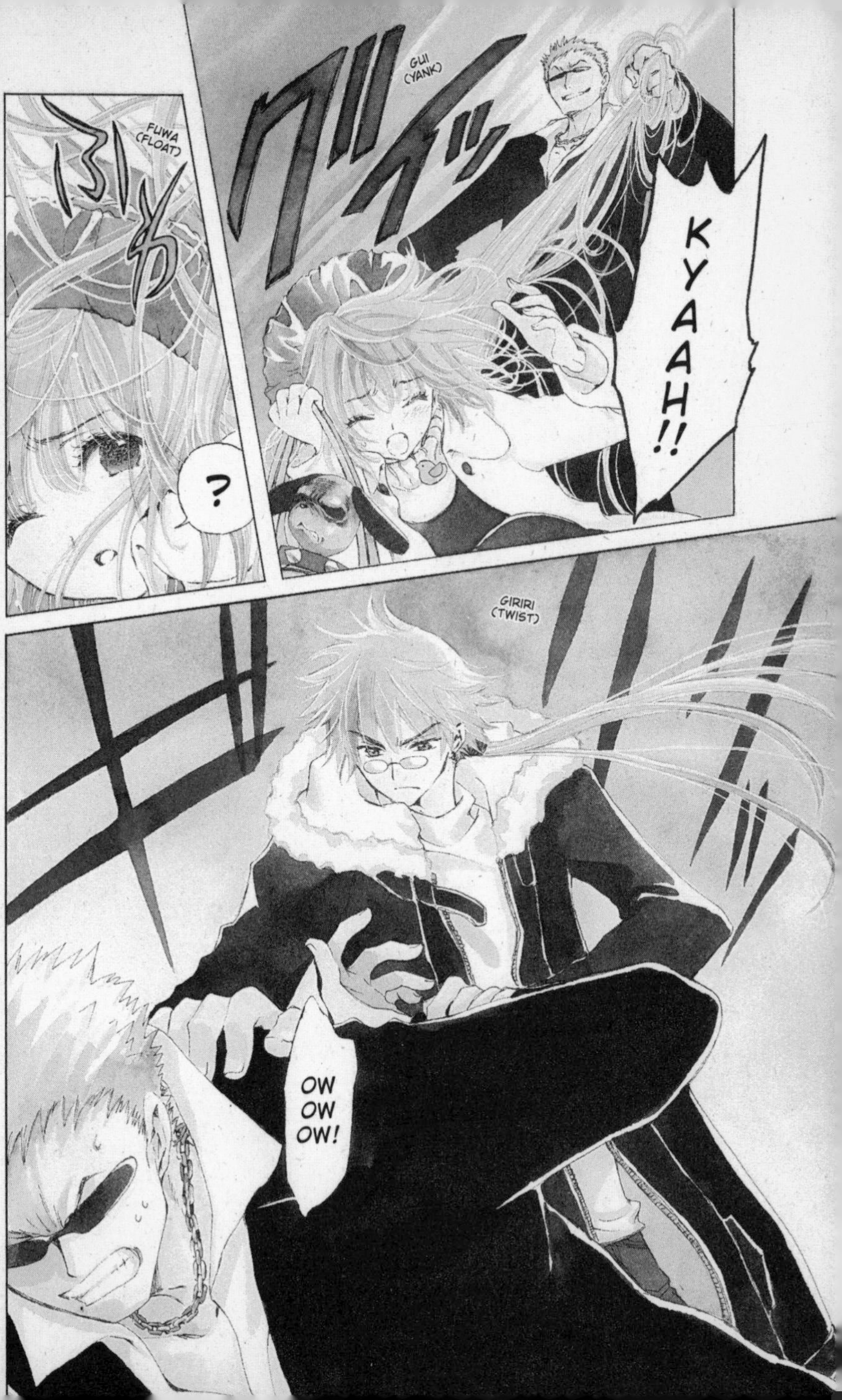
グイッ
GUI (YANK)
KYAAH!!
ふわ
FUWA (FLOAT)
?
GIRIRI (TWIST)
OW OW OW!

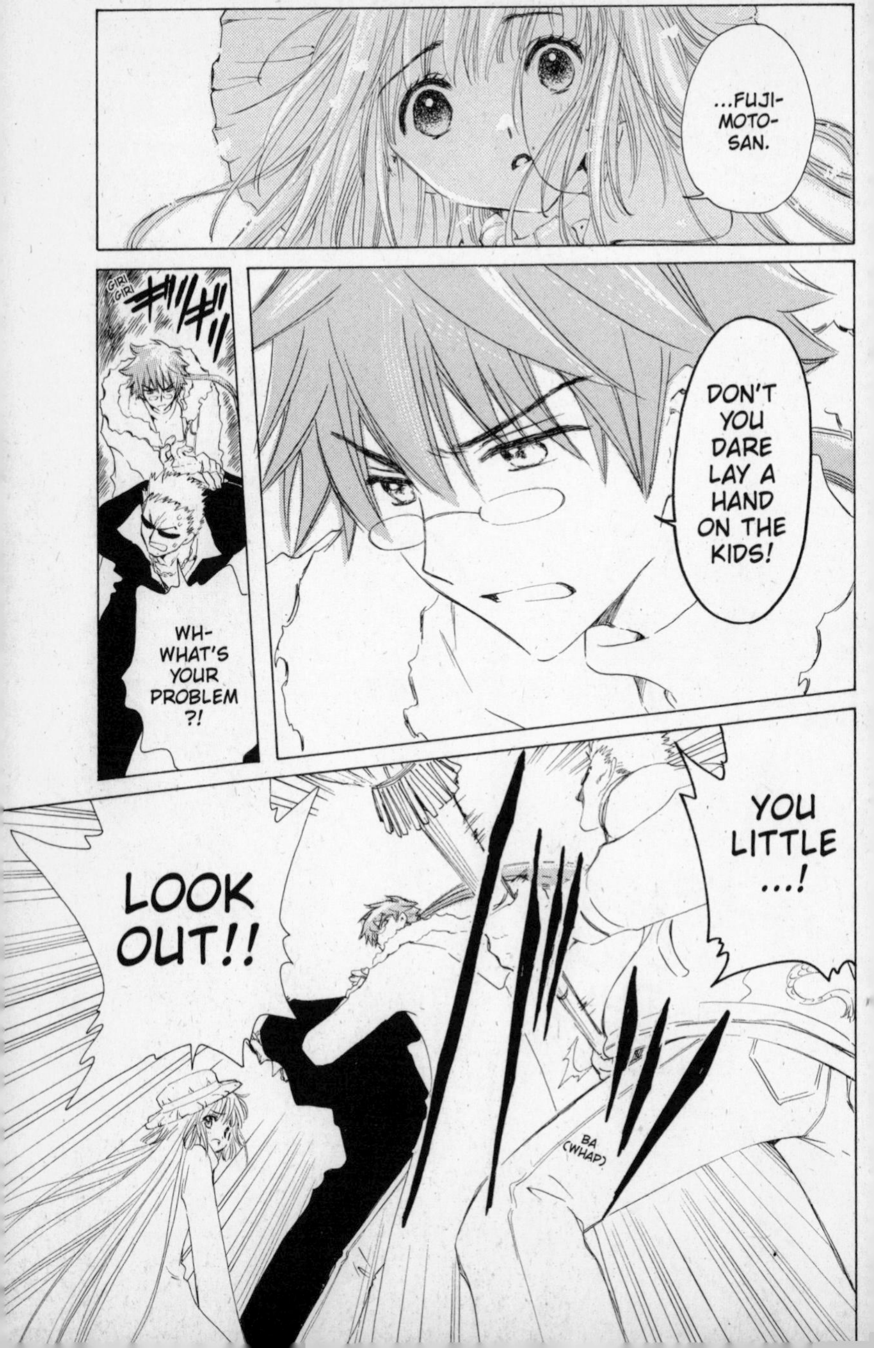
...FUJI-MOTO-SAN.
DON'T YOU DARE LAY A HAND ON THE KIDS!
ギリギリ
GIRI GIRI
WH-WHAT'S YOUR PROBLEM?!
YOU LITTLE ...!
LOOK OUT!!
BA (WHAP)

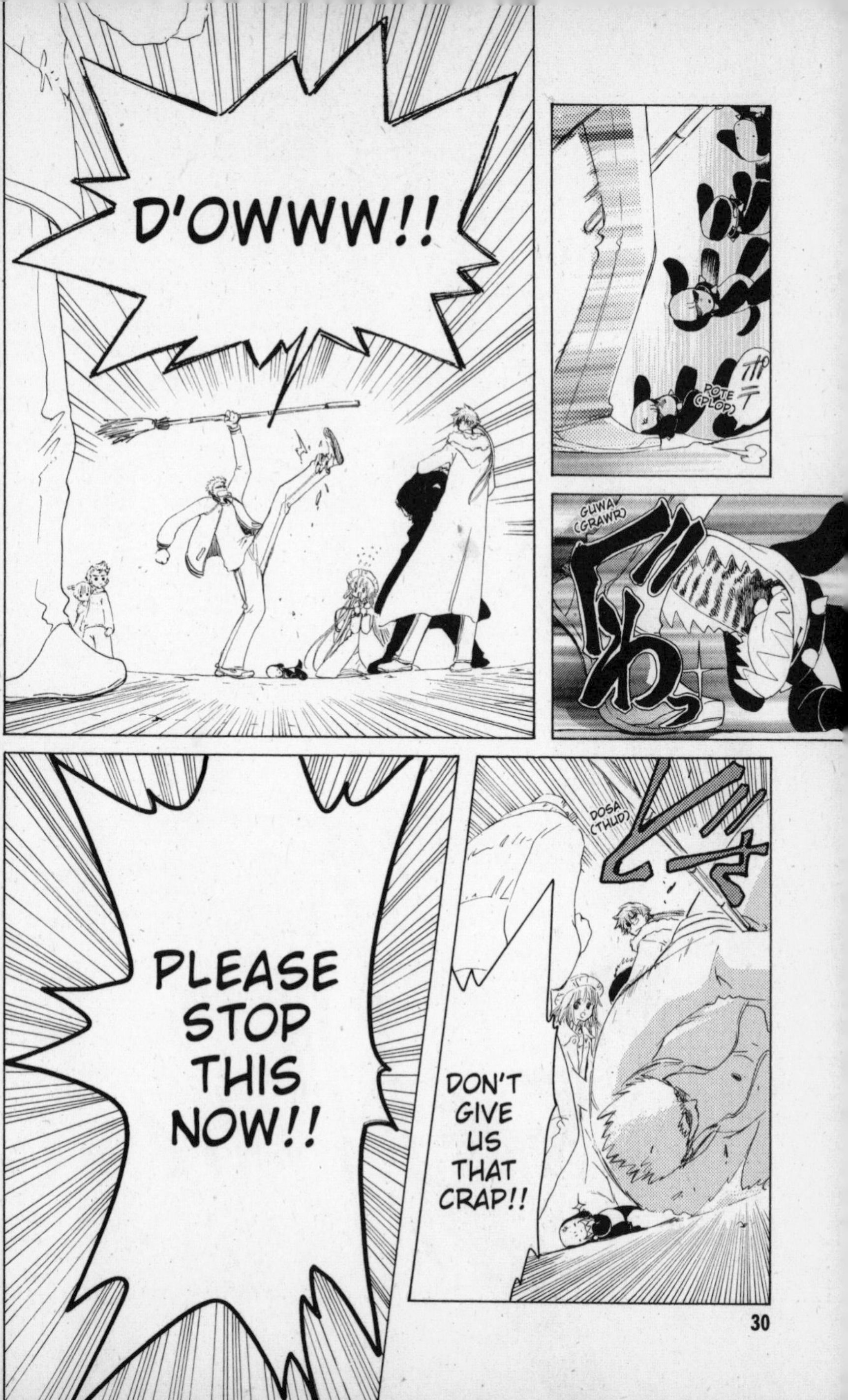
POTE (PLOP)
GUWA (GRAWR)
D'OWWW!!
DOSA (THUD)
DON'T GIVE US THAT CRAP!!
PLEASE STOP THIS NOW!!

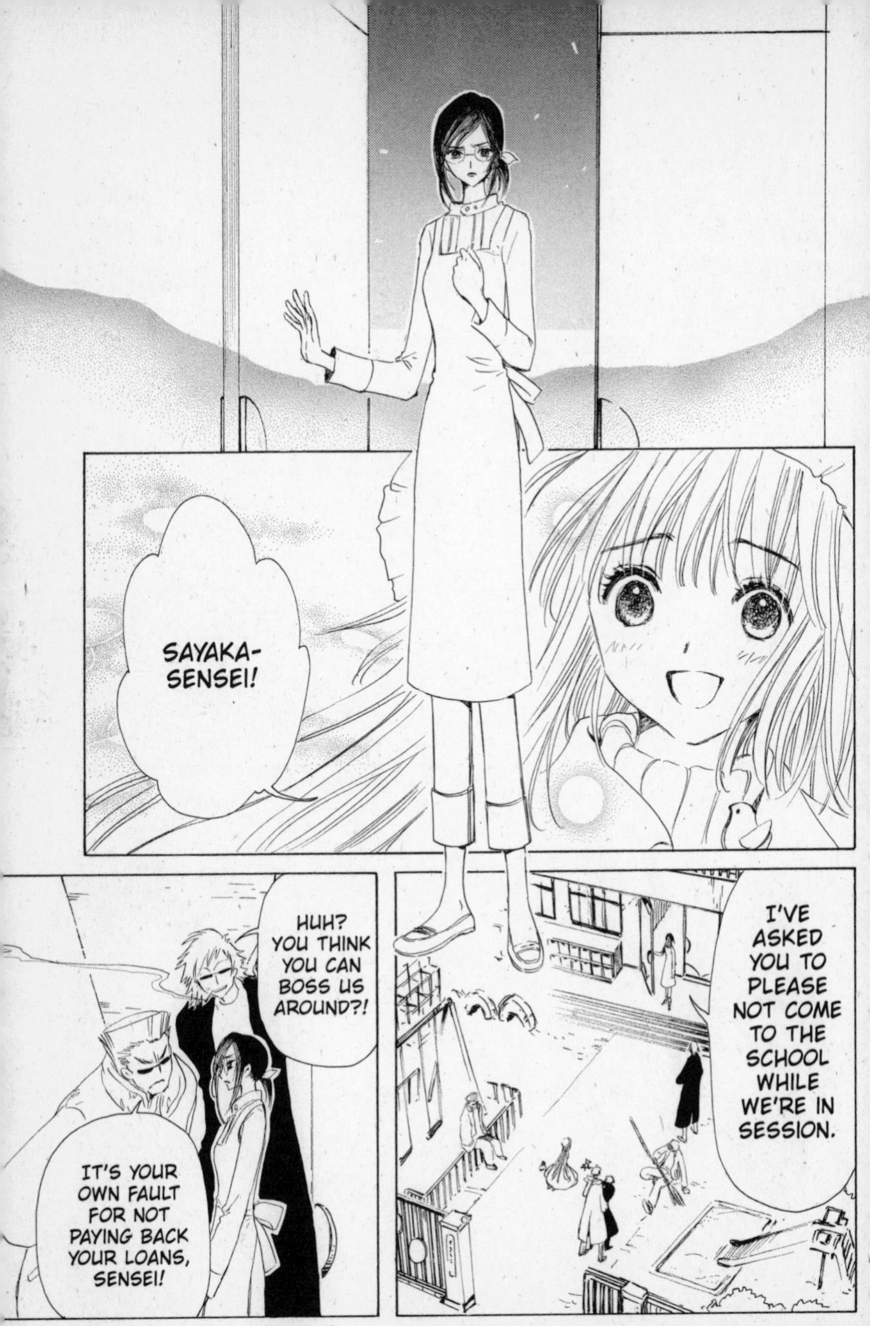
SAYAKA-SENSEI!
I'VE ASKED YOU TO PLEASE NOT COME TO THE SCHOOL WHILE WE'RE IN SESSION.
HUH? YOU THINK YOU CAN BOSS US AROUND?!
IT'S YOUR OWN FAULT FOR NOT PAYING BACK YOUR LOANS, SENSEI!

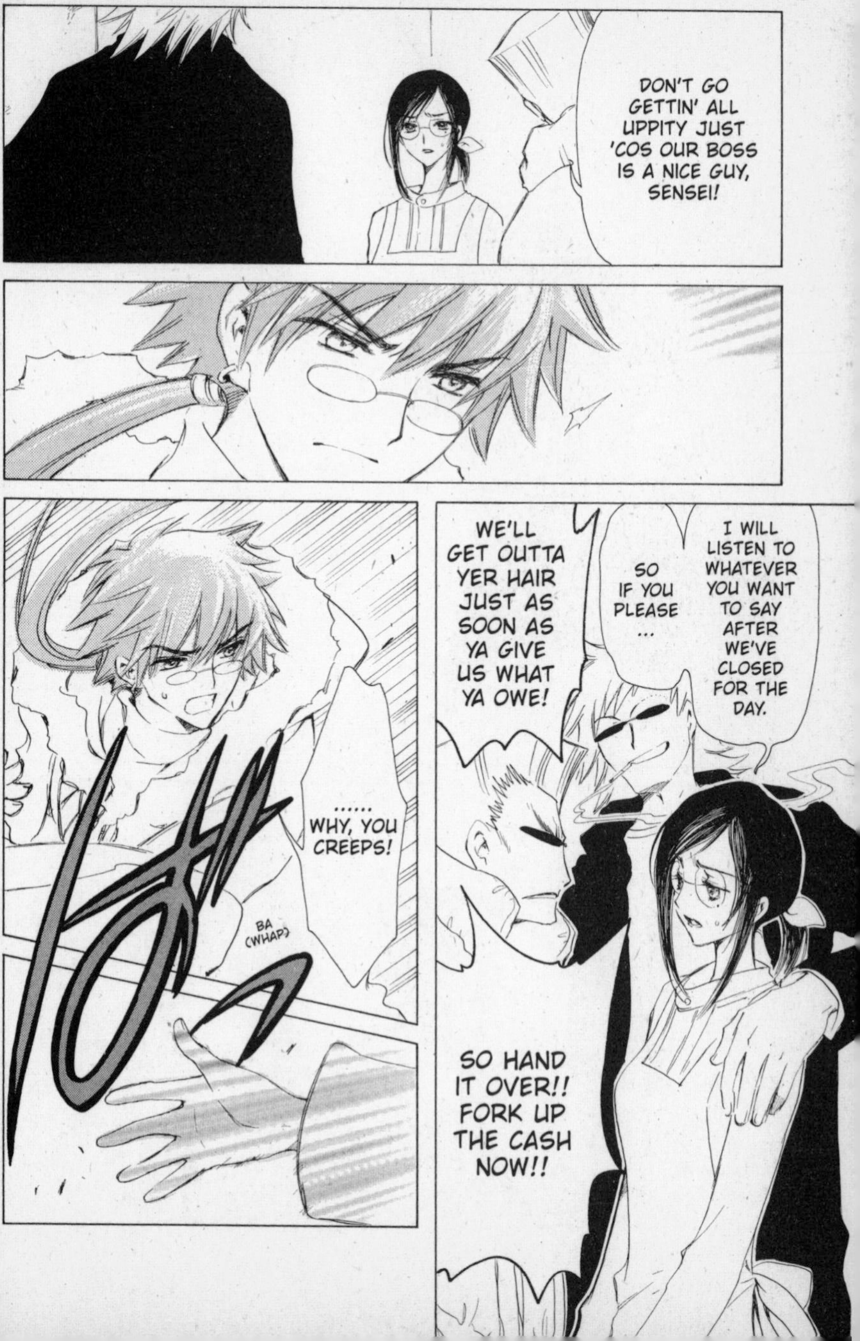
DON'T GO GETTIN' ALL UPPITY JUST 'COS OUR BOSS IS A NICE GUY, SENSEI!
I WILL LISTEN TO WHATEVER YOU WANT TO SAY AFTER WE'VE CLOSED FOR THE DAY.
SO IF YOU PLEASE ...
WE'LL GET OUTTA YER HAIR JUST AS SOON AS YA GIVE US WHAT YA OWE!
SO HAND IT OVER!! FORK UP THE CASH NOW!!
...... WHY, YOU CREEPS!
BA (WHAP)

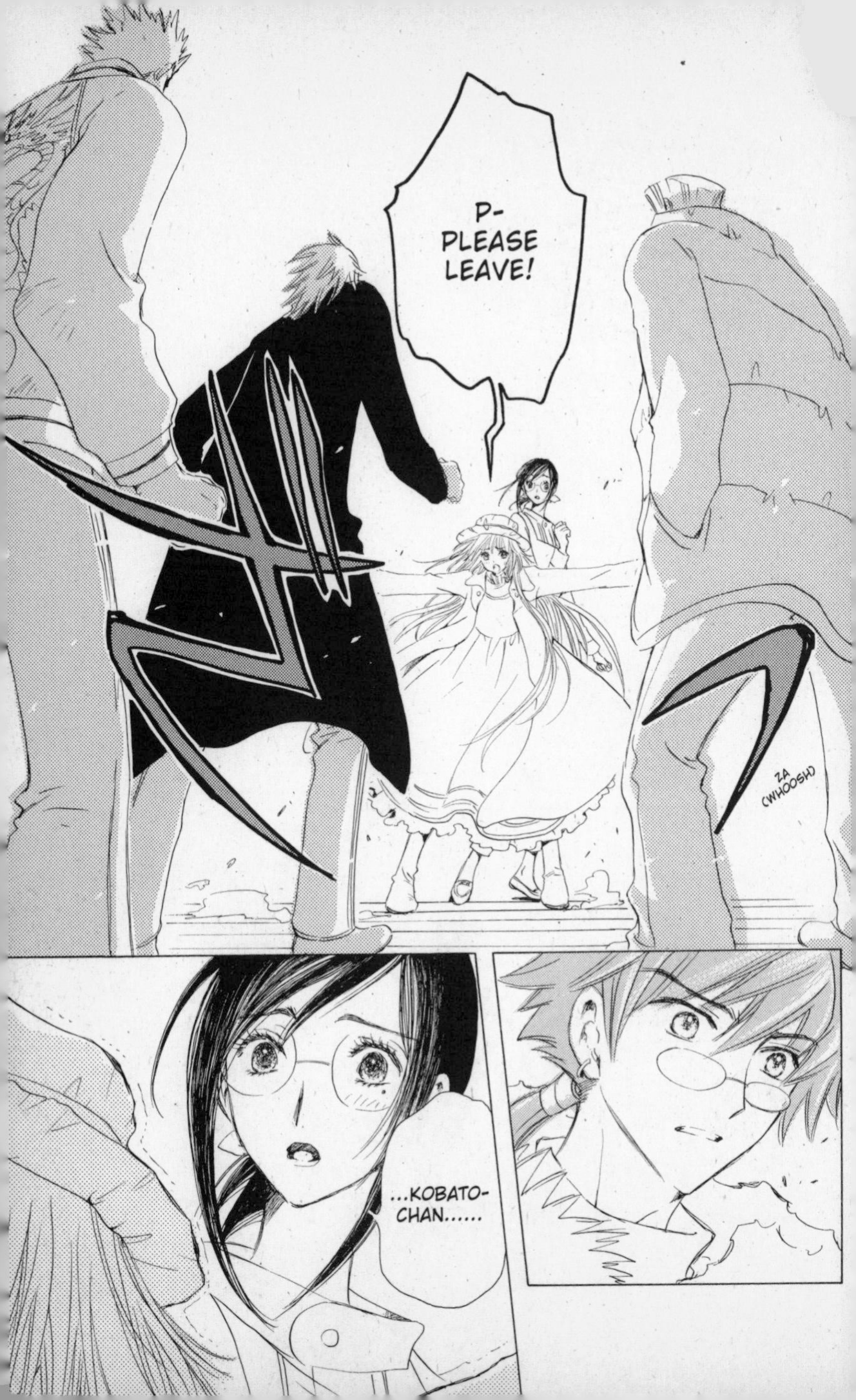
P-
PLEASE
LEAVE!
ZA
(WHOOSH)
...KOBATO-
CHAN......

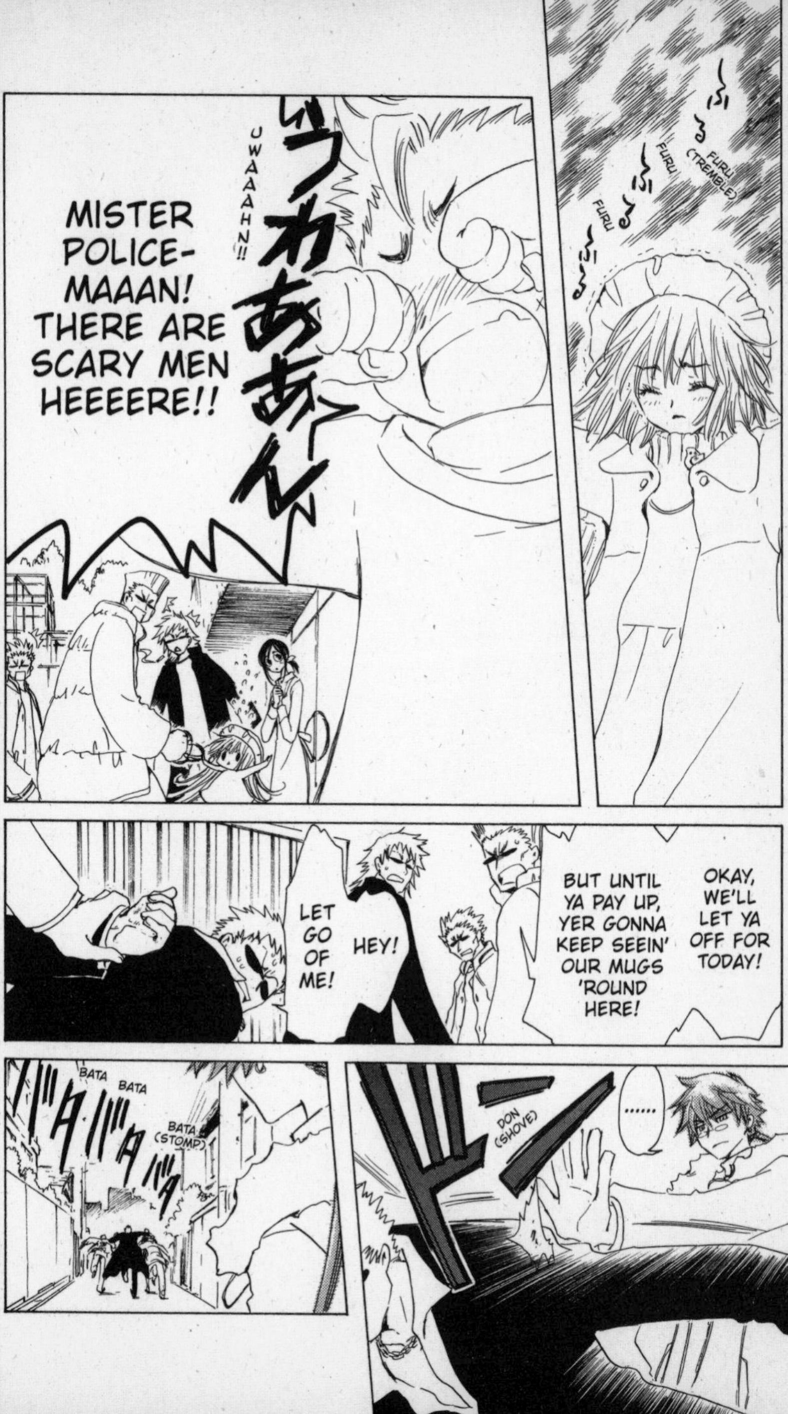
FURU (TREMBLE)
FURU
FURU
UWAAAAHN!!
MISTER POLICE-MAAAN! THERE ARE SCARY MEN HEEEEERE!!
OKAY, WE'LL LET YA OFF FOR TODAY!
BUT UNTIL YA PAY UP, YER GONNA KEEP SEEIN' OUR MUGS 'ROUND HERE!
HEY!
LET GO OF ME!
......
DON (SHOVE)
BATA
BATA
BATA (STOMP)

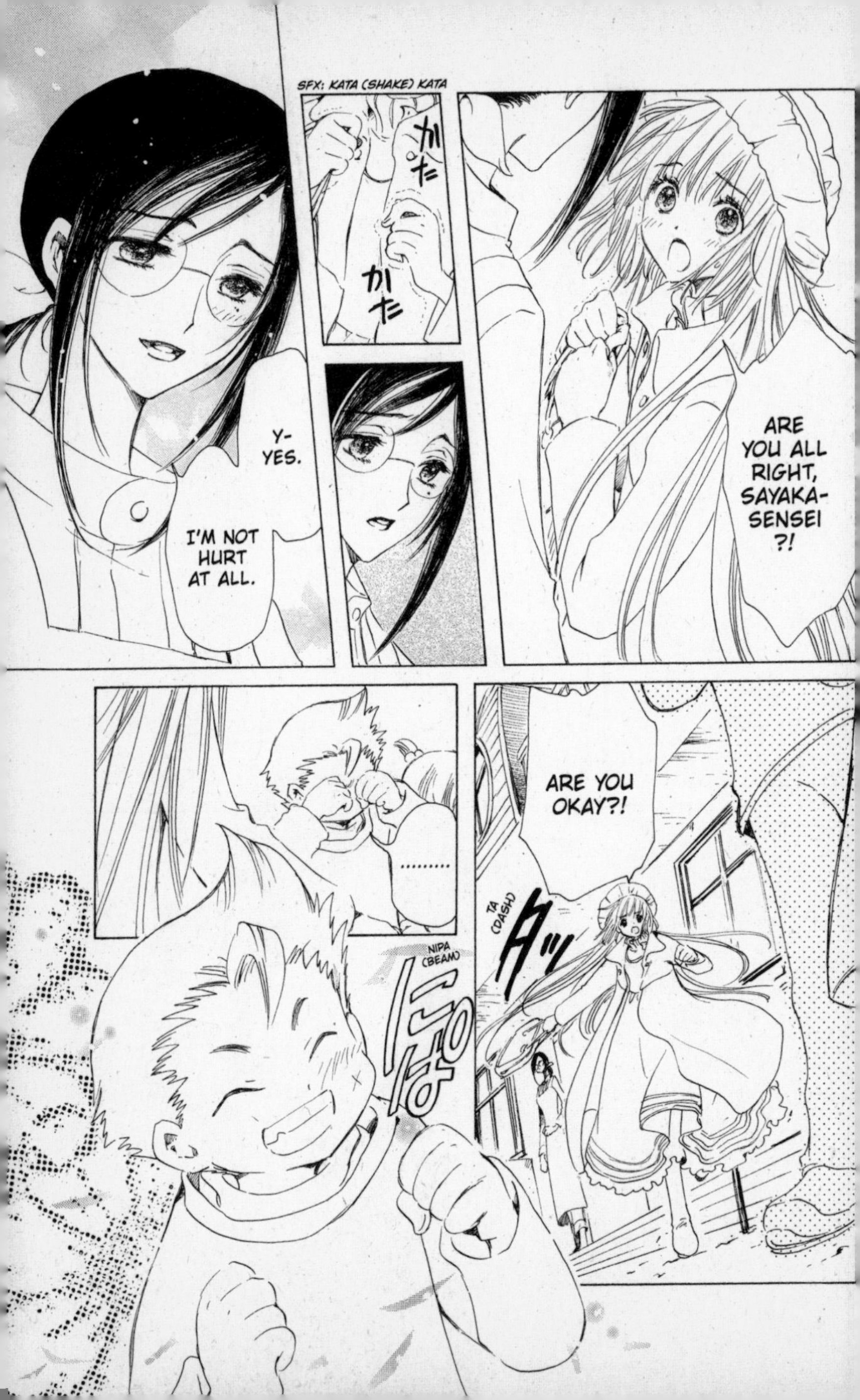
ARE YOU ALL RIGHT, SAYAKA-SENSEI?!
SFX: KATA (SHAKE) KATA
かた
かた
Y-YES.
I'M NOT HURT AT ALL.
ARE YOU OKAY?!
TA (DASH)
タッ
....
NIPA (BEAM)
にぱ

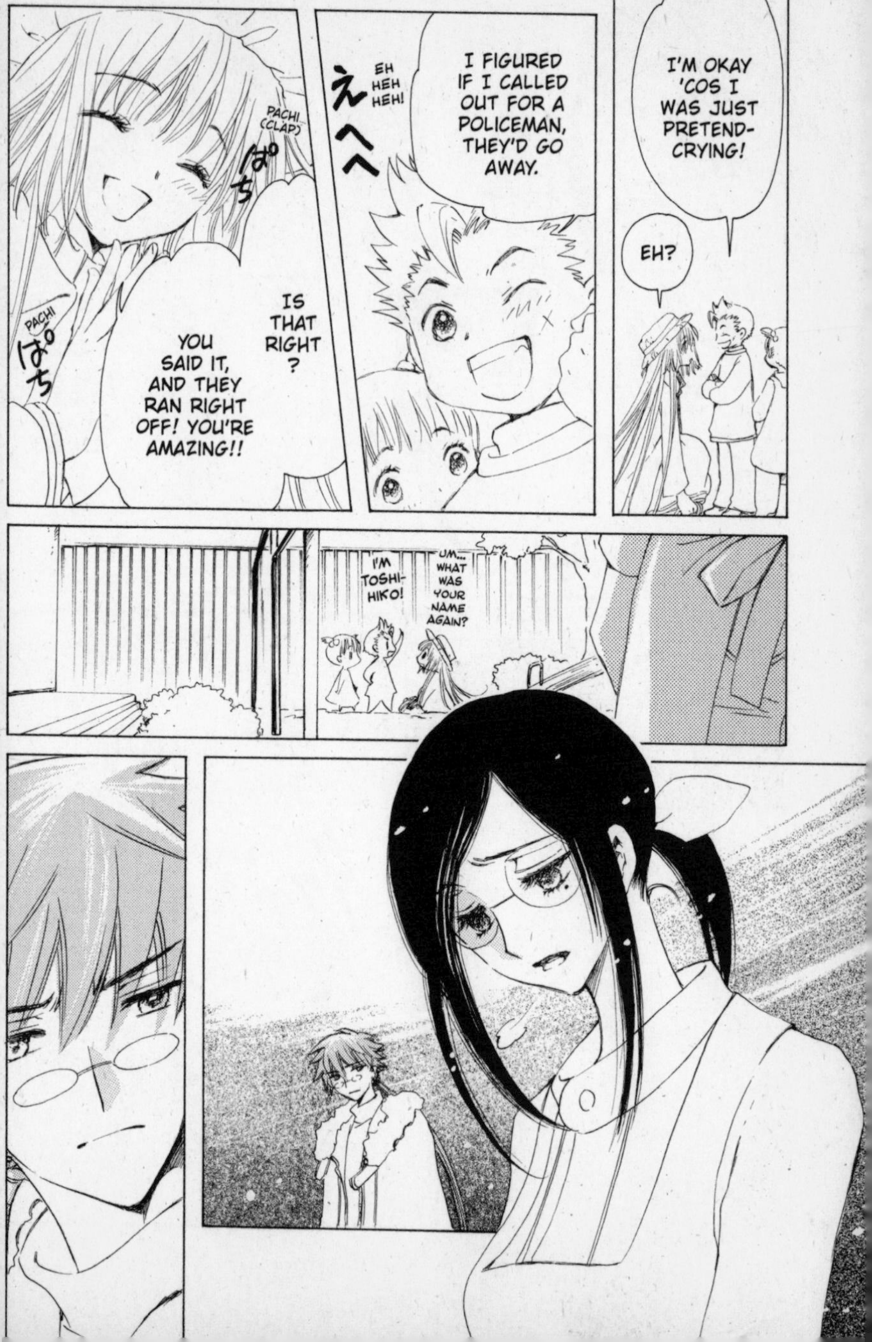
I'M OKAY 'COS I WAS JUST PRETEND-CRYING!
EH?
えへへ
EH HEH HEH!
I FIGURED IF I CALLED OUT FOR A POLICEMAN, THEY'D GO AWAY.
ぱち
PACHI (CLAP)
IS THAT RIGHT?
YOU SAID IT, AND THEY RAN RIGHT OFF! YOU'RE AMAZING!!
ぱち
PACHI
UM... WHAT WAS YOUR NAME AGAIN?
I'M TOSHIHIKO!

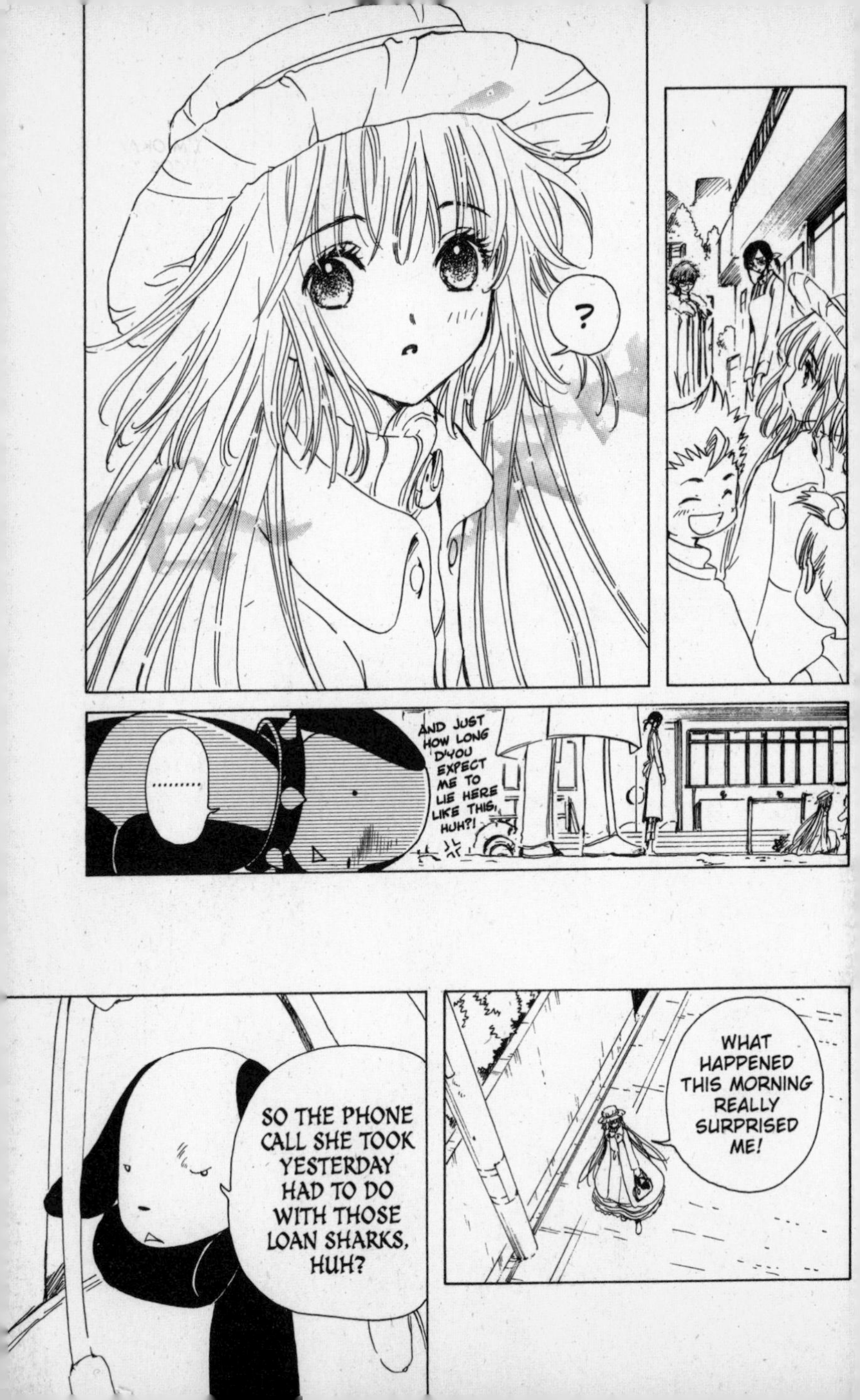
?
AND JUST HOW LONG D'YOU EXPECT ME TO LIE HERE LIKE THIS, HUH?!
....
WHAT HAPPENED THIS MORNING REALLY SURPRISED ME!
SO THE PHONE CALL SHE TOOK YESTERDAY HAD TO DO WITH THOSE LOAN SHARKS, HUH?

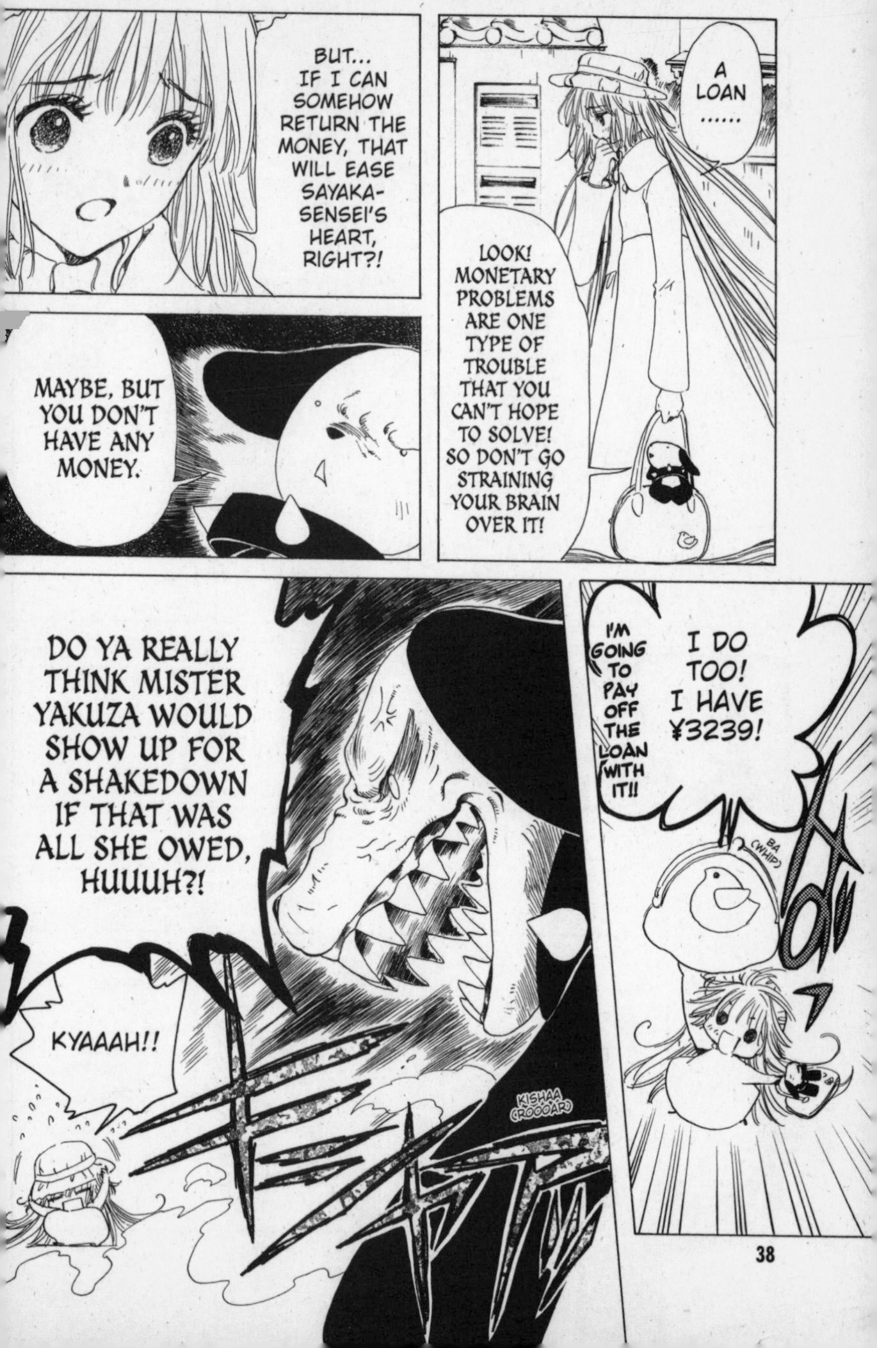
A LOAN ......
LOOK! MONETARY PROBLEMS ARE ONE TYPE OF TROUBLE THAT YOU CAN'T HOPE TO SOLVE! SO DON'T GO STRAINING YOUR BRAIN OVER IT!
BUT... IF I CAN SOMEHOW RETURN THE MONEY, THAT WILL EASE SAYAKA-SENSEI'S HEART, RIGHT?!
MAYBE, BUT YOU DON'T HAVE ANY MONEY.
I DO TOO! I HAVE ¥3239!
I'M GOING TO PAY OFF THE LOAN WITH IT!!
BA (WHIP)
DO YA REALLY THINK MISTER YAKUZA WOULD SHOW UP FOR A SHAKEDOWN IF THAT WAS ALL SHE OWED, HUUUH?!
KISHAA (ROOOAR)
KYAAAH!!

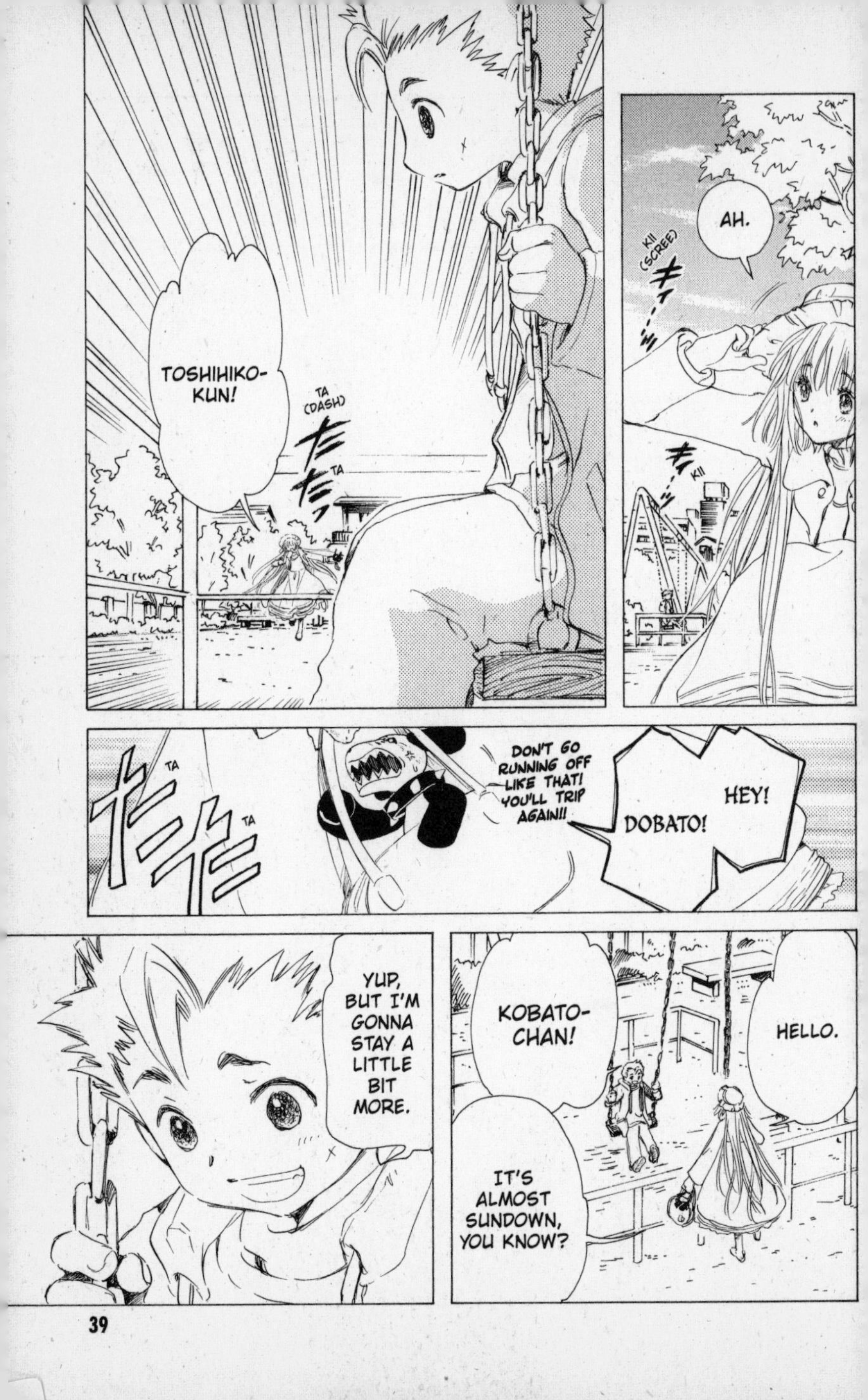
AH.
KII (SCREE)
KII
TOSHIHIKO-KUN!
TA (DASH)
TA
HEY! DOBATO!
DON'T GO RUNNING OFF LIKE THAT! YOU'LL TRIP AGAIN!!
TA
TA
HELLO.
KOBATO-CHAN!
IT'S ALMOST SUNDOWN, YOU KNOW?
YUP, BUT I'M GONNA STAY A LITTLE BIT MORE.

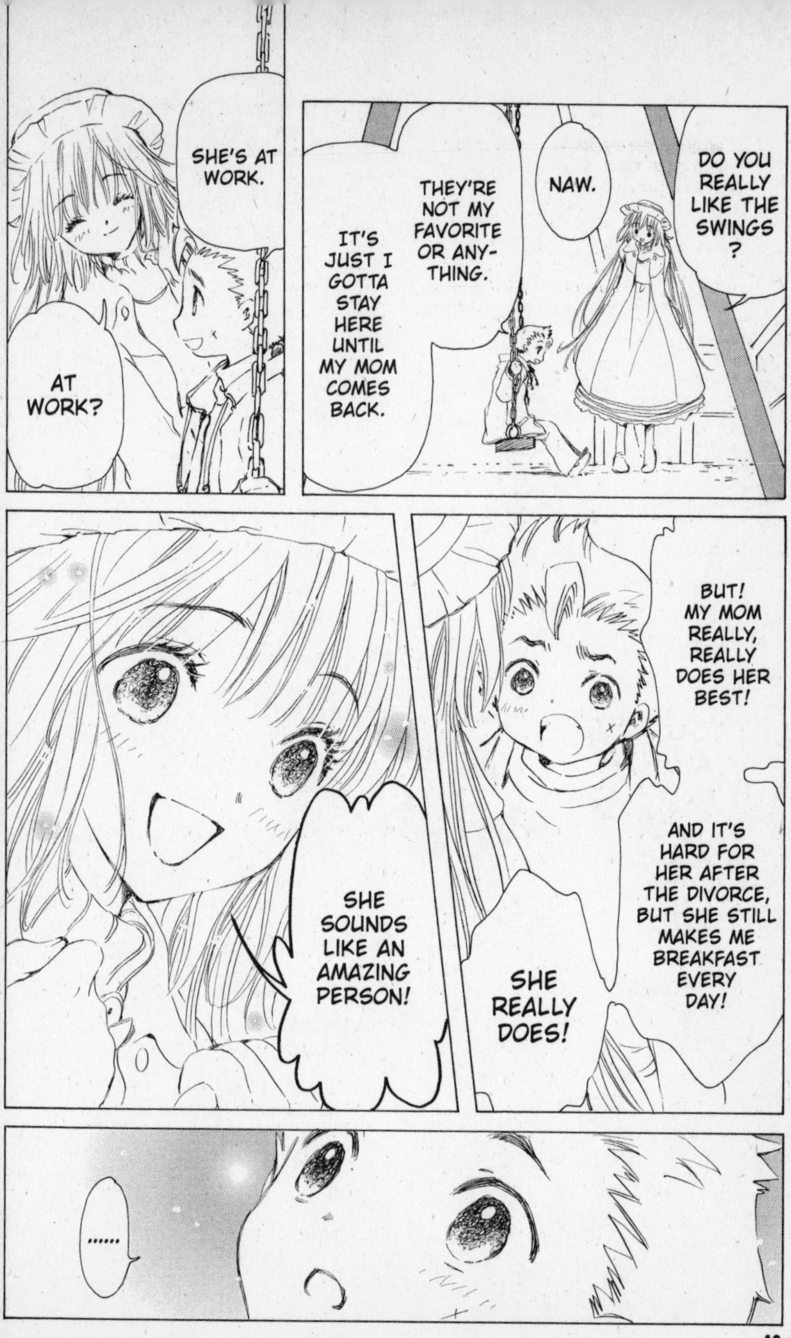
DO YOU REALLY LIKE THE SWINGS?
NAW.
THEY'RE NOT MY FAVORITE OR ANYTHING.
IT'S JUST I GOTTA STAY HERE UNTIL MY MOM COMES BACK.
SHE'S AT WORK.
AT WORK?
BUT! MY MOM REALLY, REALLY DOES HER BEST!
AND IT'S HARD FOR HER AFTER THE DIVORCE, BUT SHE STILL MAKES ME BREAKFAST EVERY DAY!
SHE REALLY DOES!
SHE SOUNDS LIKE AN AMAZING PERSON!
......

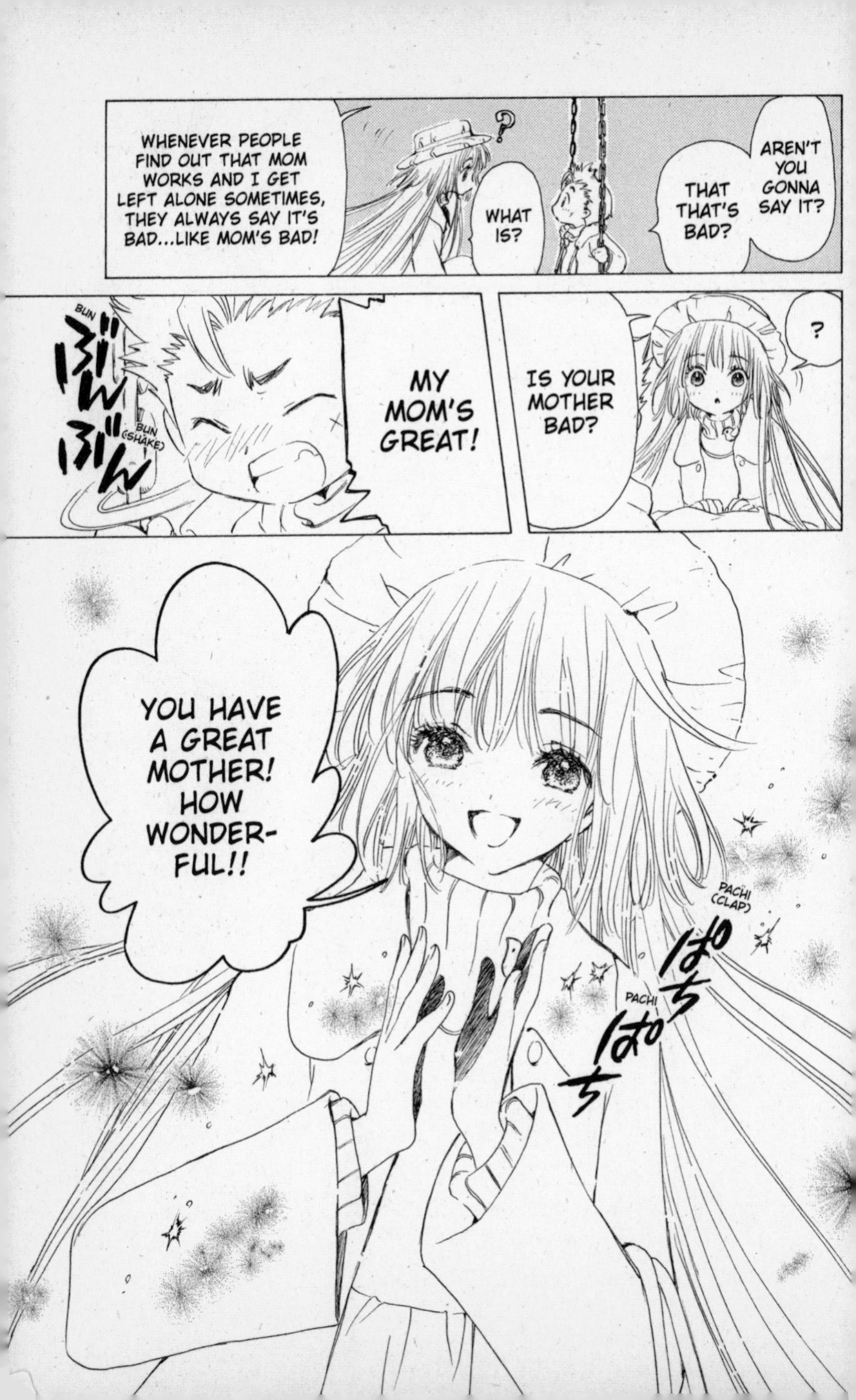
AREN'T YOU GONNA SAY IT?
THAT THAT'S BAD?
WHAT IS?
WHENEVER PEOPLE FIND OUT THAT MOM WORKS AND I GET LEFT ALONE SOMETIMES, THEY ALWAYS SAY IT'S BAD...LIKE MOM'S BAD!
?
IS YOUR MOTHER BAD?
MY MOM'S GREAT!
ぶん BUN
ぶん BUN (SHAKE)
YOU HAVE A GREAT MOTHER! HOW WONDER-FUL!!
ぱち PACHI (CLAP)
ぱち PACHI

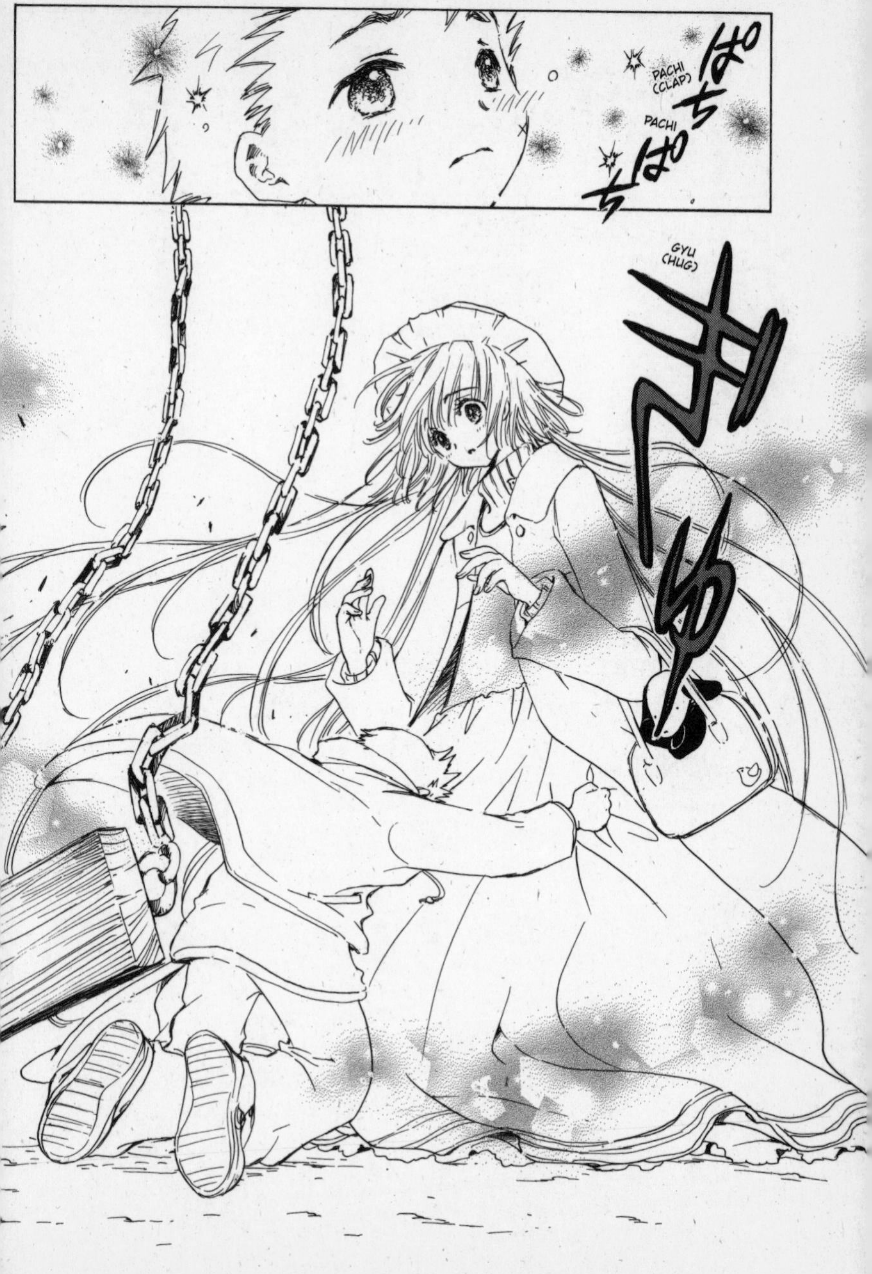
ぱち
PACHI (CLAP)
ぱち
PACHI
ぎゅ
GYU (HUG)

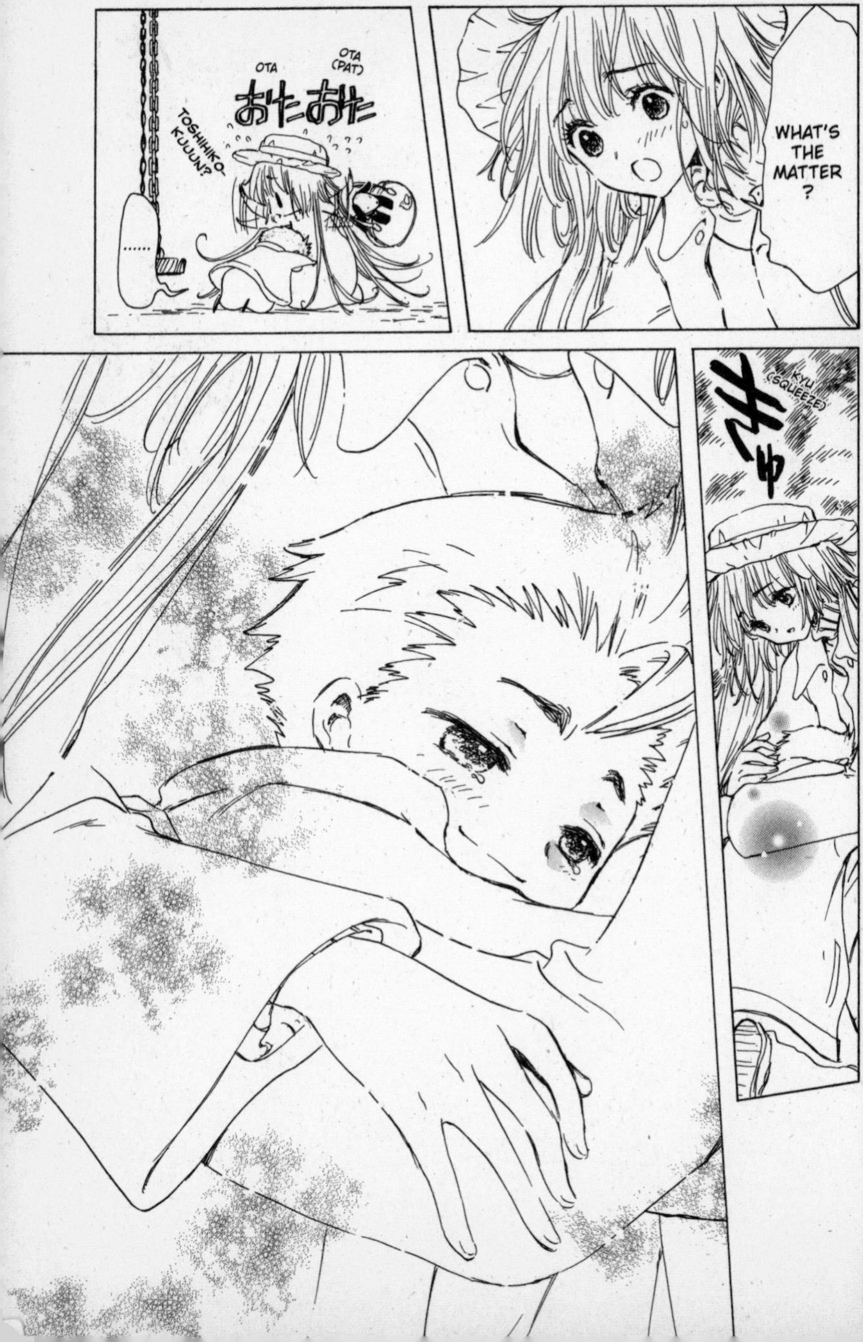
WHAT'S THE MATTER ?
OTA
OTA (PAT)
おたおた
TOSHIHIKO-KUUUN?
......
KYU (SQUEEZE)
きゅ

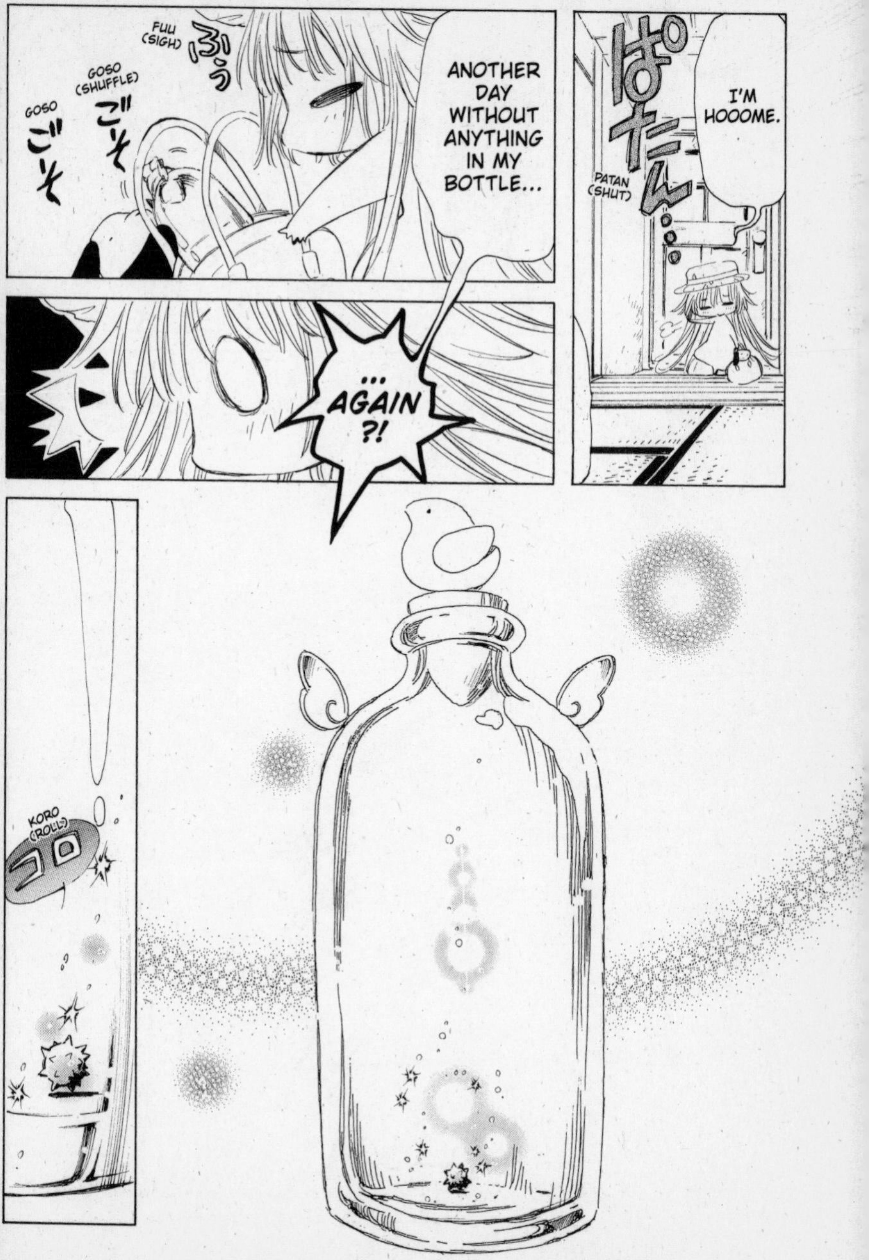
I'M HOOOME.
ぱたん
PATAN (SHUT)
ANOTHER DAY WITHOUT ANYTHING IN MY BOTTLE...
ふぅ
FUU (SIGH)
ごそ
GOSO (SHUFFLE)
ごそ
GOSO
...AGAIN?!
コロ
KORO (ROLL)

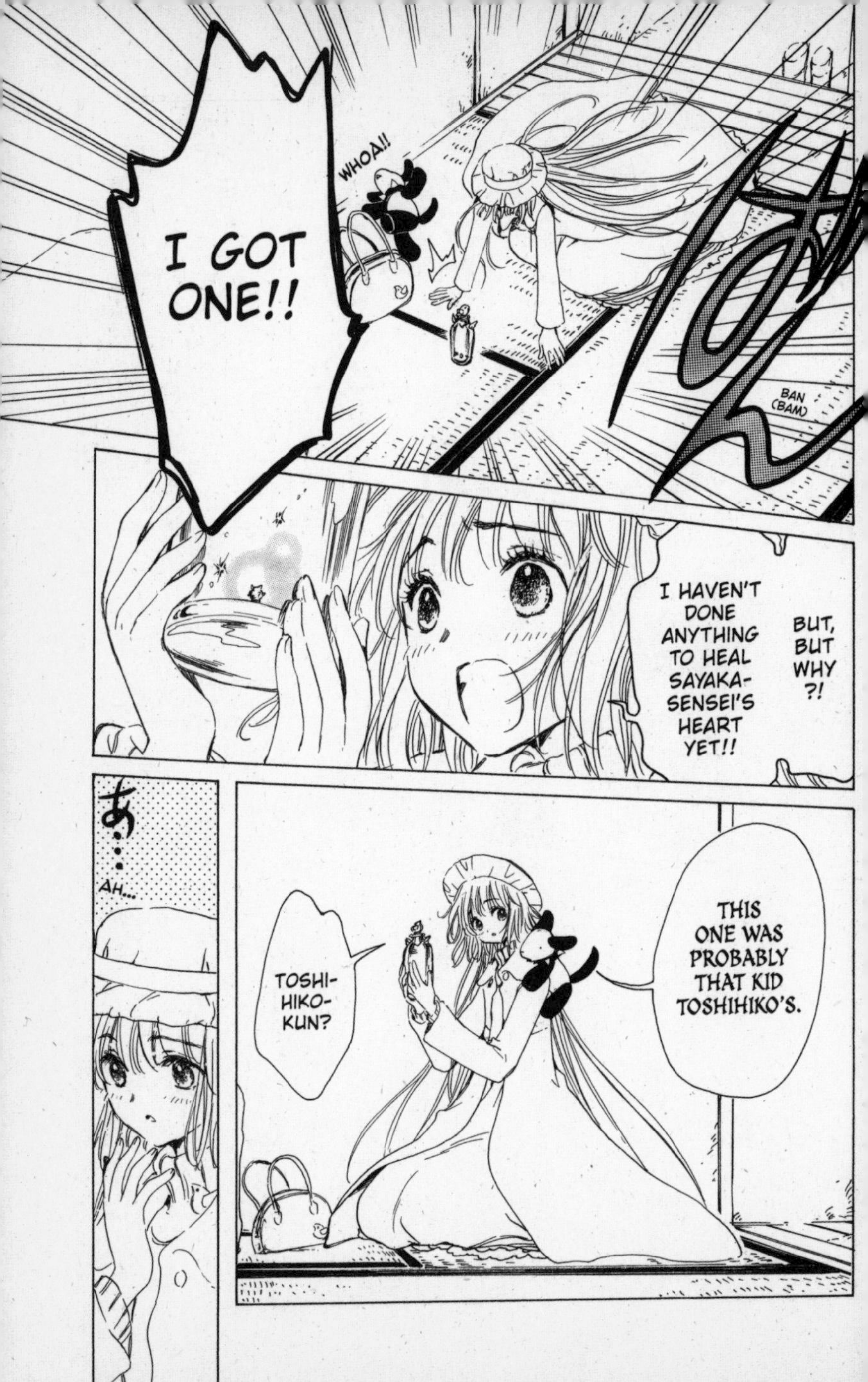
BAN (BAM)
WHOA!!
I GOT ONE!!
BUT, BUT WHY?!
I HAVEN'T DONE ANYTHING TO HEAL SAYAKA-SENSEI'S HEART YET!!
THIS ONE WAS PROBABLY THAT KID TOSHIHIKO'S.
TOSHI-HIKO-KUN?
あ…
AH...

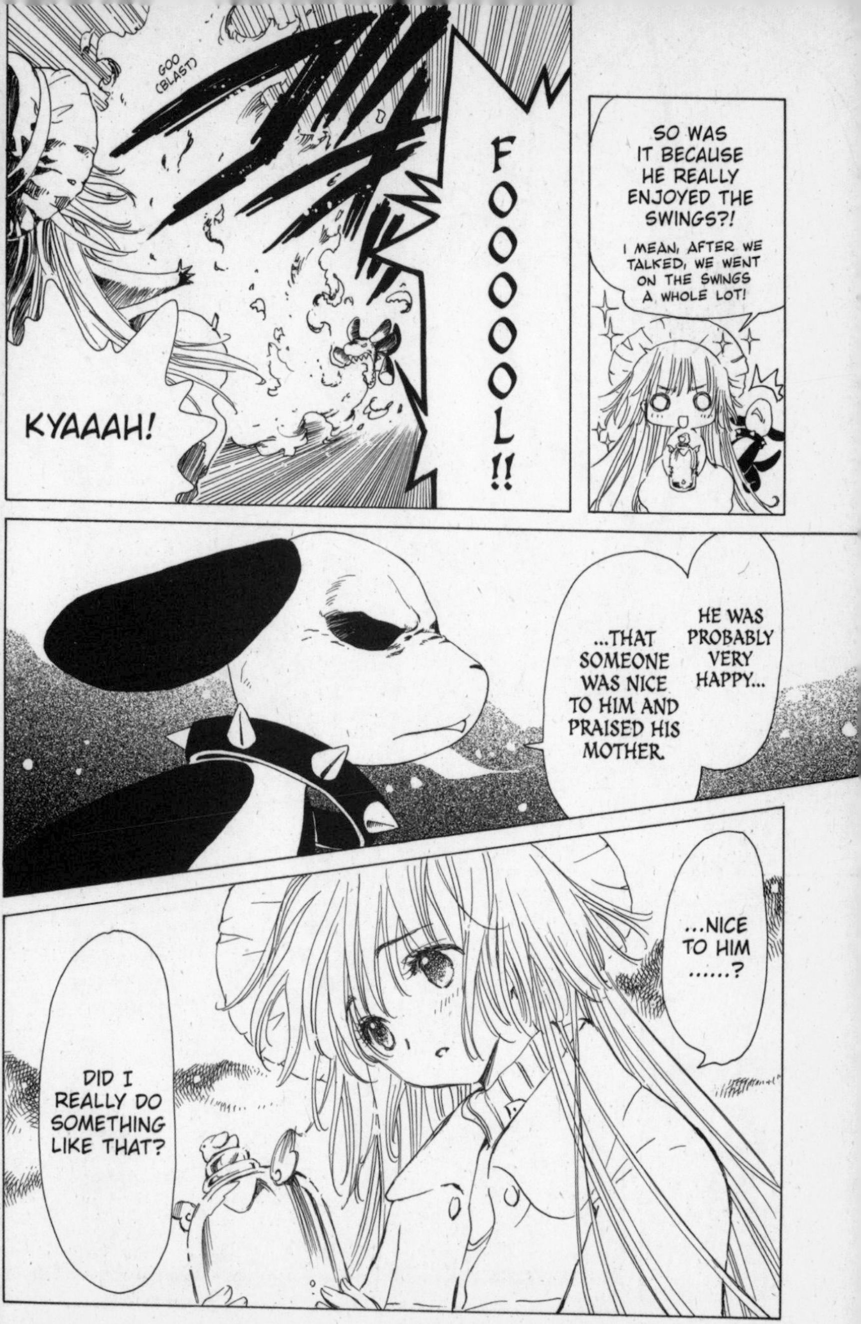
SO WAS IT BECAUSE HE REALLY ENJOYED THE SWINGS?!
I MEAN, AFTER WE TALKED, WE WENT ON THE SWINGS A WHOLE LOT!
FOOOOOL!!
GOO (BLAST)
KYAAAH!
HE WAS PROBABLY VERY HAPPY...
...THAT SOMEONE WAS NICE TO HIM AND PRAISED HIS MOTHER.
...NICE TO HIM ......?
DID I REALLY DO SOMETHING LIKE THAT?

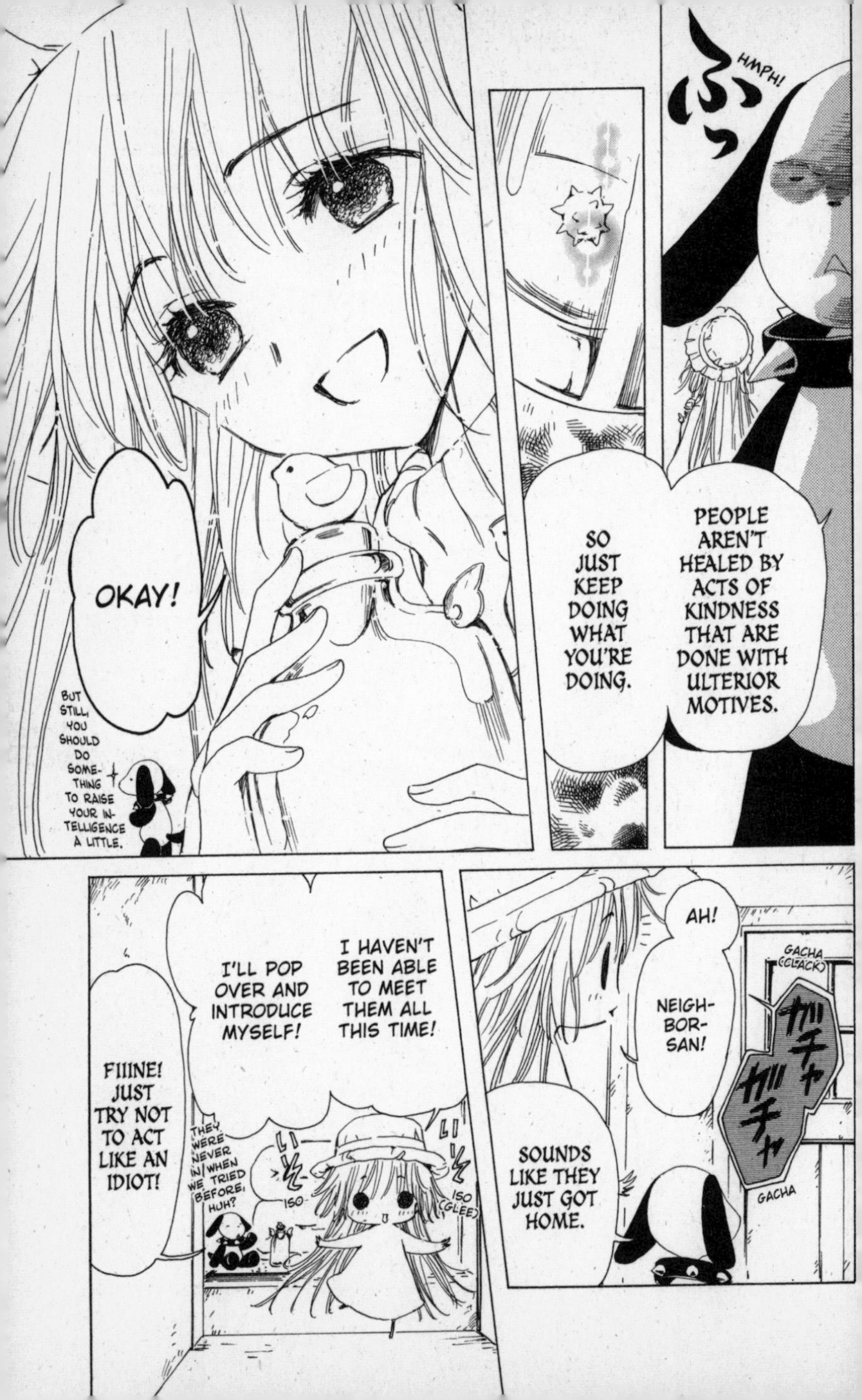
ふっ
HMPH!
PEOPLE AREN'T HEALED BY ACTS OF KINDNESS THAT ARE DONE WITH ULTERIOR MOTIVES.
SO JUST KEEP DOING WHAT YOU'RE DOING.
OKAY!
BUT STILL, YOU SHOULD DO SOME-THING TO RAISE YOUR IN-TELLIGENCE A LITTLE.
AH!
NEIGH-BOR-SAN!
ガチャ
ガチャ
GACHA (CLACK)
GACHA
SOUNDS LIKE THEY JUST GOT HOME.
I HAVEN'T BEEN ABLE TO MEET THEM ALL THIS TIME!
I'LL POP OVER AND INTRODUCE MYSELF!
ISO-
ISO (GLEE)
THEY WERE NEVER IN WHEN WE TRIED BEFORE, HUH?
FIIINE! JUST TRY NOT TO ACT LIKE AN IDIOT!

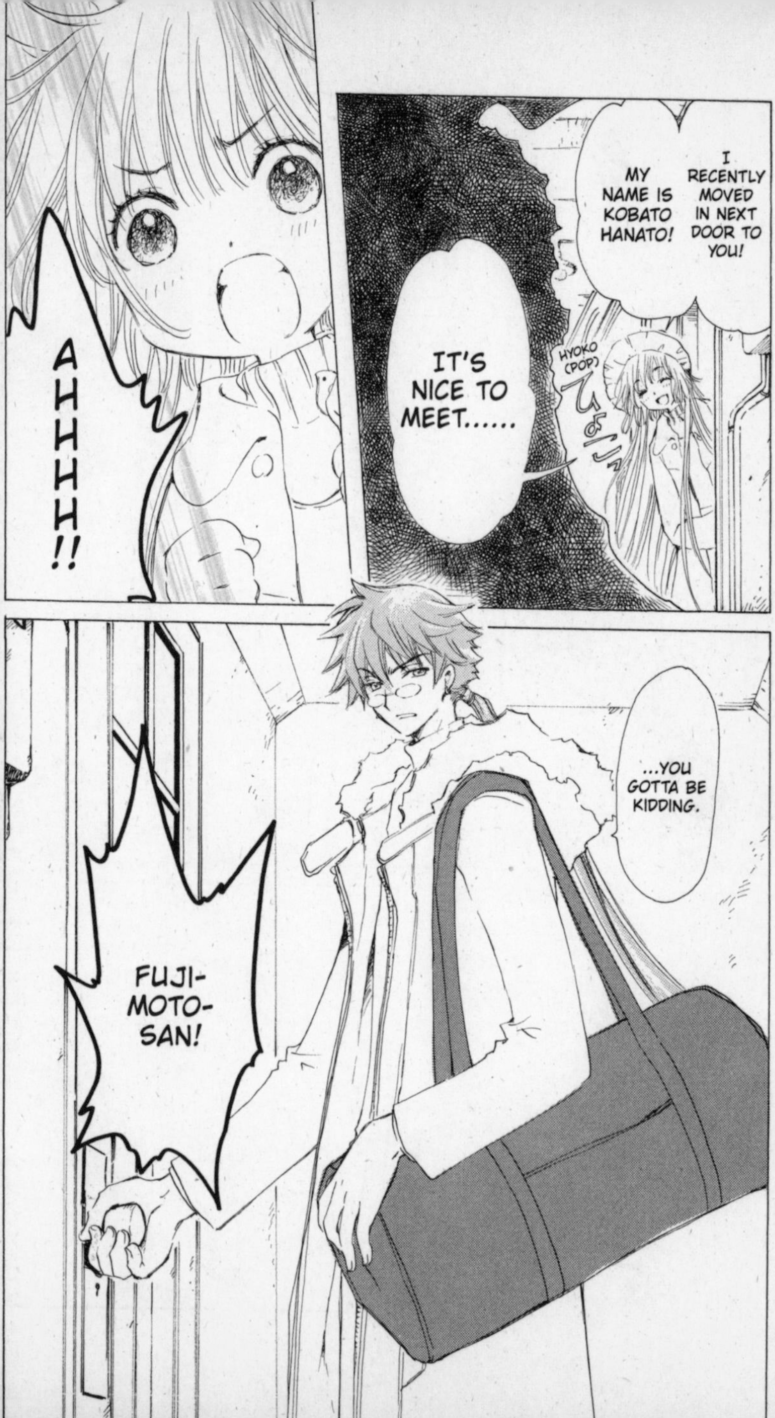
MY NAME IS KOBATO HANATO! I RECENTLY MOVED IN NEXT DOOR TO YOU!
HYOKO (POP)
ひょこ
IT'S NICE TO MEET......
AHHHHH!!
...YOU GOTTA BE KIDDING.
FUJI-MOTO-SAN!

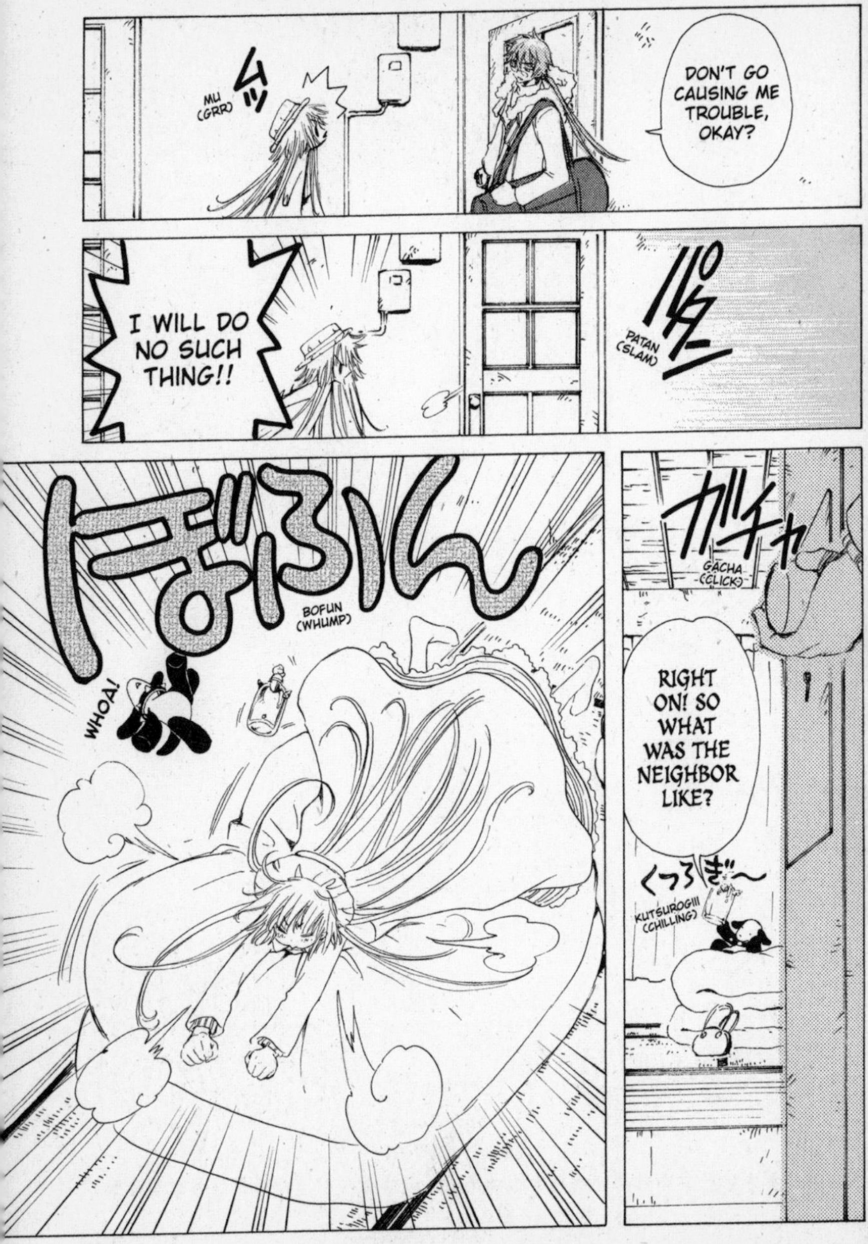
DON'T GO CAUSING ME TROUBLE, OKAY?
ムッ
MU (GRR)
パタン
PATAN (SLAM)
I WILL DO NO SUCH THING!!
ガチャ
GACHA (CLICK)
RIGHT ON! SO WHAT WAS THE NEIGHBOR LIKE?
くつろぎ～
KUTSUROGIII (CHILLING)
ぼふん
BOFUN (WHUMP)
WHOA!

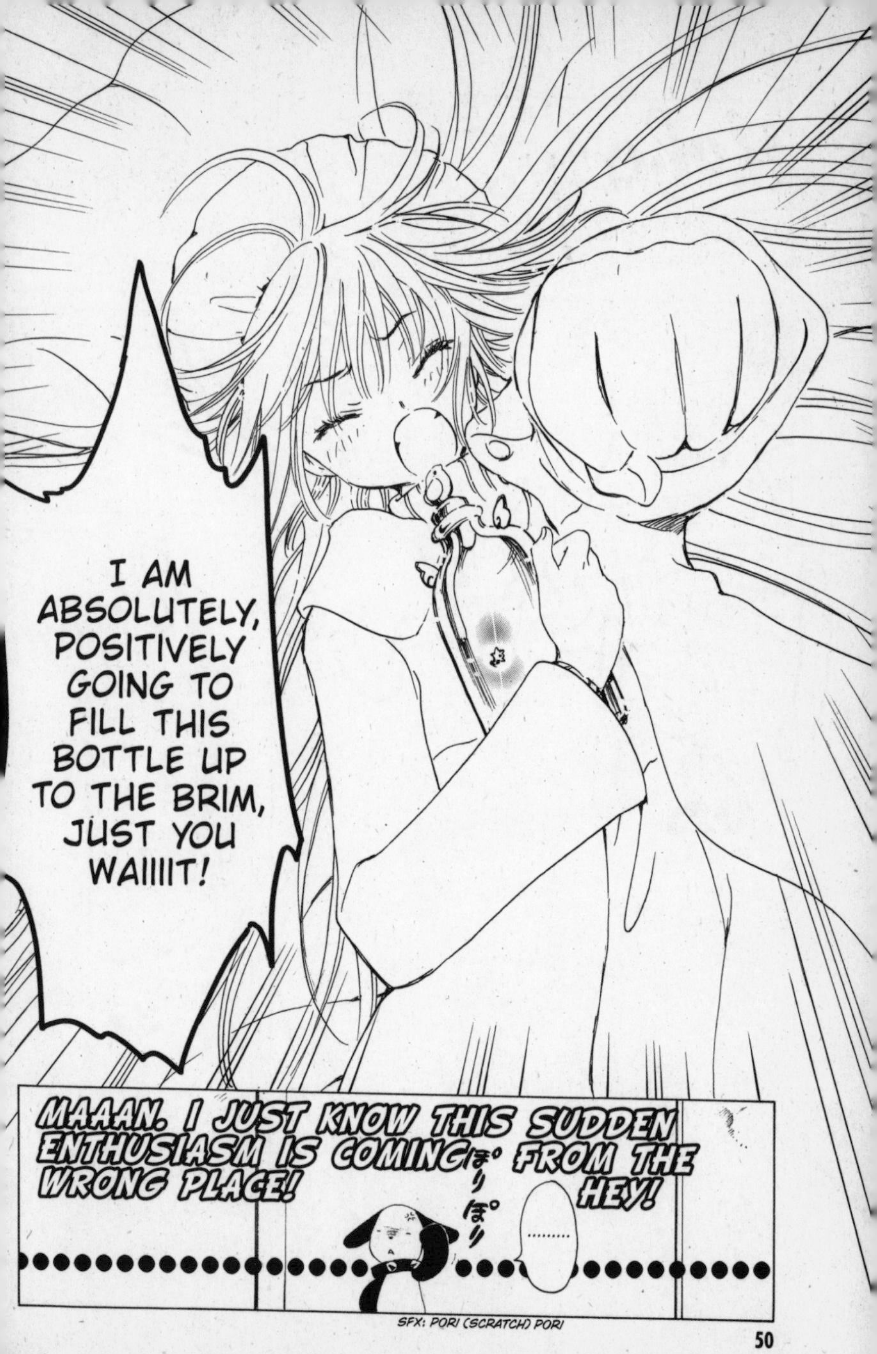
I AM ABSOLUTELY, POSITIVELY GOING TO FILL THIS BOTTLE UP TO THE BRIM, JUST YOU WAIIIIT!
HEY!
....
ぽりぽり
MAAAN. I JUST KNOW THIS SUDDEN ENTHUSIASM IS COMING FROM THE WRONG PLACE!
••••••••••••••••••••••••••••••••••••••
SFX: PORI (SCRATCH) PORI

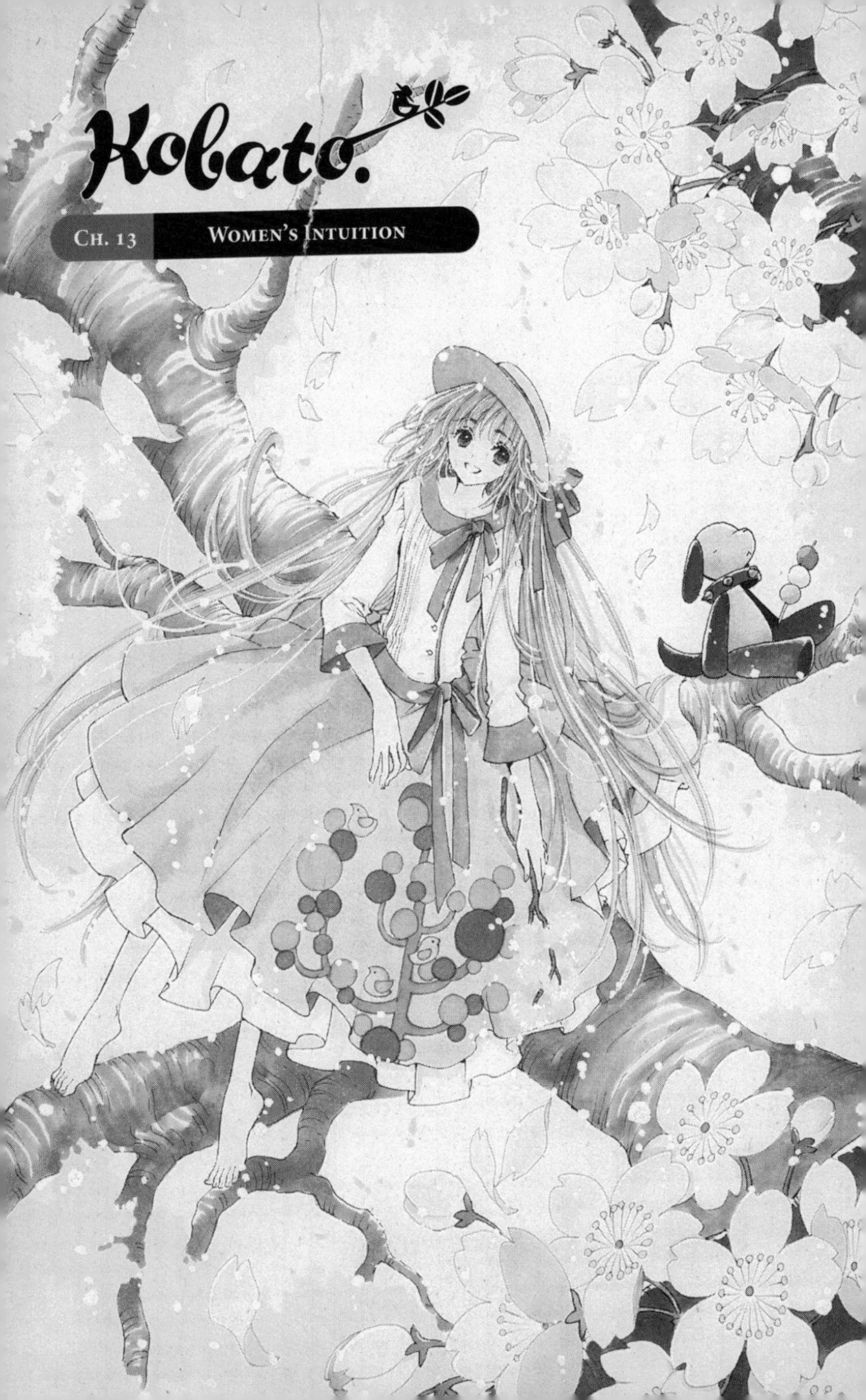
Kobato.
Ch. 13
Women's Intuition

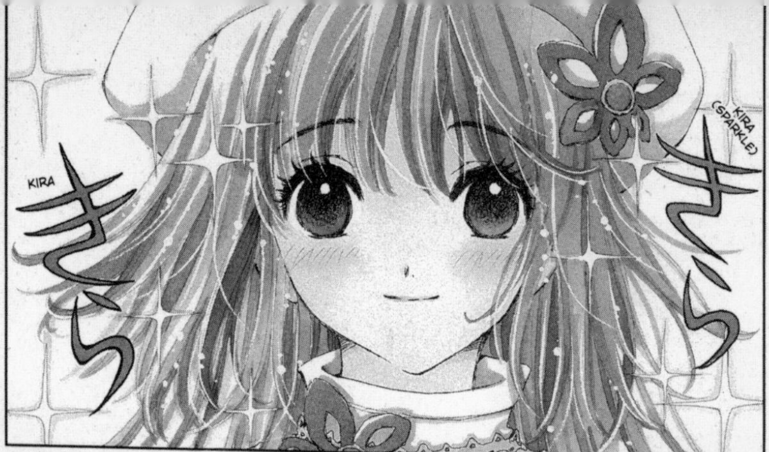
きら
KIRA (SPARKLE)
きら
KIRA

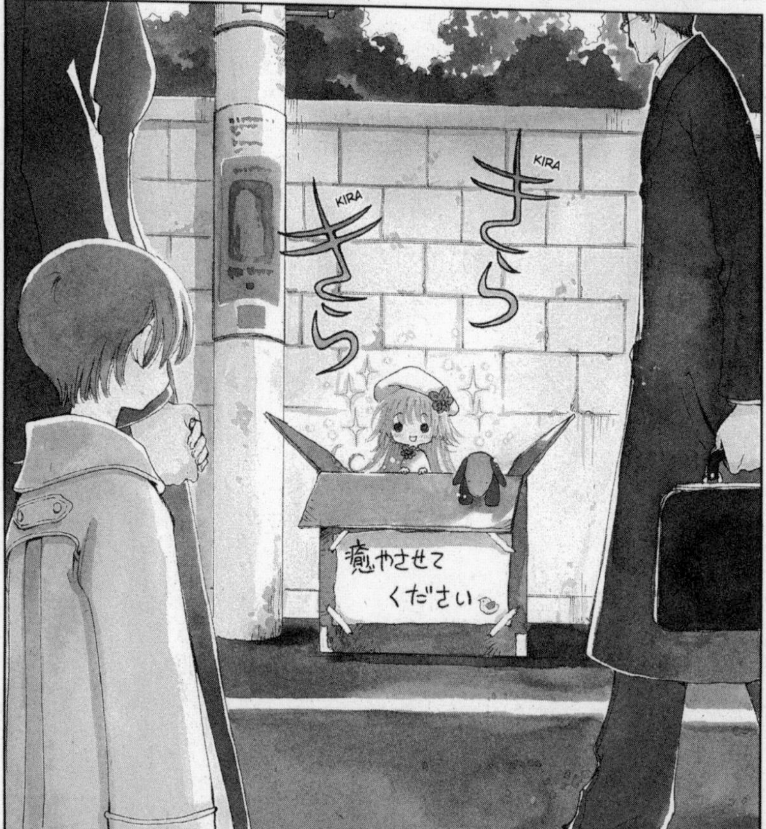
きら
KIRA
きら
KIRA
癒やさせて
ください

BOX: PLEASE LET ME HEAL YOU!

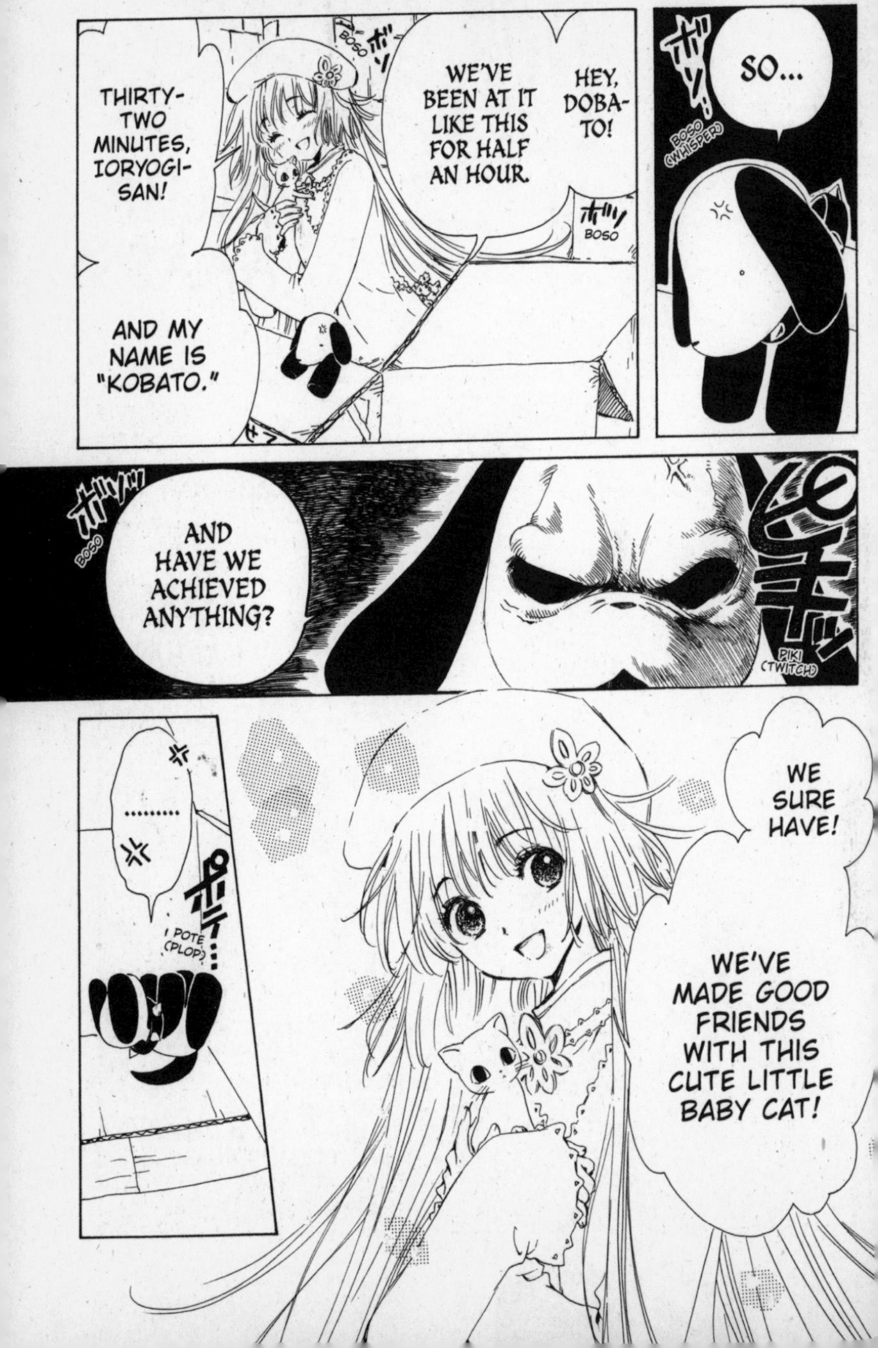
SO...
BOSO (WHISPER)
HEY, DOBA-TO!
BOSO
WE'VE BEEN AT IT LIKE THIS FOR HALF AN HOUR.
BOSO
THIRTY-TWO MINUTES, IORYOGI-SAN!
AND MY NAME IS "KOBATO."
PIKI (TWITCH)
BOSO
AND HAVE WE ACHIEVED ANYTHING?
WE SURE HAVE!
WE'VE MADE GOOD FRIENDS WITH THIS CUTE LITTLE BABY CAT!
....
POTE (PLOP)

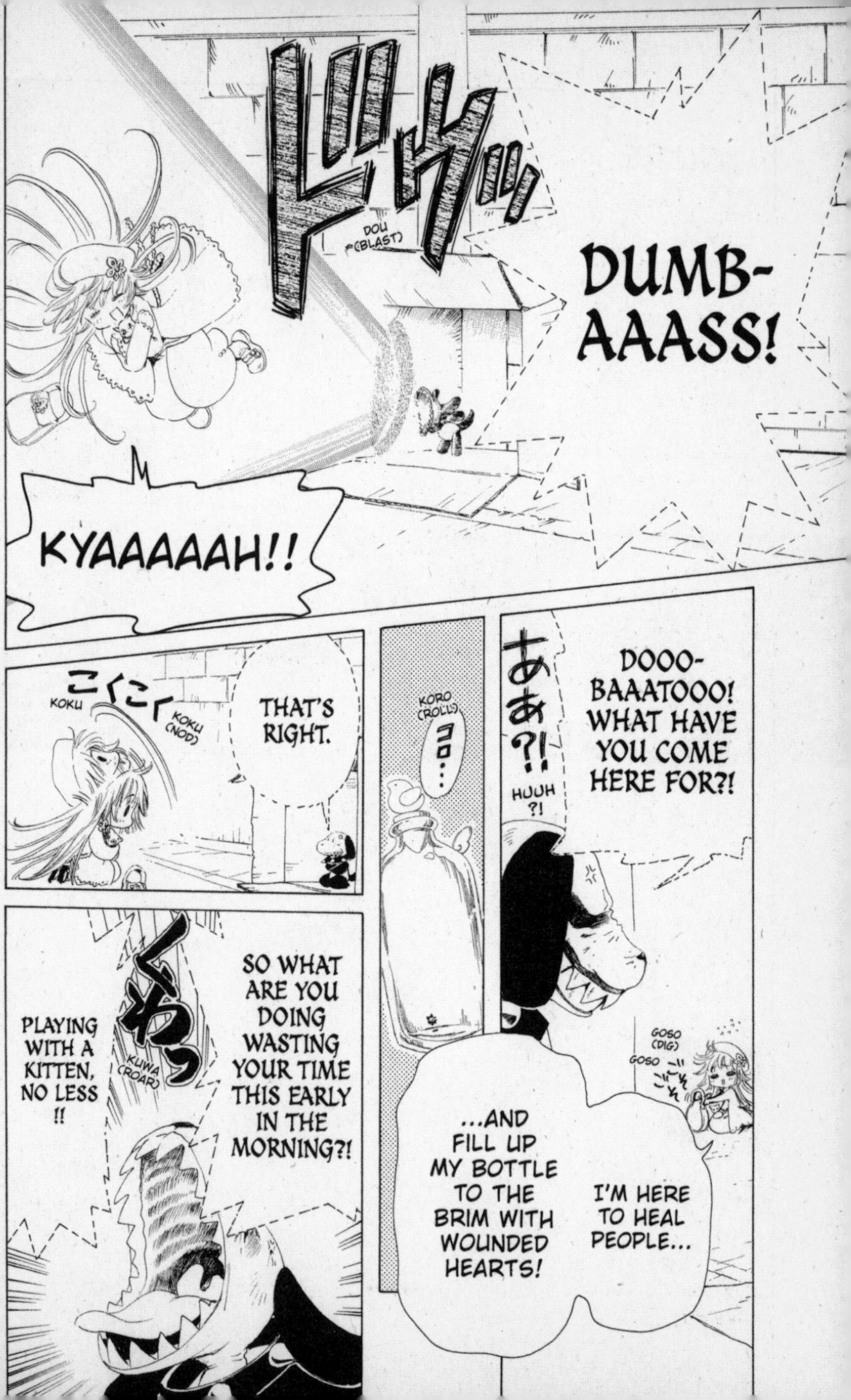
ドゥッ
DOU (BLAST)
DUMB-AAASS!
KYAAAAAH!!
あぁ?!
HUUH ?!
DOOO-BAAATOOO! WHAT HAVE YOU COME HERE FOR?!
ごそごそ
GOSO (DIG) GOSO
I'M HERE TO HEAL PEOPLE...
...AND FILL UP MY BOTTLE TO THE BRIM WITH WOUNDED HEARTS!
コロ…
KORO (ROLL)
THAT'S RIGHT.
こくこく
KOKU KOKU (NOD)
SO WHAT ARE YOU DOING WASTING YOUR TIME THIS EARLY IN THE MORNING?!
くわっ
KUWA (ROAR)
PLAYING WITH A KITTEN, NO LESS!!

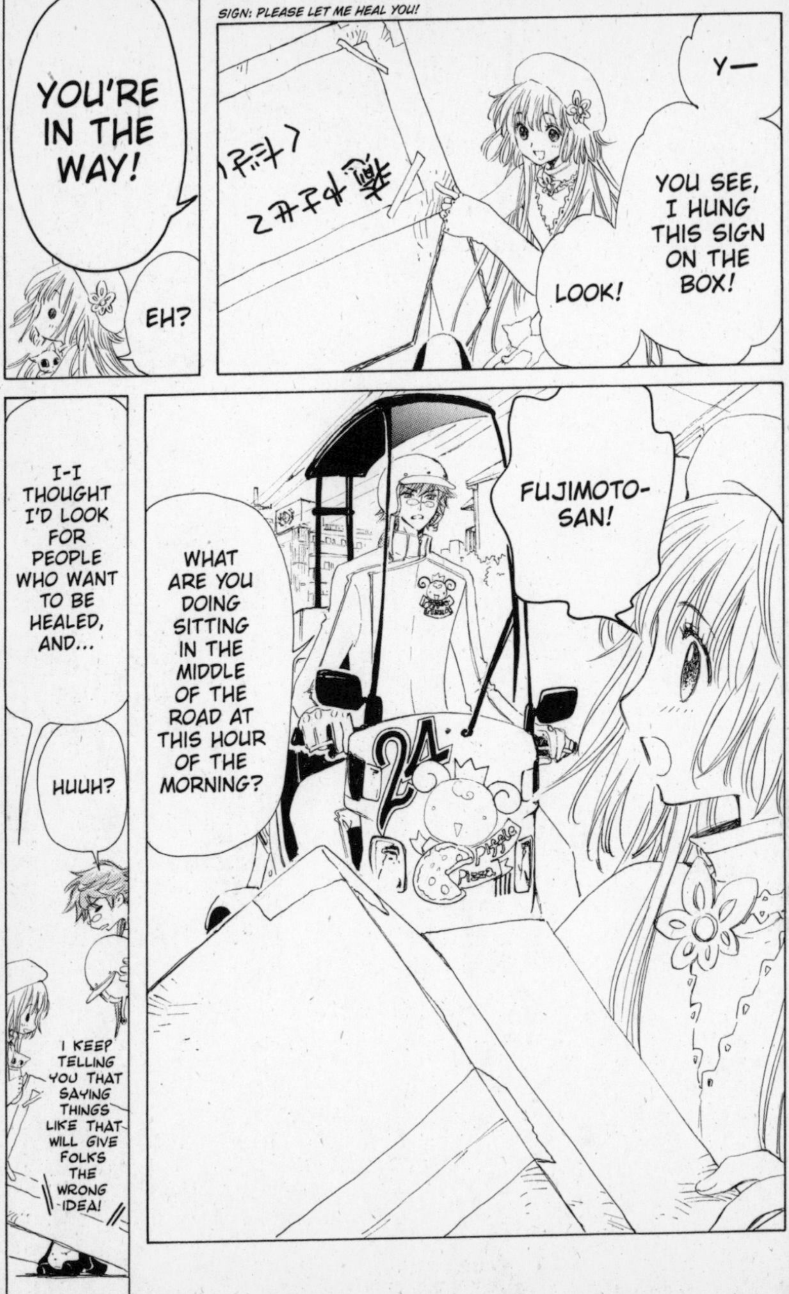
SIGN: PLEASE LET ME HEAL YOU!
Y—
YOU SEE, I HUNG THIS SIGN ON THE BOX!
LOOK!
YOU'RE IN THE WAY!
EH?
FUJIMOTO-SAN!
WHAT ARE YOU DOING SITTING IN THE MIDDLE OF THE ROAD AT THIS HOUR OF THE MORNING?
I-I THOUGHT I'D LOOK FOR PEOPLE WHO WANT TO BE HEALED, AND...
HUUH?
I KEEP TELLING YOU THAT SAYING THINGS LIKE THAT WILL GIVE FOLKS THE WRONG IDEA!

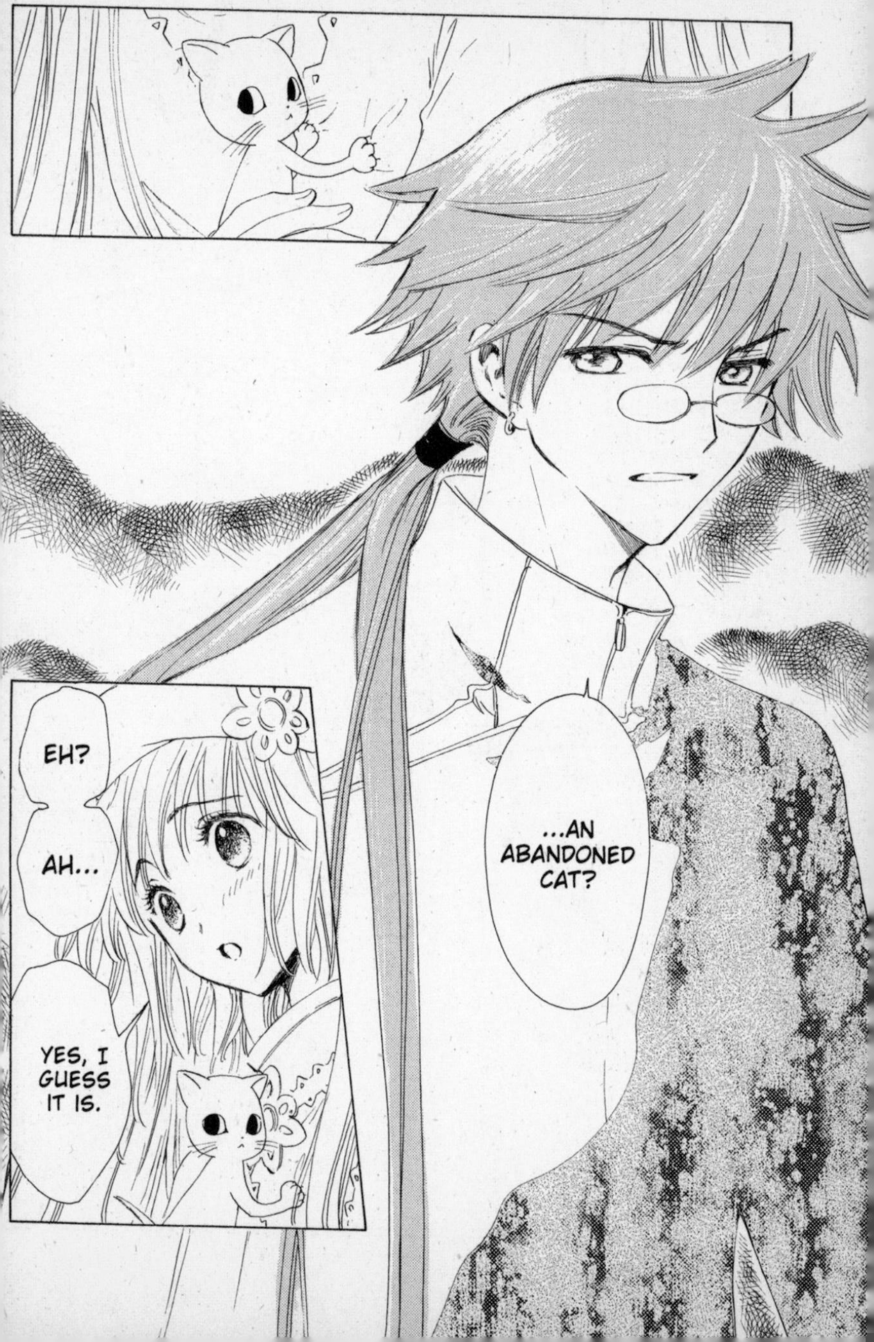
...AN ABANDONED CAT?
EH?
AH...
YES, I GUESS IT IS.

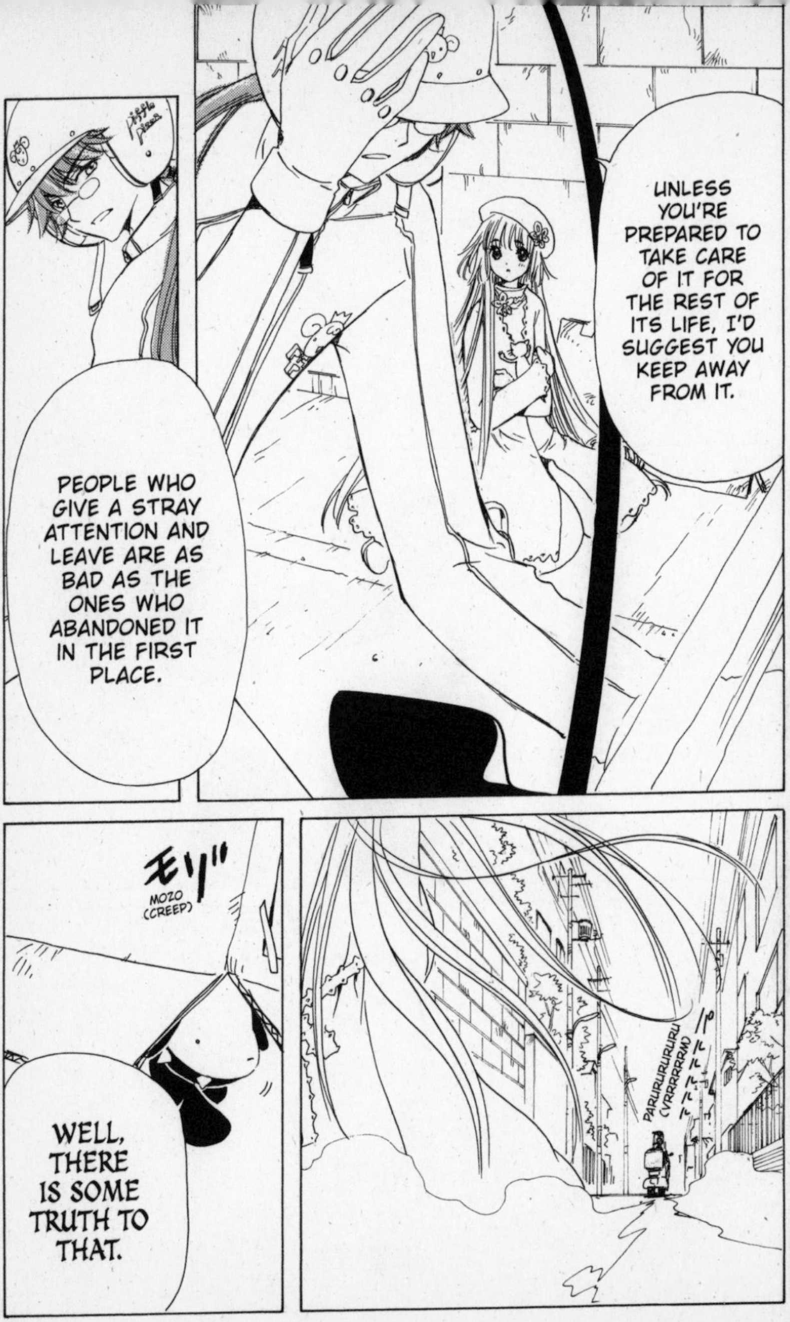

UNLESS YOU'RE PREPARED TO TAKE CARE OF IT FOR THE REST OF ITS LIFE, I'D SUGGEST YOU KEEP AWAY FROM IT.
PEOPLE WHO GIVE A STRAY ATTENTION AND LEAVE ARE AS BAD AS THE ONES WHO ABANDONED IT IN THE FIRST PLACE.
パルルルルルル
PARURURURURU (VRRRRRRM)
モゾ
MOZO (CREEP)
WELL, THERE IS SOME TRUTH TO THAT.

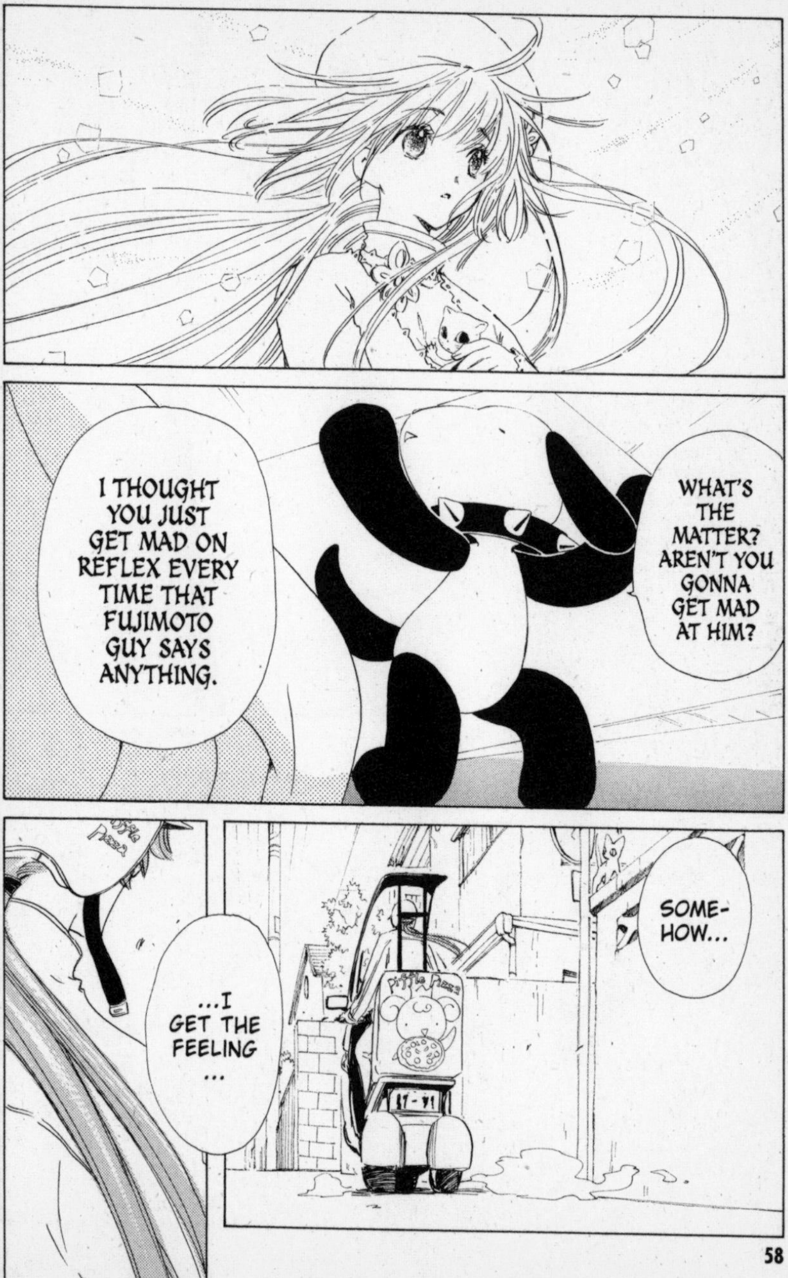
WHAT'S THE MATTER? AREN'T YOU GONNA GET MAD AT HIM?
I THOUGHT YOU JUST GET MAD ON REFLEX EVERY TIME THAT FUJIMOTO GUY SAYS ANYTHING.
SOME-HOW...
...I GET THE FEELING ...

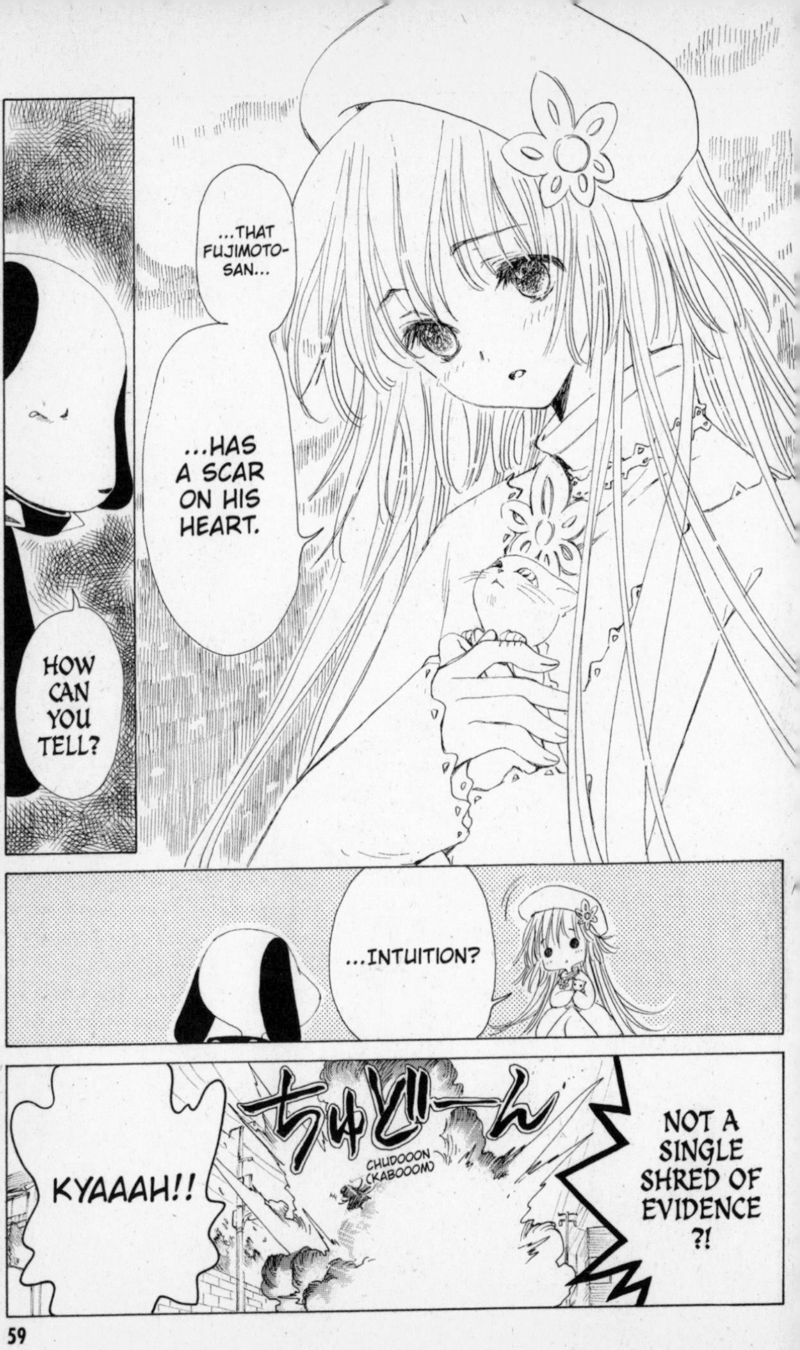
...THAT FUJIMOTO-SAN...
...HAS A SCAR ON HIS HEART.
HOW CAN YOU TELL?
...INTUITION?
NOT A SINGLE SHRED OF EVIDENCE ?!
ちゅどーん
CHUDOOON (KABOOOM)
KYAAAH!!

SIGN: YOMOGI KINDERGARTEN

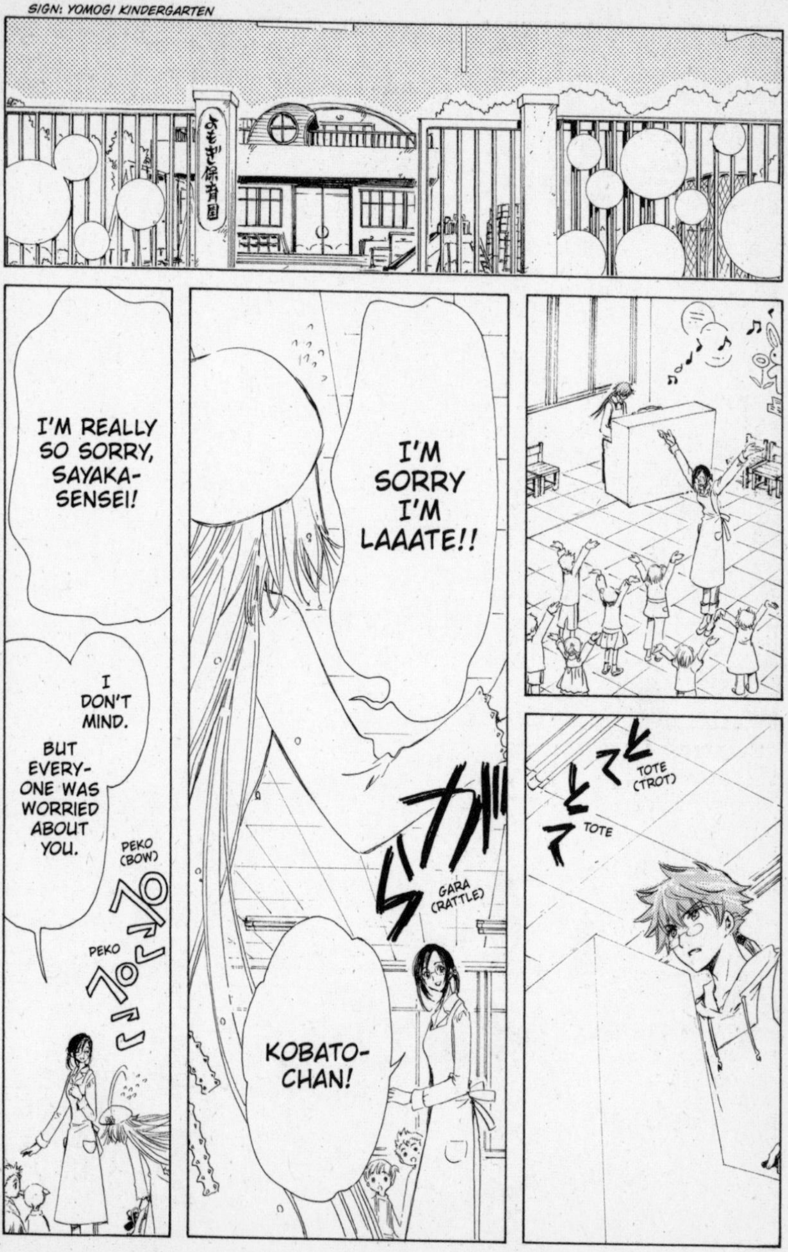

よもぎ保育園
TOTE (TROT)
TOTE
I'M SORRY I'M LAAATE!!
GARA (RATTLE)
KOBATO-CHAN!
I'M REALLY SO SORRY, SAYAKA-SENSEI!
I DON'T MIND.
BUT EVERYONE WAS WORRIED ABOUT YOU.
PEKO (BOW)
PEKO

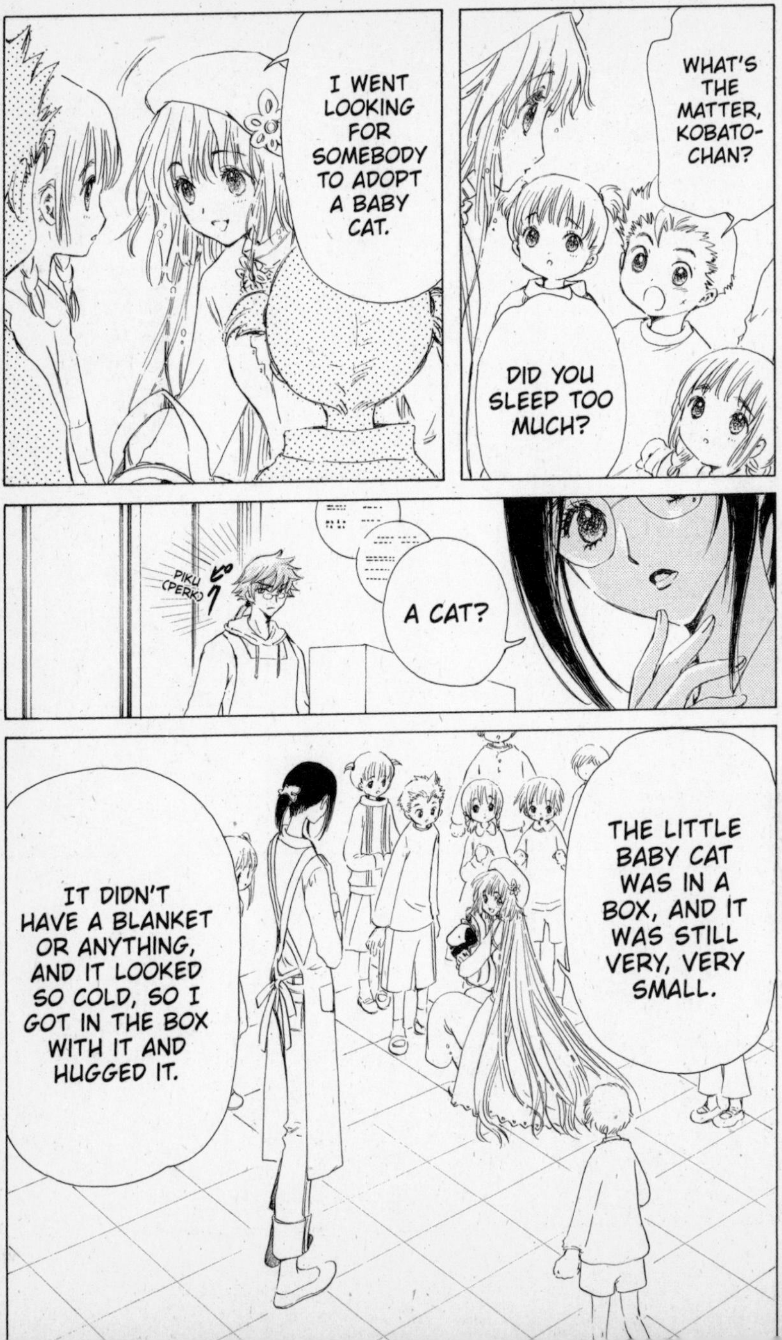
WHAT'S THE MATTER, KOBATO-CHAN?
DID YOU SLEEP TOO MUCH?
I WENT LOOKING FOR SOMEBODY TO ADOPT A BABY CAT.
A CAT?
PIKU (PERK)
THE LITTLE BABY CAT WAS IN A BOX, AND IT WAS STILL VERY, VERY SMALL.
IT DIDN'T HAVE A BLANKET OR ANYTHING, AND IT LOOKED SO COLD, SO I GOT IN THE BOX WITH IT AND HUGGED IT.

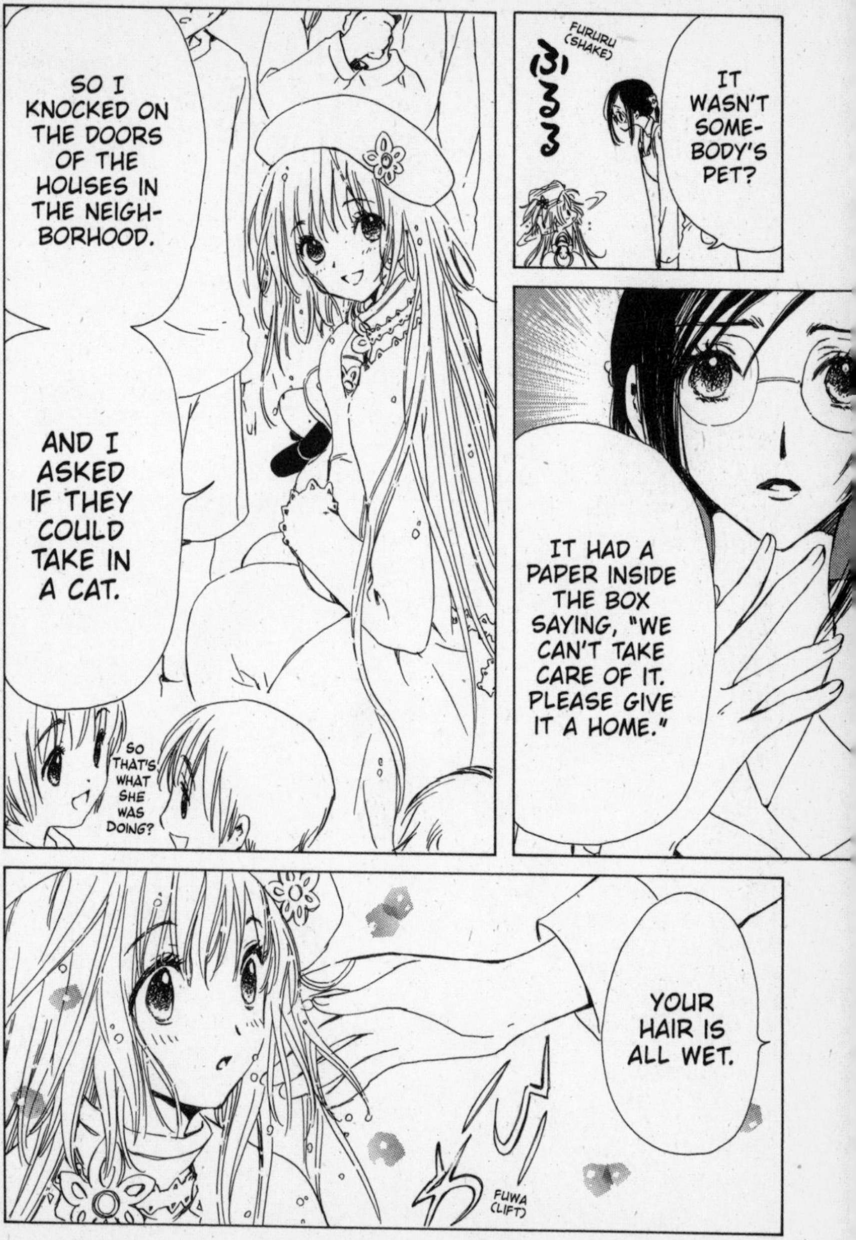
FURURU (SHAKE)
IT WASN'T SOME-BODY'S PET?
IT HAD A PAPER INSIDE THE BOX SAYING, "WE CAN'T TAKE CARE OF IT. PLEASE GIVE IT A HOME."
SO I KNOCKED ON THE DOORS OF THE HOUSES IN THE NEIGH-BORHOOD.
AND I ASKED IF THEY COULD TAKE IN A CAT.
SO THAT'S WHAT SHE WAS DOING?
YOUR HAIR IS ALL WET.
FUWA (LIFT)

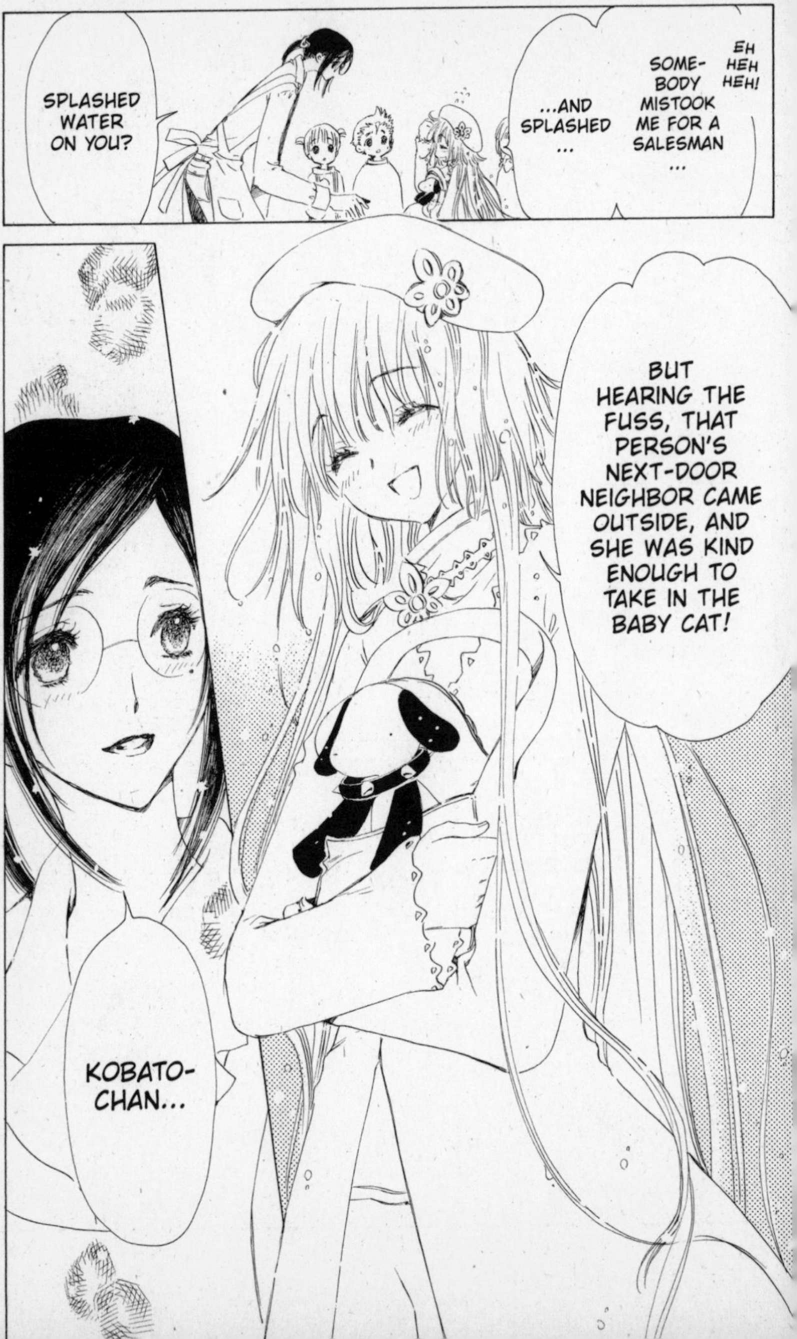
EH HEH HEH!
SOME-BODY MISTOOK ME FOR A SALESMAN ...
...AND SPLASHED ...
SPLASHED WATER ON YOU?
BUT HEARING THE FUSS, THAT PERSON'S NEXT-DOOR NEIGHBOR CAME OUTSIDE, AND SHE WAS KIND ENOUGH TO TAKE IN THE BABY CAT!
KOBATO-CHAN...

SFX: GYUMU (HUG) GYUMU

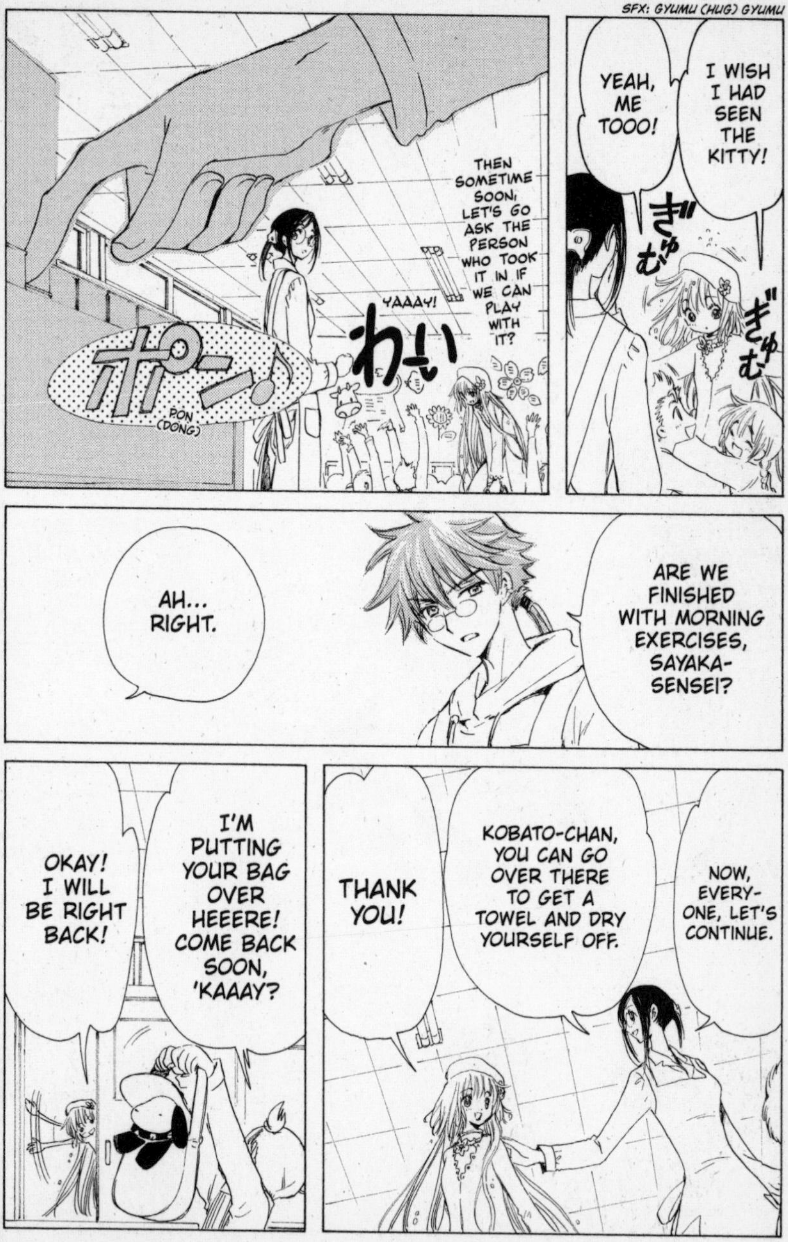
I WISH I HAD SEEN THE KITTY!
YEAH, ME TOOO!
ぎゅむ
ぎゅむ
THEN SOMETIME SOON, LET'S GO ASK THE PERSON WHO TOOK IT IN IF WE CAN PLAY WITH IT?
YAAAY!
わーい
ポーン♪
PON (DONG)
ARE WE FINISHED WITH MORNING EXERCISES, SAYAKA-SENSEI?
AH... RIGHT.
NOW, EVERY-ONE, LET'S CONTINUE.
KOBATO-CHAN, YOU CAN GO OVER THERE TO GET A TOWEL AND DRY YOURSELF OFF.
THANK YOU!
I'M PUTTING YOUR BAG OVER HEEERE! COME BACK SOON, 'KAAAY?
OKAY! I WILL BE RIGHT BACK!

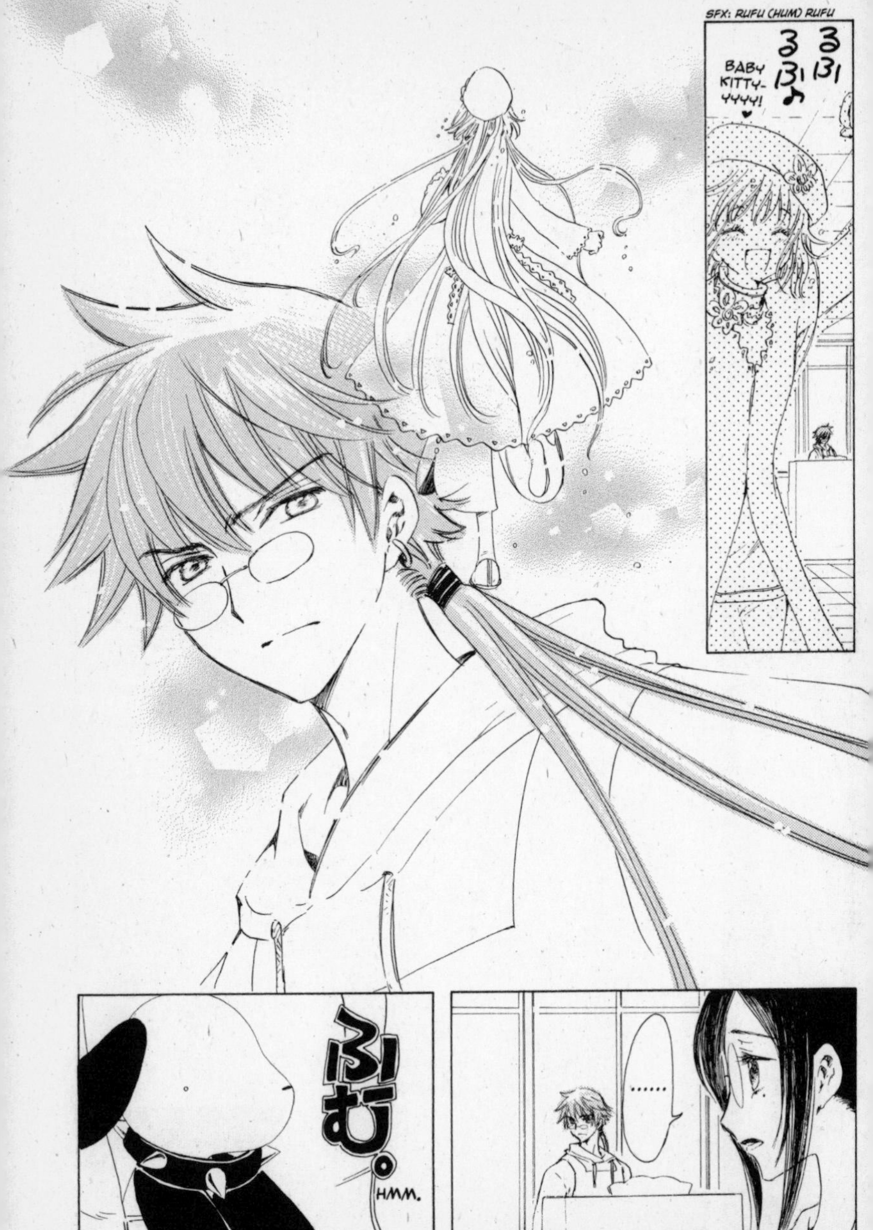
SFX: RUFU (HUM) RUFU
るふるふ♪
BABY KITTY-YYYY! ♥
......
ふむ。
HMM.

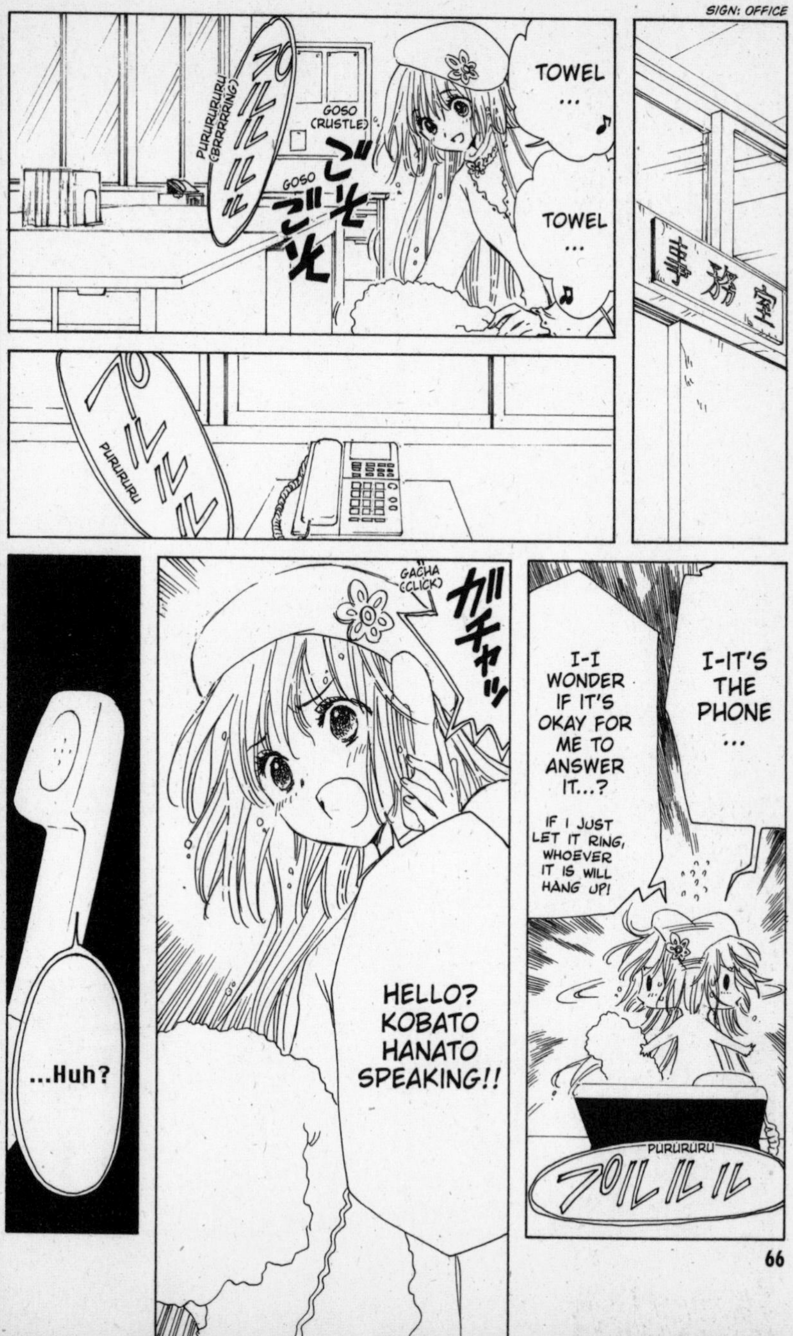
SIGN: OFFICE
事務室
TOWEL ... ♪
TOWEL ... ♪
PURURURURU (BRRRRRING)
GOSO (RUSTLE)
GOSO
PURURURU
I-IT'S THE PHONE ...
I-I WONDER IF IT'S OKAY FOR ME TO ANSWER IT...?
IF I JUST LET IT RING, WHOEVER IT IS WILL HANG UP!
PURURURU
GACHA (CLICK)
HELLO? KOBATO HANATO SPEAKING!!
...Huh?

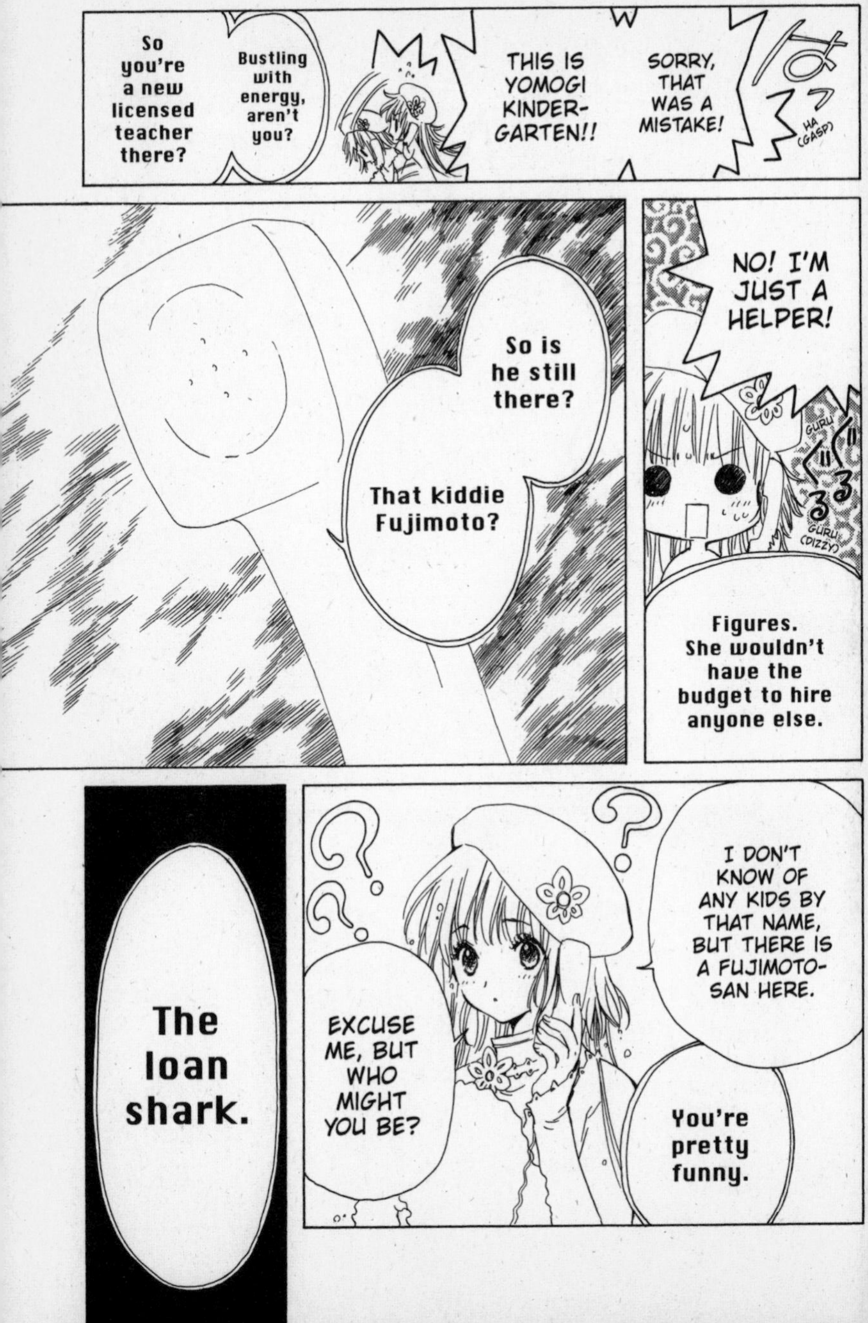
はっ
HA (GASP)
SORRY, THAT WAS A MISTAKE!
THIS IS YOMOGI KINDERGARTEN!!
Bustling with energy, aren't you?
So you're a new licensed teacher there?
NO! I'M JUST A HELPER!
ぐるぐる
GURU GURU (DIZZY)
Figures. She wouldn't have the budget to hire anyone else.
So is he still there?
That kiddie Fujimoto?
I DON'T KNOW OF ANY KIDS BY THAT NAME, BUT THERE IS A FUJIMOTO-SAN HERE.
You're pretty funny.
EXCUSE ME, BUT WHO MIGHT YOU BE?
The loan shark.

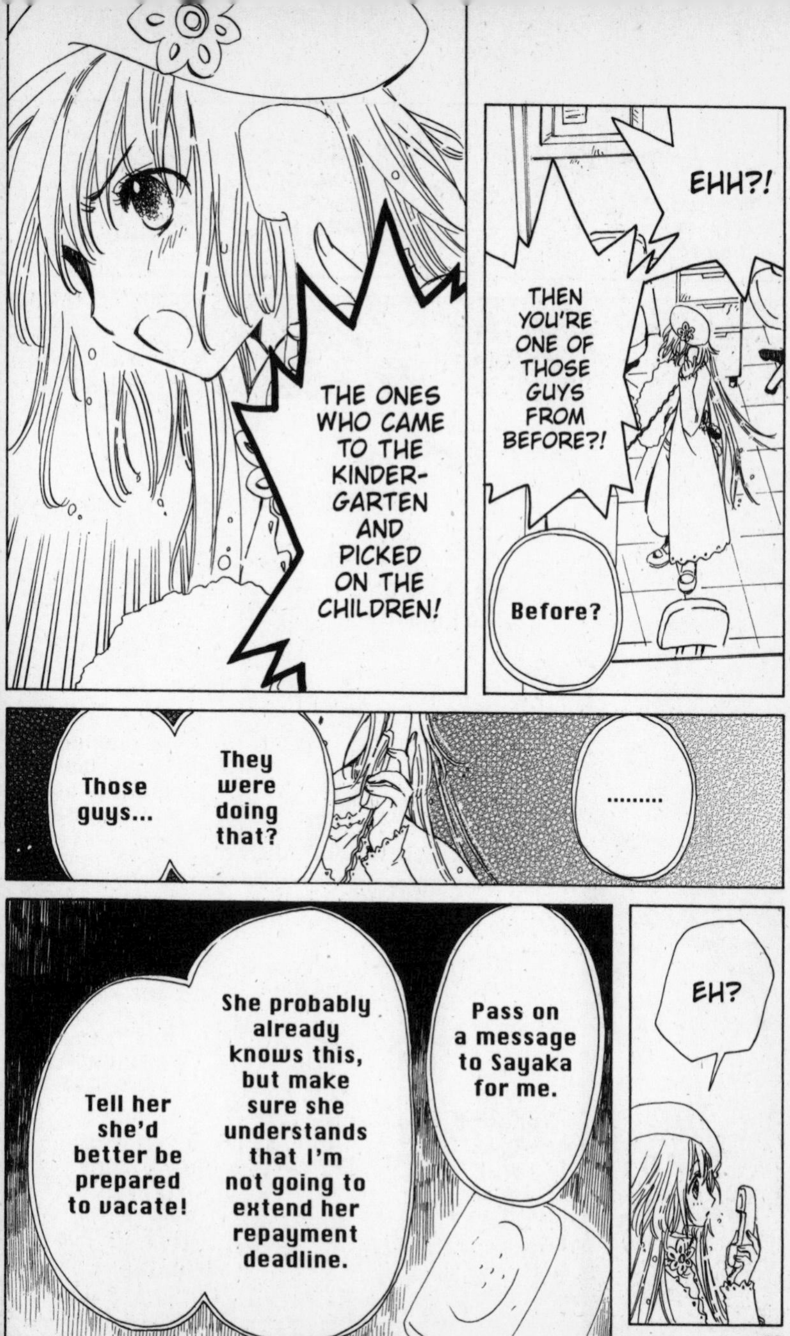
EHH?!
THEN YOU'RE ONE OF THOSE GUYS FROM BEFORE?!
Before?
THE ONES WHO CAME TO THE KINDER-GARTEN AND PICKED ON THE CHILDREN!
....
Those guys... They were doing that?
EH?
Pass on a message to Sayaka for me.
She probably already knows this, but make sure she understands that I'm not going to extend her repayment deadline.
Tell her she'd better be prepared to vacate!

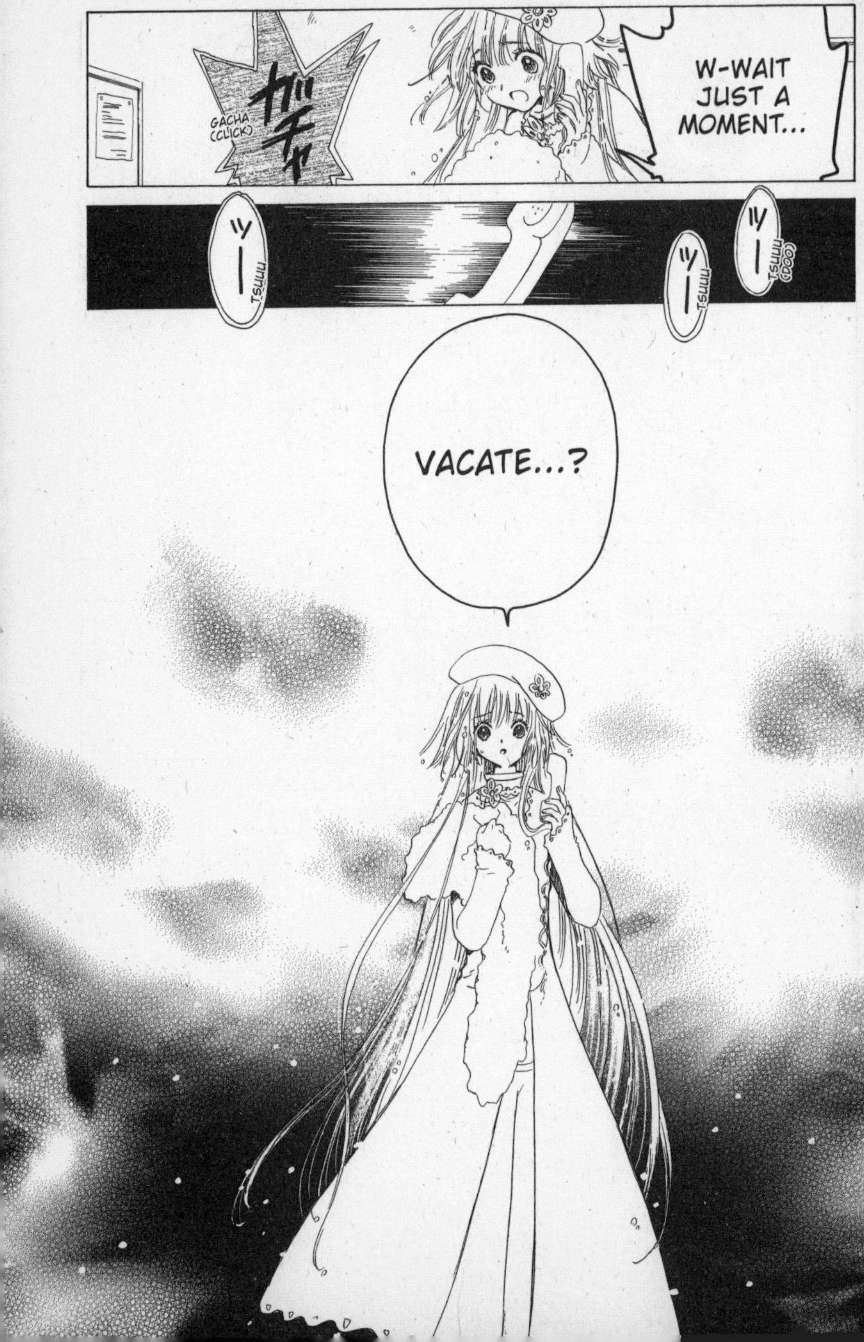

W-WAIT JUST A MOMENT...
ガチャ
GACHA (CLICK)
ツー
TSUUU (BOOO)
ツー
TSUUU
ツー
TSUUU
VACATE...?

SFX: TOBO (TRUDGE) TOBO

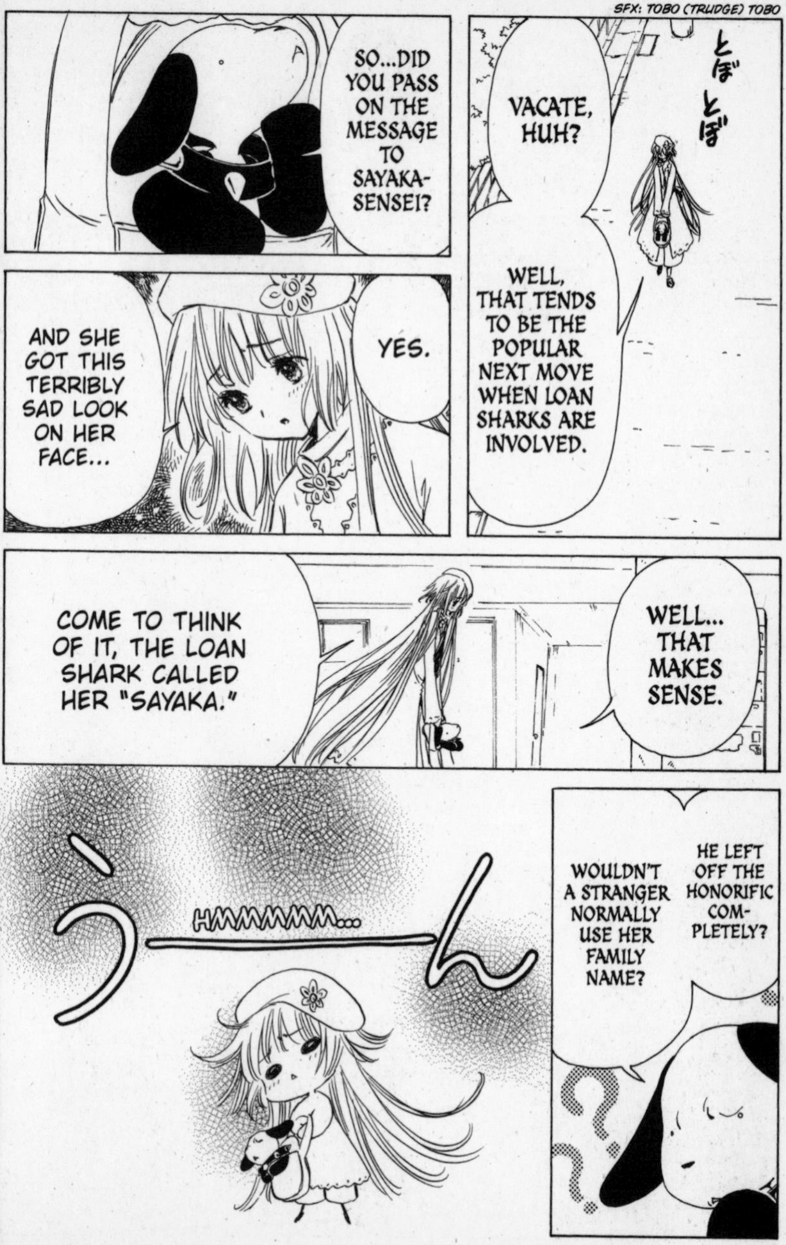

とぼ とぼ
VACATE, HUH?
WELL, THAT TENDS TO BE THE POPULAR NEXT MOVE WHEN LOAN SHARKS ARE INVOLVED.
SO...DID YOU PASS ON THE MESSAGE TO SAYAKA-SENSEI?
YES.
AND SHE GOT THIS TERRIBLY SAD LOOK ON HER FACE...
WELL... THAT MAKES SENSE.
COME TO THINK OF IT, THE LOAN SHARK CALLED HER "SAYAKA."
HE LEFT OFF THE HONORIFIC COM-PLETELY?
WOULDN'T A STRANGER NORMALLY USE HER FAMILY NAME?
うーん
HMMMMM...

SFX: TOTE (TROT) TOTE

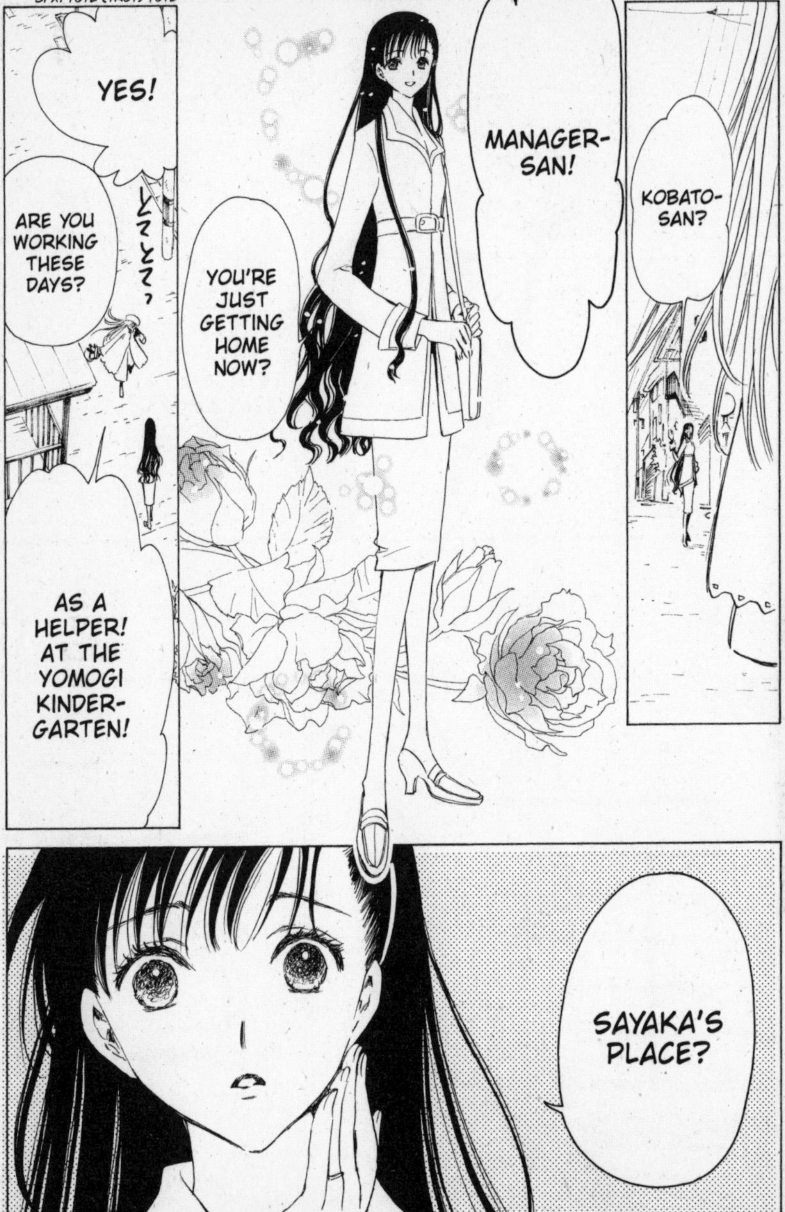
KOBATO-SAN?
MANAGER-SAN!
YOU'RE JUST GETTING HOME NOW?
YES!
ARE YOU WORKING THESE DAYS?
AS A HELPER! AT THE YOMOGI KINDERGARTEN!
SAYAKA'S PLACE?

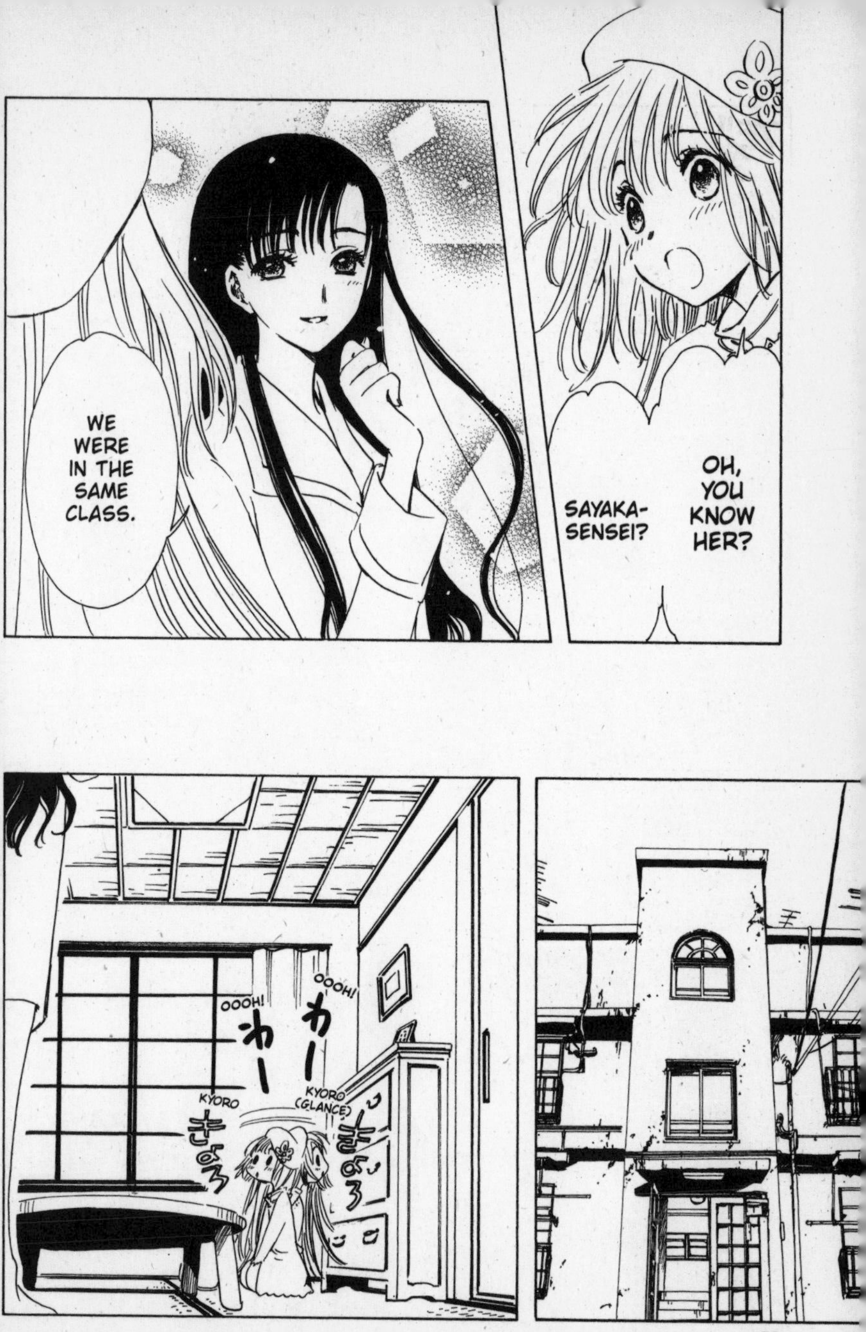
OH, YOU KNOW HER?
SAYAKA-SENSEI?
WE WERE IN THE SAME CLASS.
OOOH!
わー
OOOH!
わー
KYORO (GLANCE)
きょろ
KYORO
きょろ

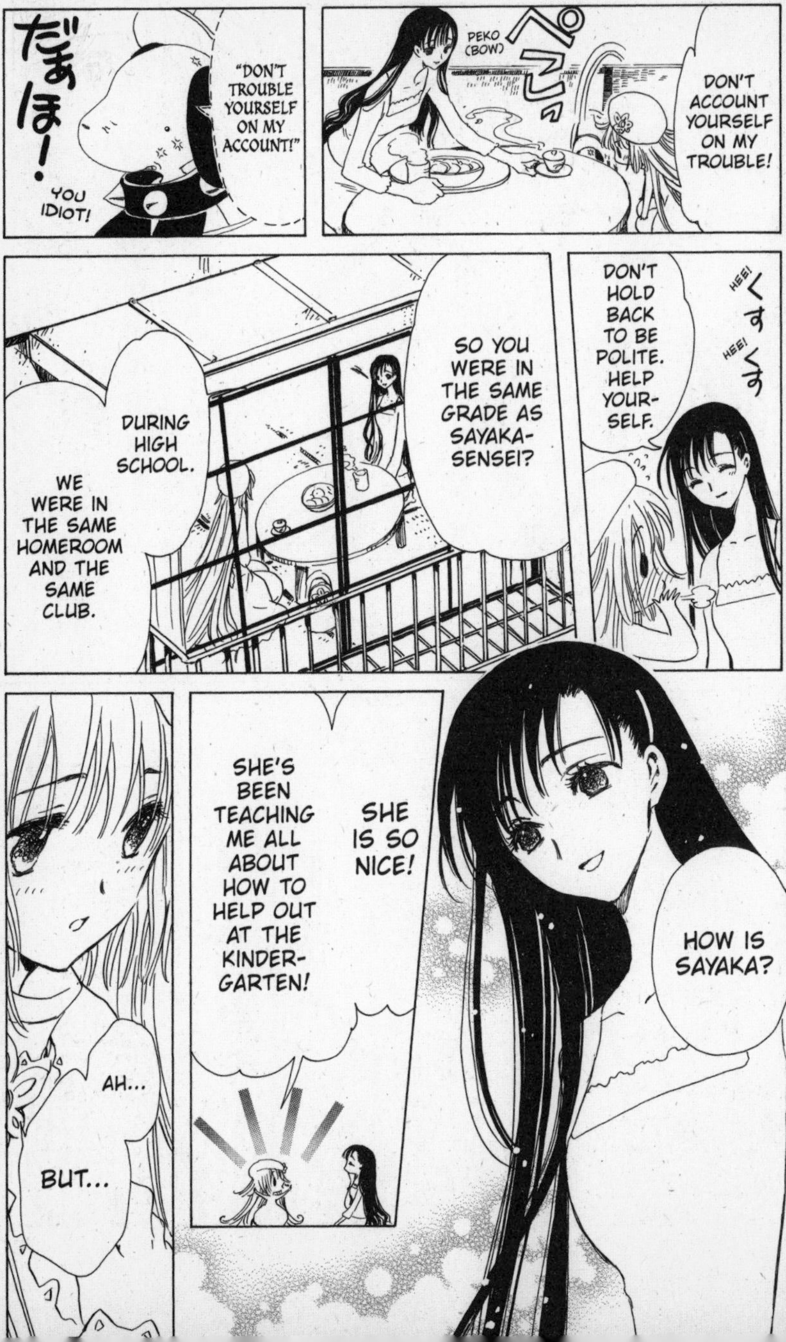
PEKO (BOW)
ペこっ
DON'T ACCOUNT YOURSELF ON MY TROUBLE!
だぁほ!
YOU IDIOT!
"DON'T TROUBLE YOURSELF ON MY ACCOUNT!"
くすくす
HEE! HEE!
DON'T HOLD BACK TO BE POLITE. HELP YOUR-SELF.
SO YOU WERE IN THE SAME GRADE AS SAYAKA-SENSEI?
DURING HIGH SCHOOL.
WE WERE IN THE SAME HOMEROOM AND THE SAME CLUB.
HOW IS SAYAKA?
SHE'S BEEN TEACHING ME ALL ABOUT HOW TO HELP OUT AT THE KINDER-GARTEN!
SHE IS SO NICE!
AH...
BUT...

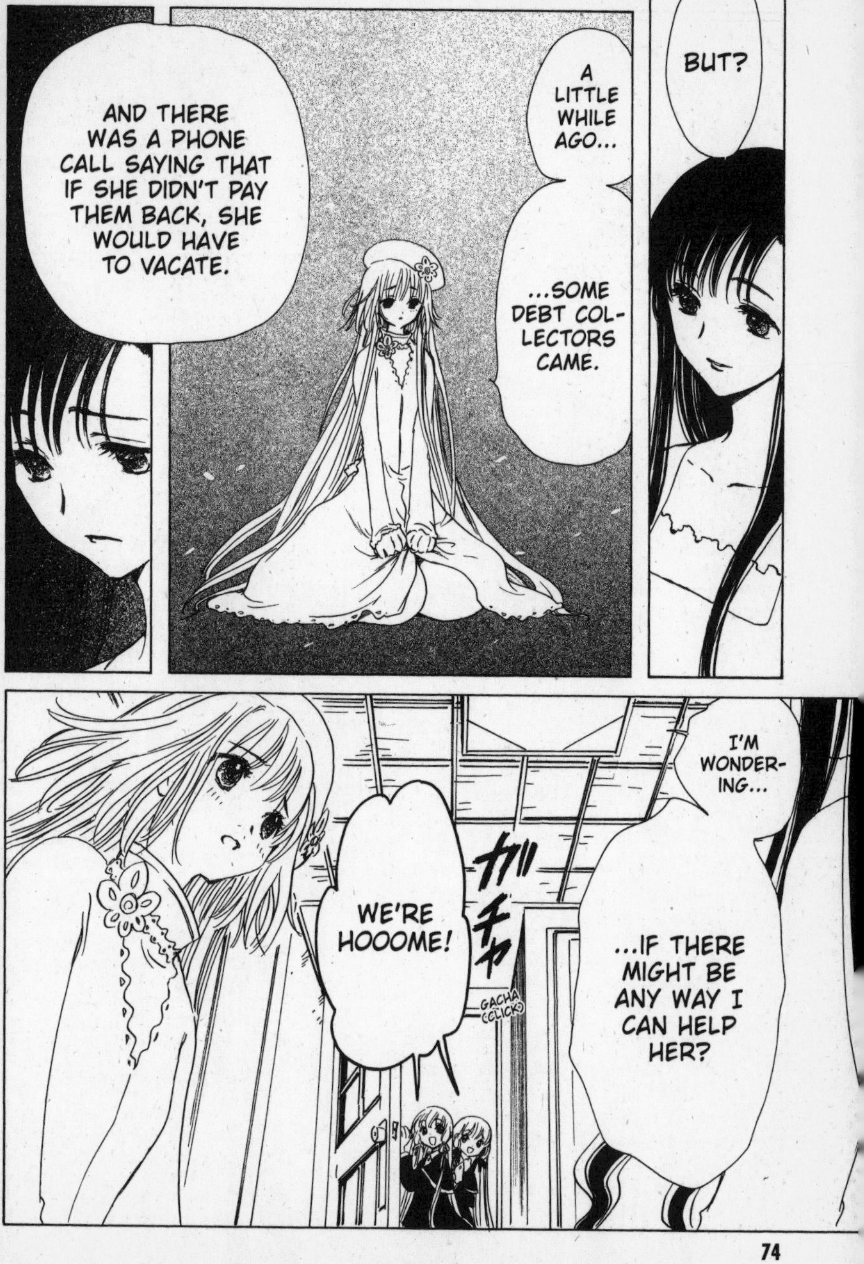
BUT?
A LITTLE WHILE AGO...
...SOME DEBT COL-LECTORS CAME.
AND THERE WAS A PHONE CALL SAYING THAT IF SHE DIDN'T PAY THEM BACK, SHE WOULD HAVE TO VACATE.
I'M WONDER-ING...
...IF THERE MIGHT BE ANY WAY I CAN HELP HER?
WE'RE HOOOME!
ガチャ
GACHA (CLICK)

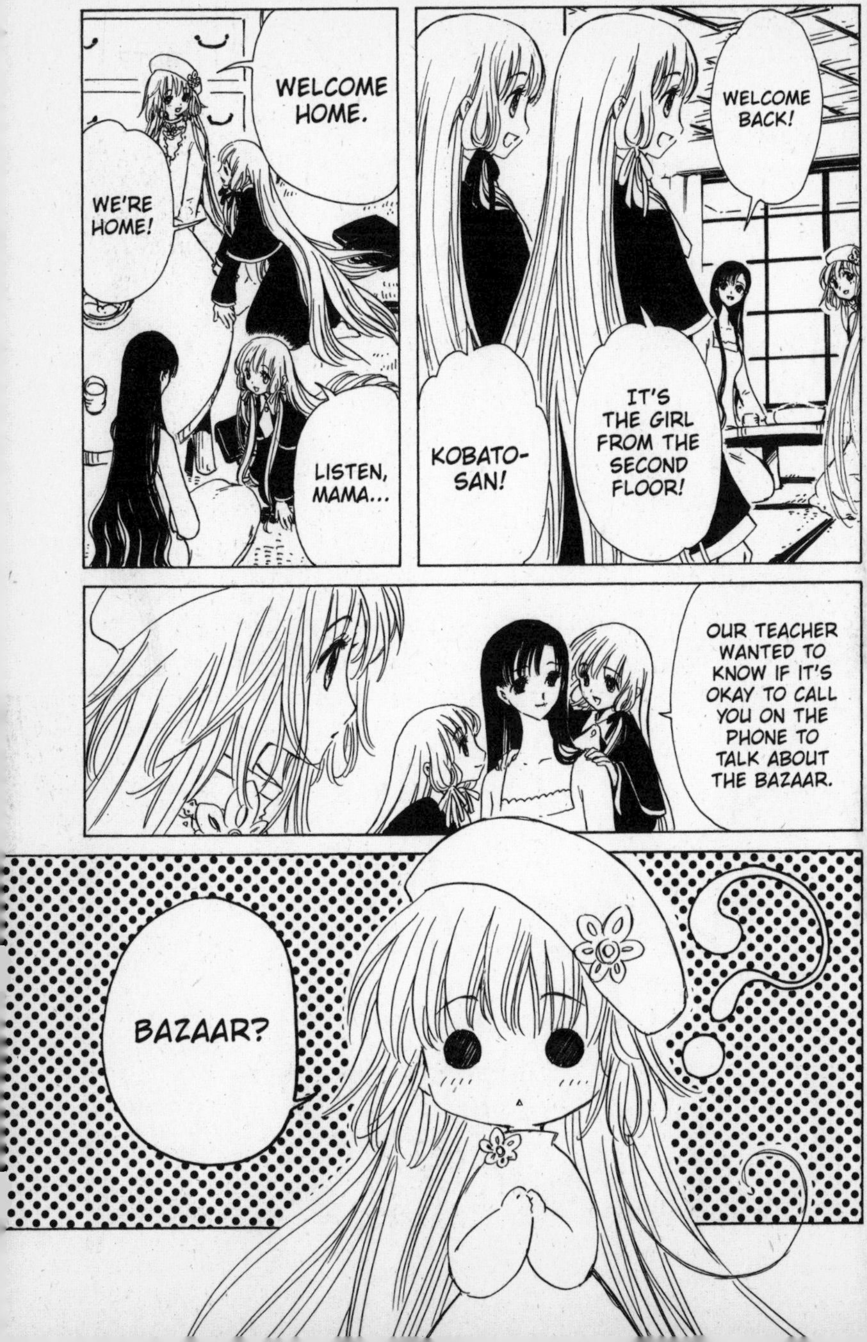
WELCOME BACK!
IT'S THE GIRL FROM THE SECOND FLOOR!
KOBATO-SAN!
WELCOME HOME.
WE'RE HOME!
LISTEN, MAMA...
OUR TEACHER WANTED TO KNOW IF IT'S OKAY TO CALL YOU ON THE PHONE TO TALK ABOUT THE BAZAAR.
BAZAAR?

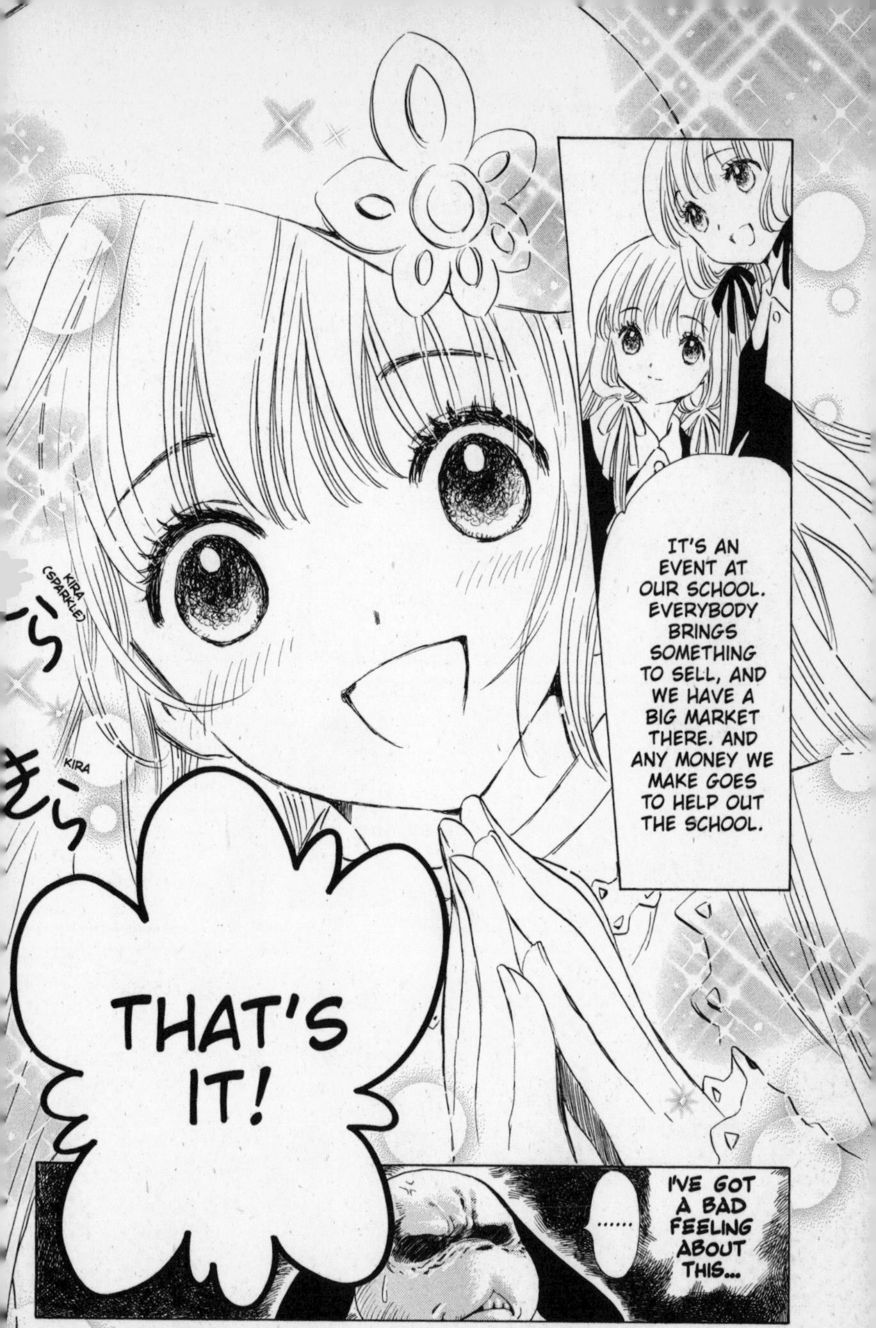
IT'S AN EVENT AT OUR SCHOOL. EVERYBODY BRINGS SOMETHING TO SELL, AND WE HAVE A BIG MARKET THERE. AND ANY MONEY WE MAKE GOES TO HELP OUT THE SCHOOL.
KIRA (SPARKLE)
KIRA
THAT'S IT!
......
I'VE GOT A BAD FEELING ABOUT THIS...

Kobato.

Ch. 14 Let's Have a Bazaar

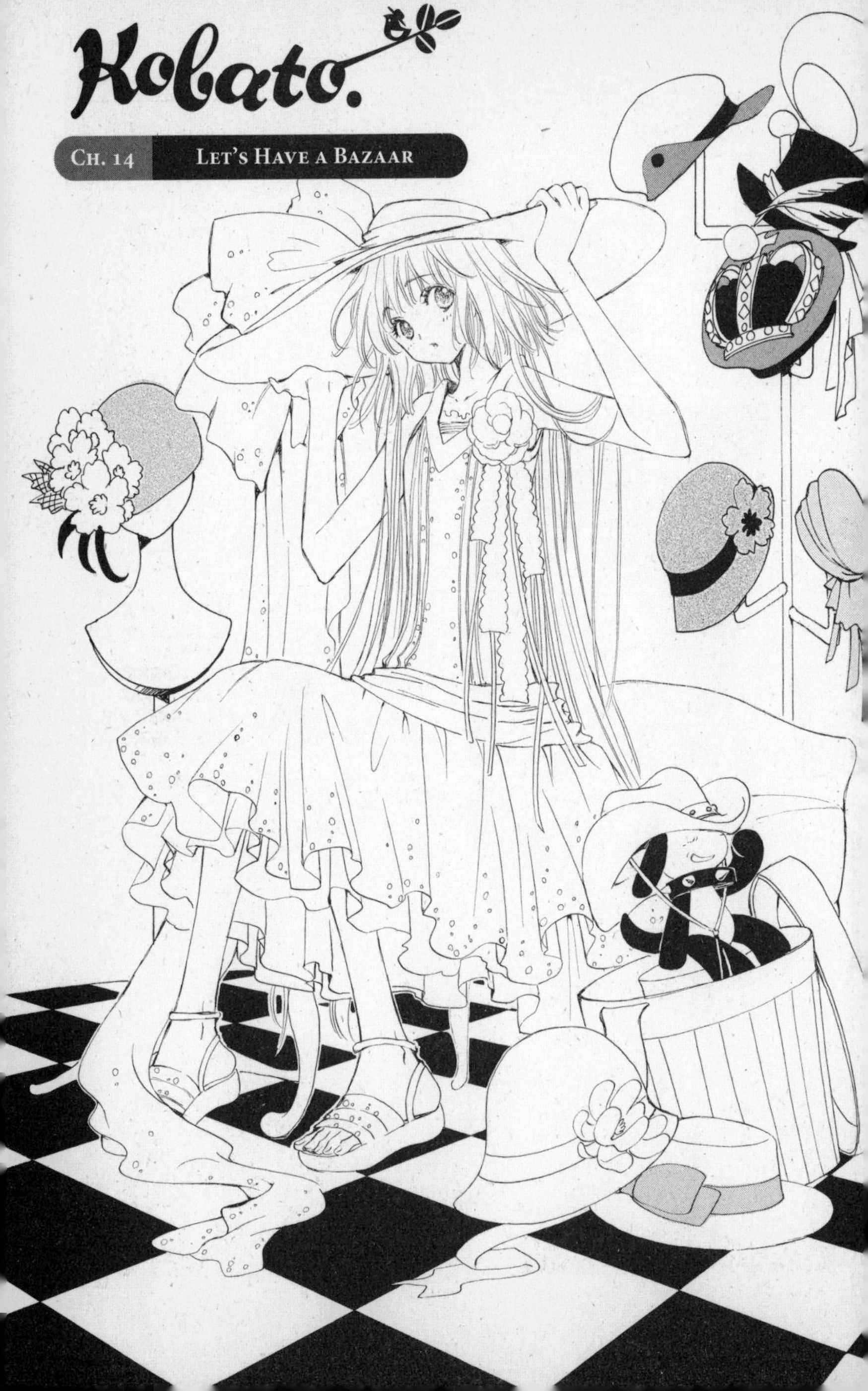

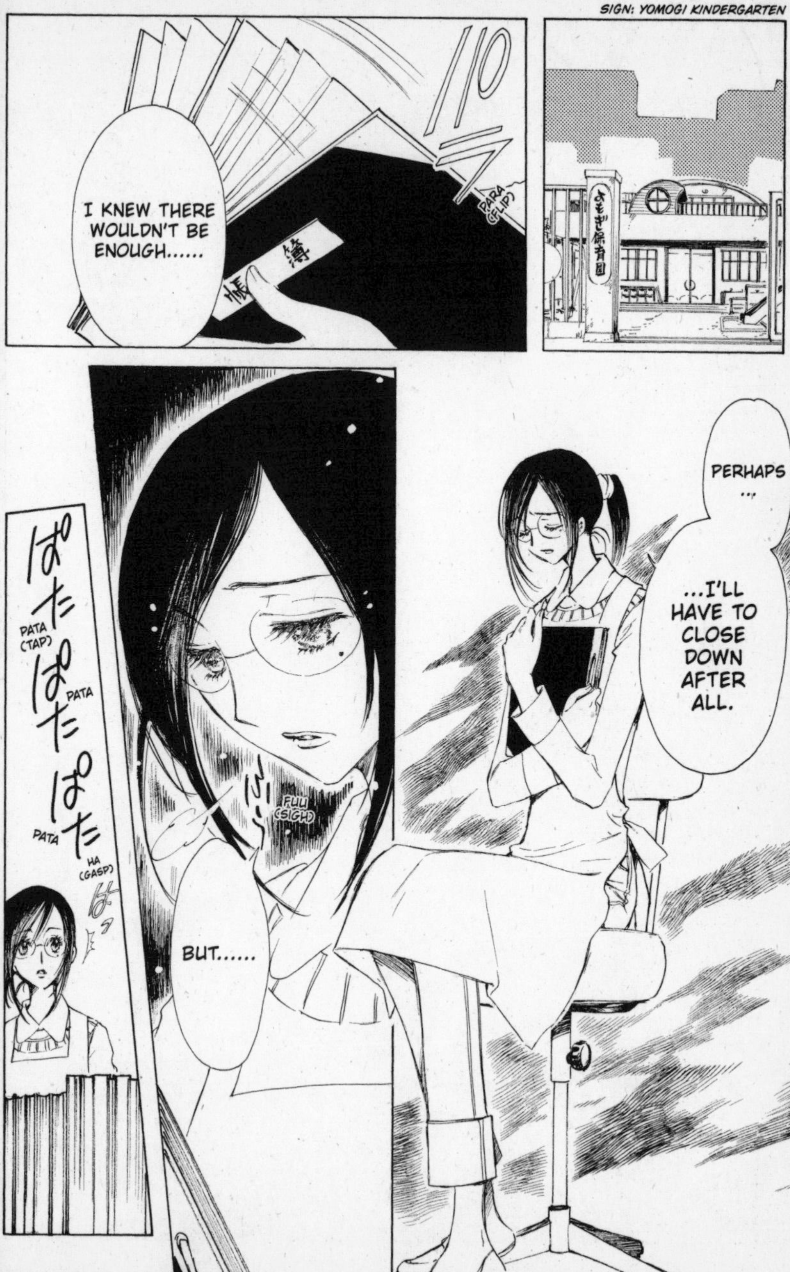
SIGN: YOMOGI KINDERGARTEN
PARA (FLIP)
I KNEW THERE WOULDN'T BE ENOUGH......
PERHAPS ...
...I'LL HAVE TO CLOSE DOWN AFTER ALL.
FUU (SIGH)
BUT......
PATA (TAP) PATA PATA
HA (GASP)

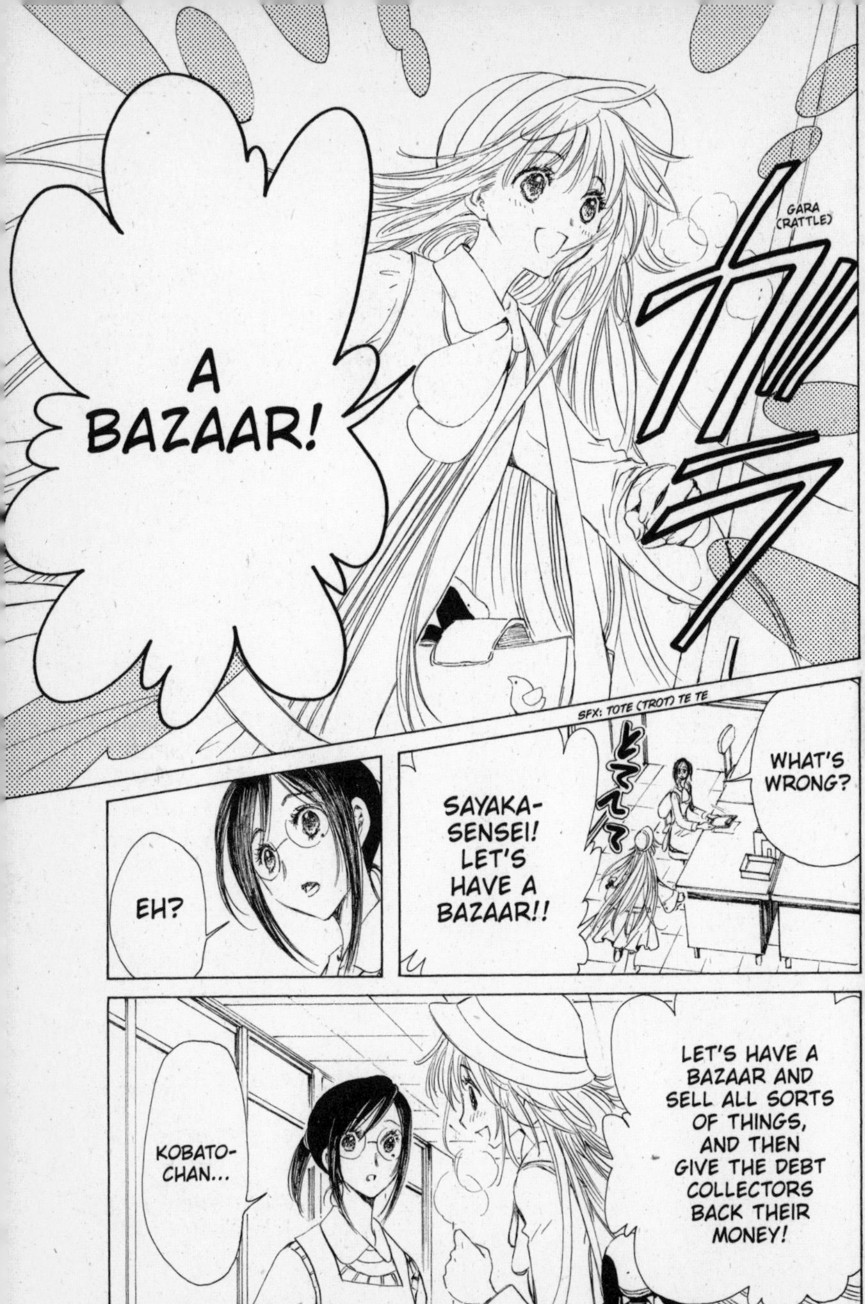
GARA (RATTLE)
A BAZAAR!
SFX: TOTE (TROT) TE TE
WHAT'S WRONG?
SAYAKA-SENSEI! LET'S HAVE A BAZAAR!!
EH?
LET'S HAVE A BAZAAR AND SELL ALL SORTS OF THINGS, AND THEN GIVE THE DEBT COLLECTORS BACK THEIR MONEY!
KOBATO-CHAN...

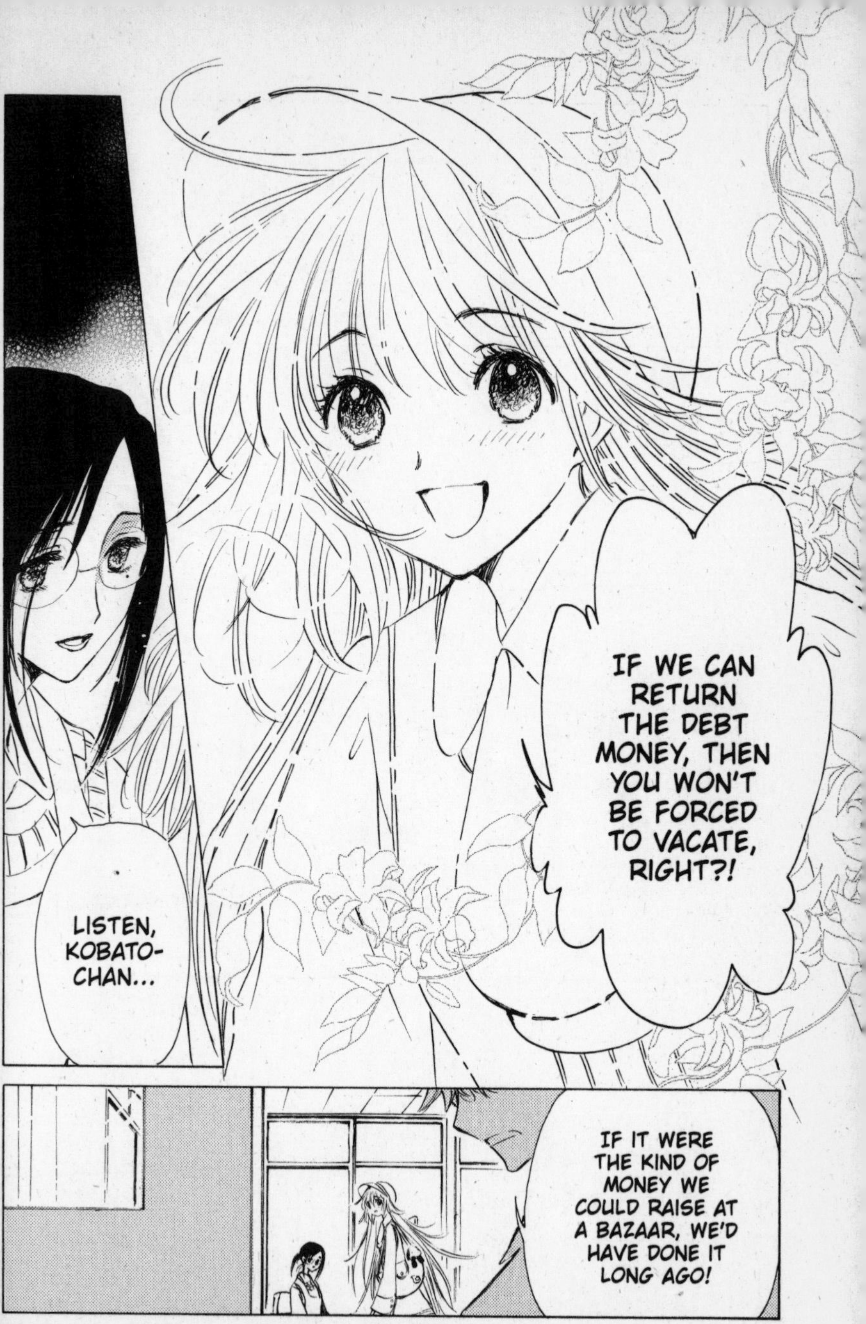
IF WE CAN RETURN THE DEBT MONEY, THEN YOU WON'T BE FORCED TO VACATE, RIGHT?!
LISTEN, KOBATO-CHAN...
IF IT WERE THE KIND OF MONEY WE COULD RAISE AT A BAZAAR, WE'D HAVE DONE IT LONG AGO!

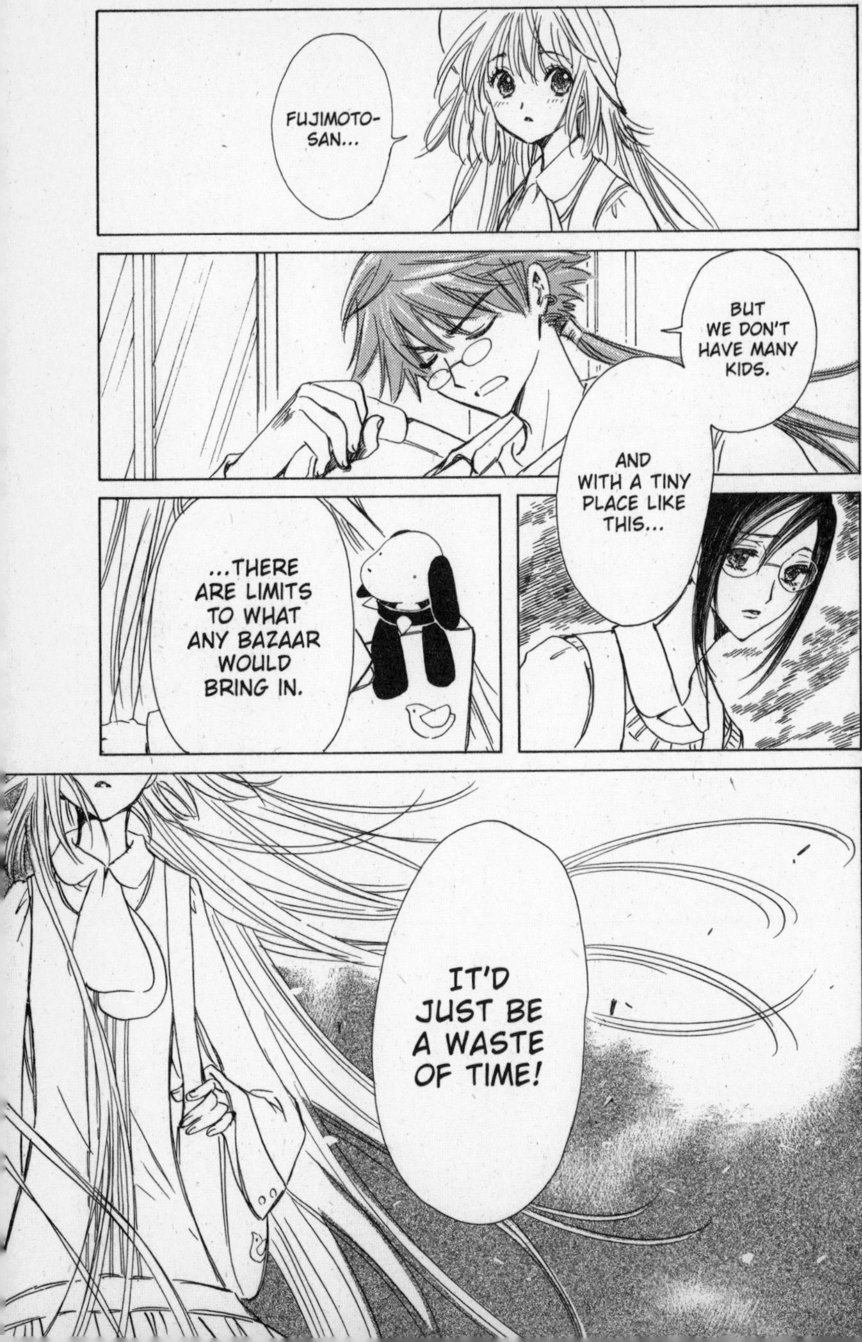
FUJIMOTO-SAN...
BUT WE DON'T HAVE MANY KIDS.
AND WITH A TINY PLACE LIKE THIS...
...THERE ARE LIMITS TO WHAT ANY BAZAAR WOULD BRING IN.
IT'D JUST BE A WASTE OF TIME!

EH HEH HEH!

I'M SORRY! I JUST GOT MYSELF ALL WORKED UP OVER NOTHING, HUH?

TOKE (TROMP)

TOKE

TOKE

I'LL GO CLEAN UP OUTSIDE!

......

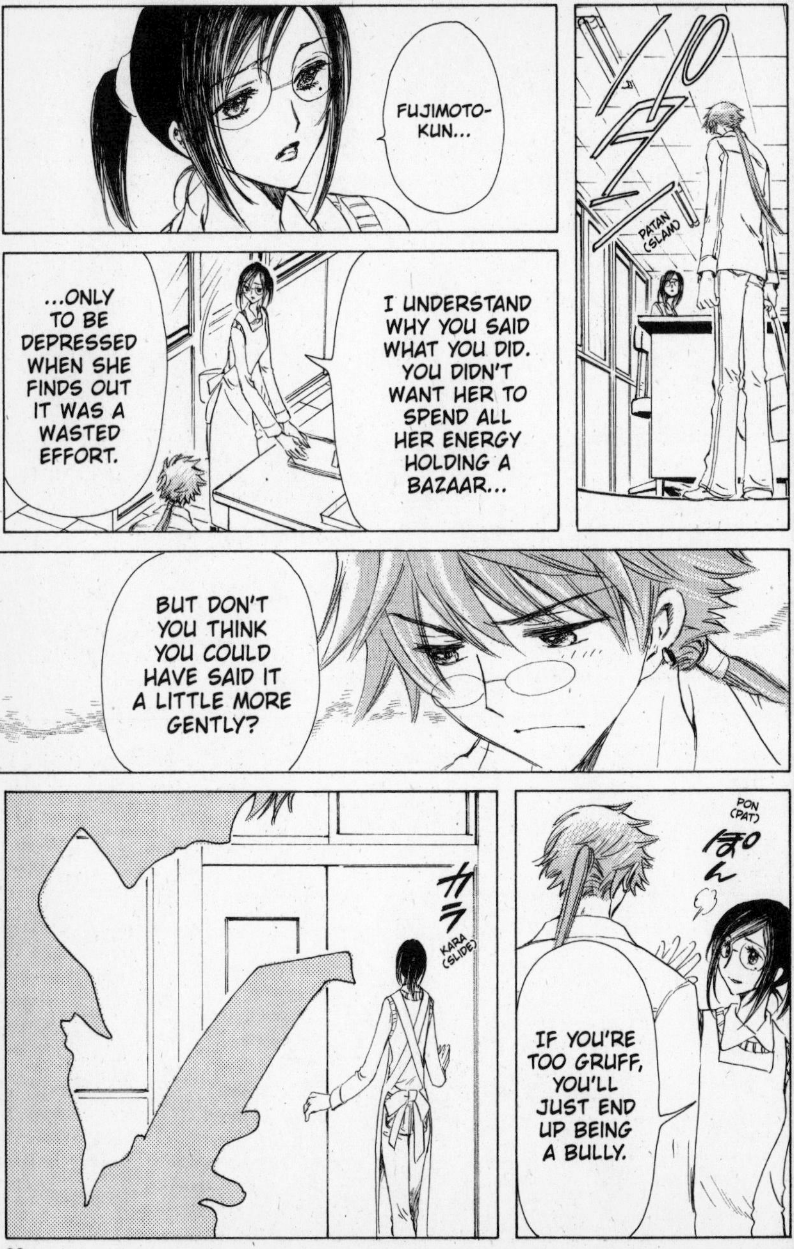
PATAN (SLAM)
FUJIMOTO-KUN...
I UNDERSTAND WHY YOU SAID WHAT YOU DID. YOU DIDN'T WANT HER TO SPEND ALL HER ENERGY HOLDING A BAZAAR...
...ONLY TO BE DEPRESSED WHEN SHE FINDS OUT IT WAS A WASTED EFFORT.
BUT DON'T YOU THINK YOU COULD HAVE SAID IT A LITTLE MORE GENTLY?
PON (PAT)
IF YOU'RE TOO GRUFF, YOU'LL JUST END UP BEING A BULLY.
KARA (SLIDE)

BOOK: CLASS ROLL

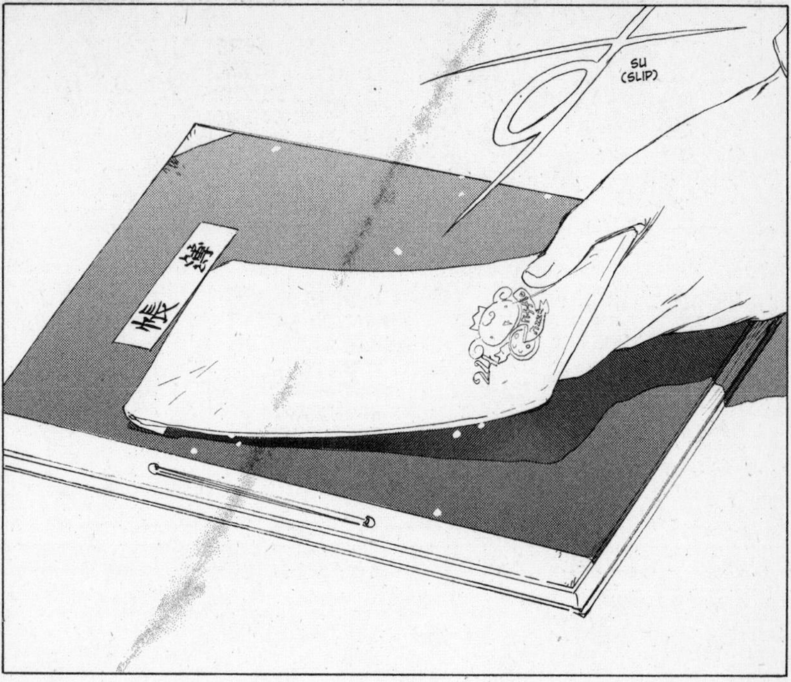
SU
(SLIP)

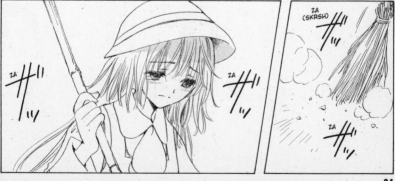

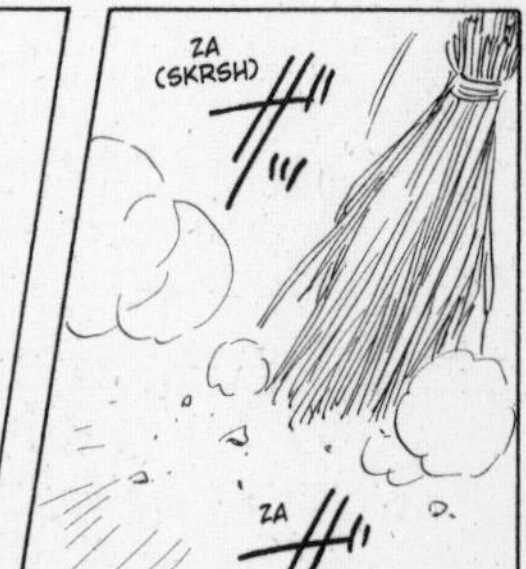
ZA
(SKRSH)
ZA

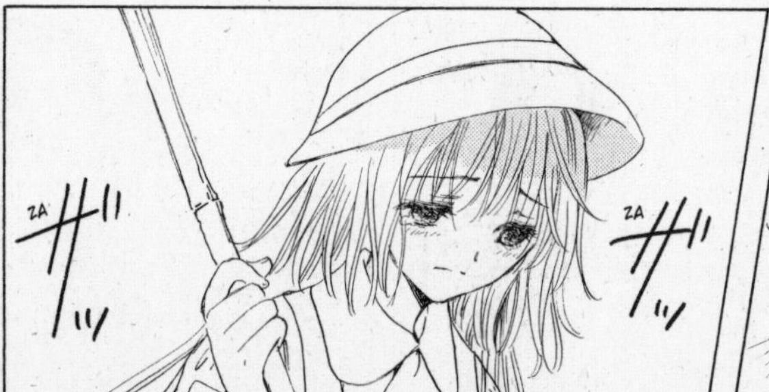
ZA
ZA

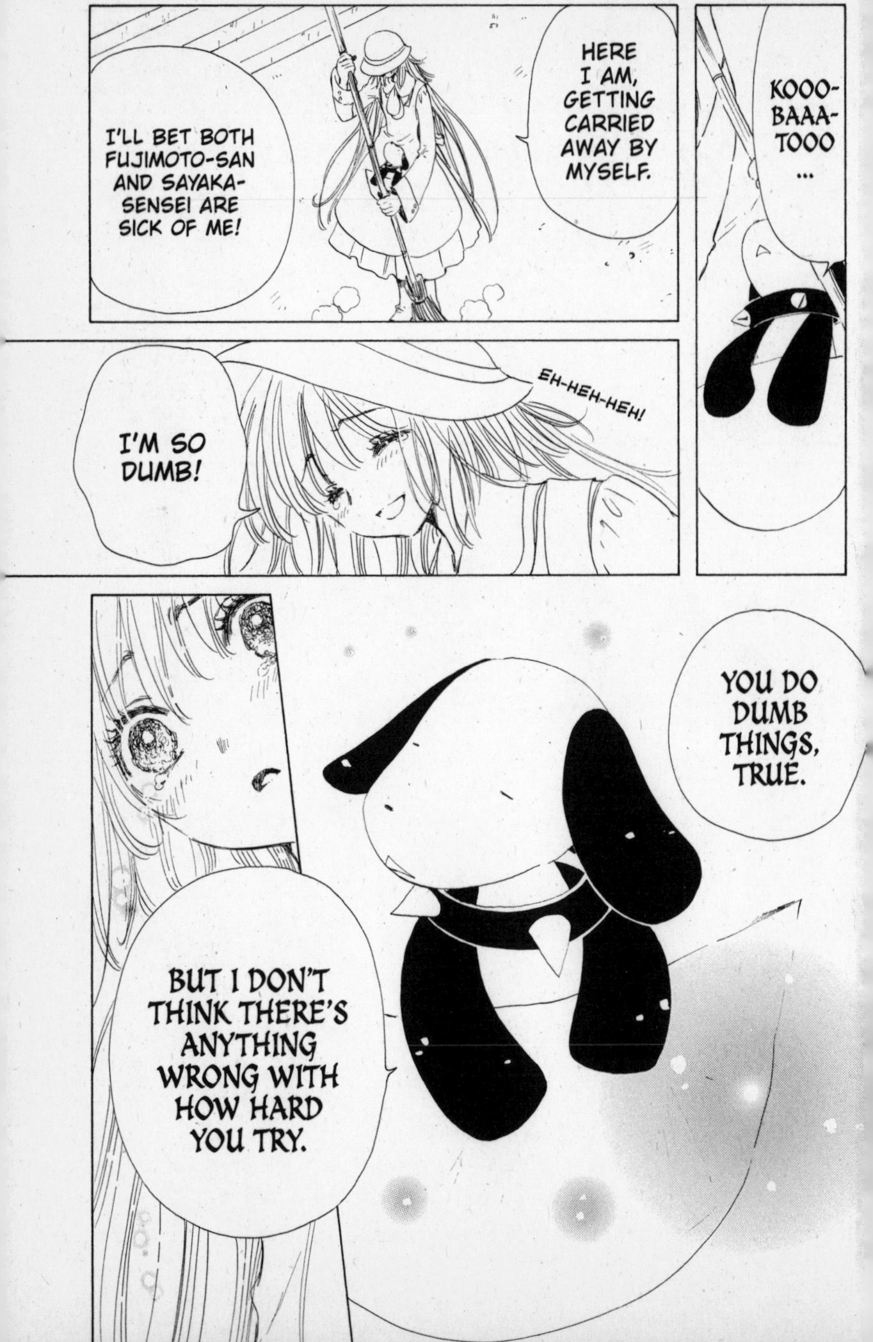
KOOO-BAAA-TOOO ...
HERE I AM, GETTING CARRIED AWAY BY MYSELF.
I'LL BET BOTH FUJIMOTO-SAN AND SAYAKA-SENSEI ARE SICK OF ME!
EH-HEH-HEH!
I'M SO DUMB!
YOU DO DUMB THINGS, TRUE.
BUT I DON'T THINK THERE'S ANYTHING WRONG WITH HOW HARD YOU TRY.

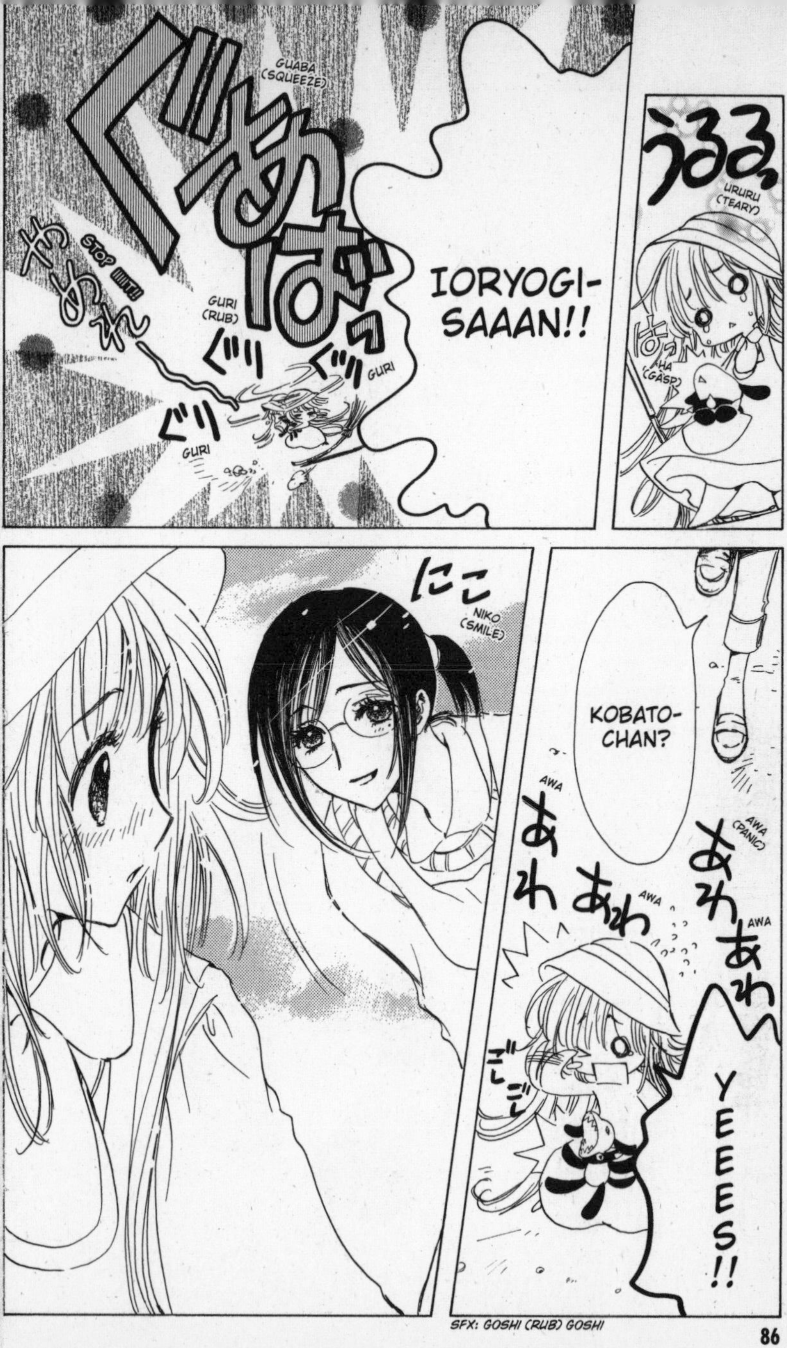
URURU (TEARY)
HA (GASP)
GUABA (SQUEEZE)
IORYOGI-SAAAN!!
STOP IIIIT!!
GURI (RUB)
GURI
GURI
KOBATO-CHAN?
AWA (PANIC)
AWA
AWA
AWA
YEEES!!
NIKO (SMILE)
SFX: GOSHI (RUB) GOSHI

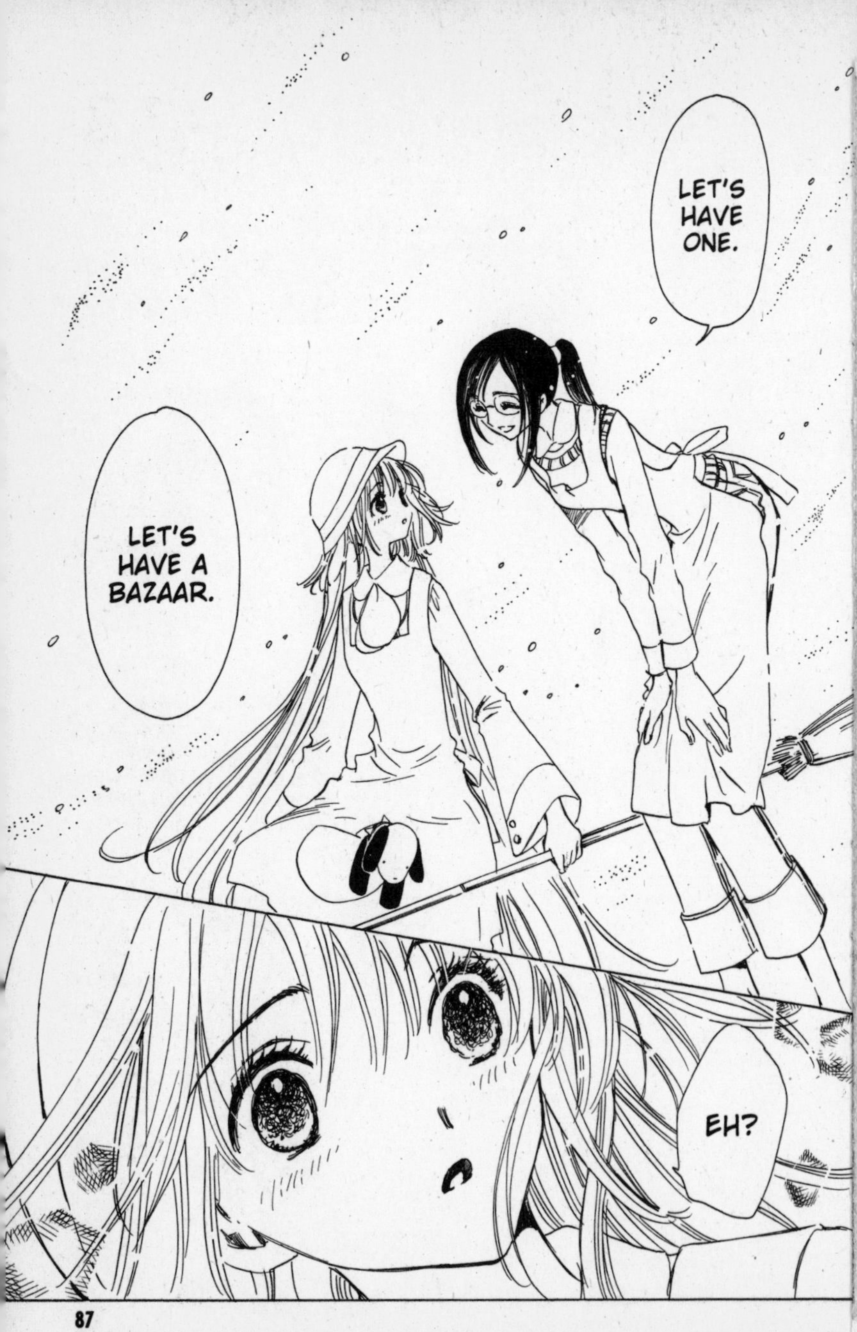
LET'S HAVE ONE.
LET'S HAVE A BAZAAR.
EH?

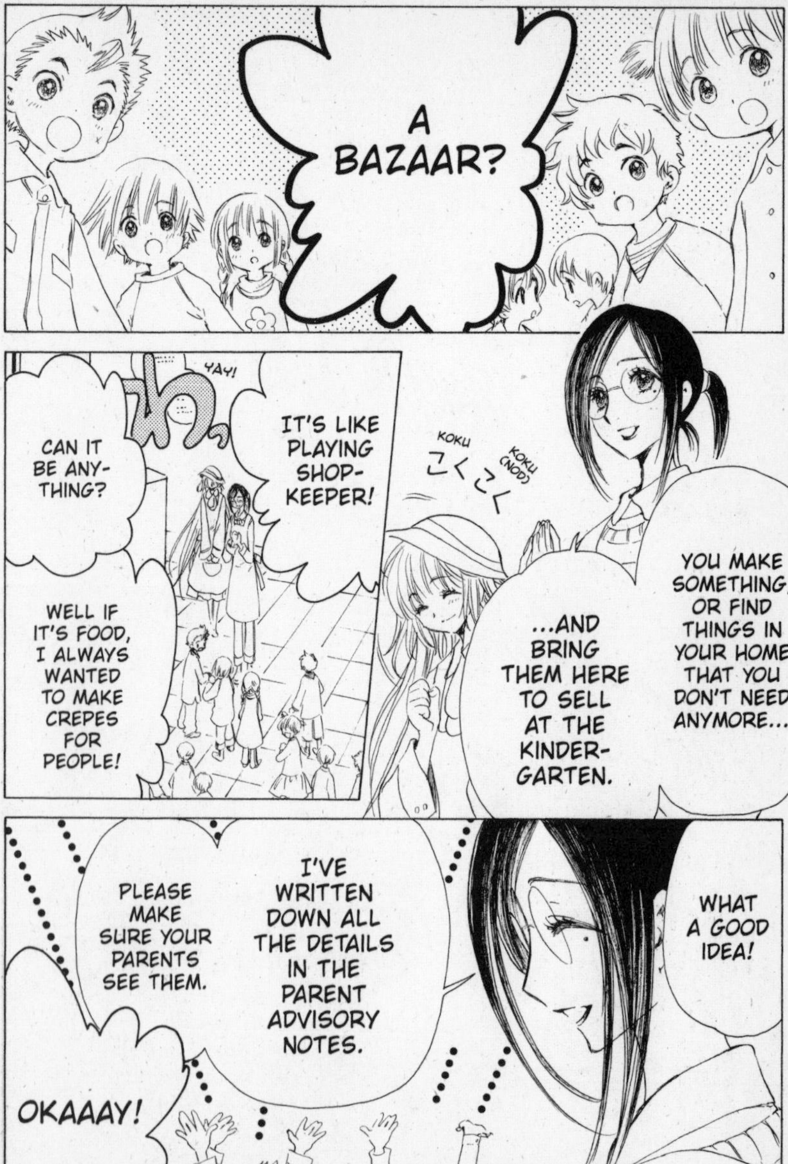
A BAZAAR?
YOU MAKE SOMETHING, OR FIND THINGS IN YOUR HOME THAT YOU DON'T NEED ANYMORE...
...AND BRING THEM HERE TO SELL AT THE KINDERGARTEN.
KOKU
こくこく
KOKU (NOD)
YAY!
わ
IT'S LIKE PLAYING SHOP-KEEPER!
CAN IT BE ANY-THING?
WELL IF IT'S FOOD, I ALWAYS WANTED TO MAKE CREPES FOR PEOPLE!
WHAT A GOOD IDEA!
I'VE WRITTEN DOWN ALL THE DETAILS IN THE PARENT ADVISORY NOTES.
PLEASE MAKE SURE YOUR PARENTS SEE THEM.
OKAAAY!

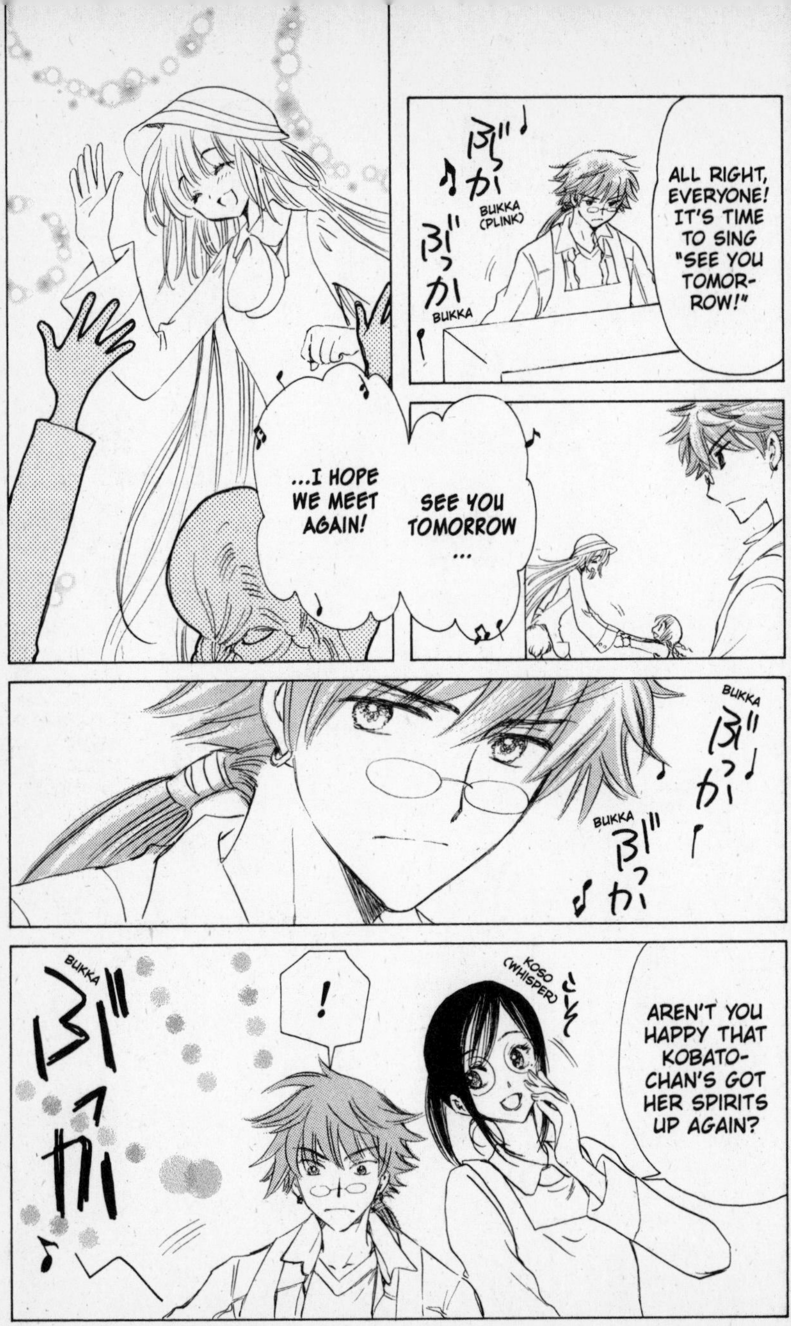
ALL RIGHT, EVERYONE! IT'S TIME TO SING "SEE YOU TOMORROW!"
ぶっか
BUKKA (PLINK)
ぶっか
BUKKA
SEE YOU TOMORROW ...
...I HOPE WE MEET AGAIN!
ぶっか
BUKKA
ぶっか
BUKKA
ARE'NT YOU HAPPY THAT KOBATO-CHAN'S GOT HER SPIRITS UP AGAIN?
こそ
KOSO (WHISPER)
!
ぶっか
BUKKA

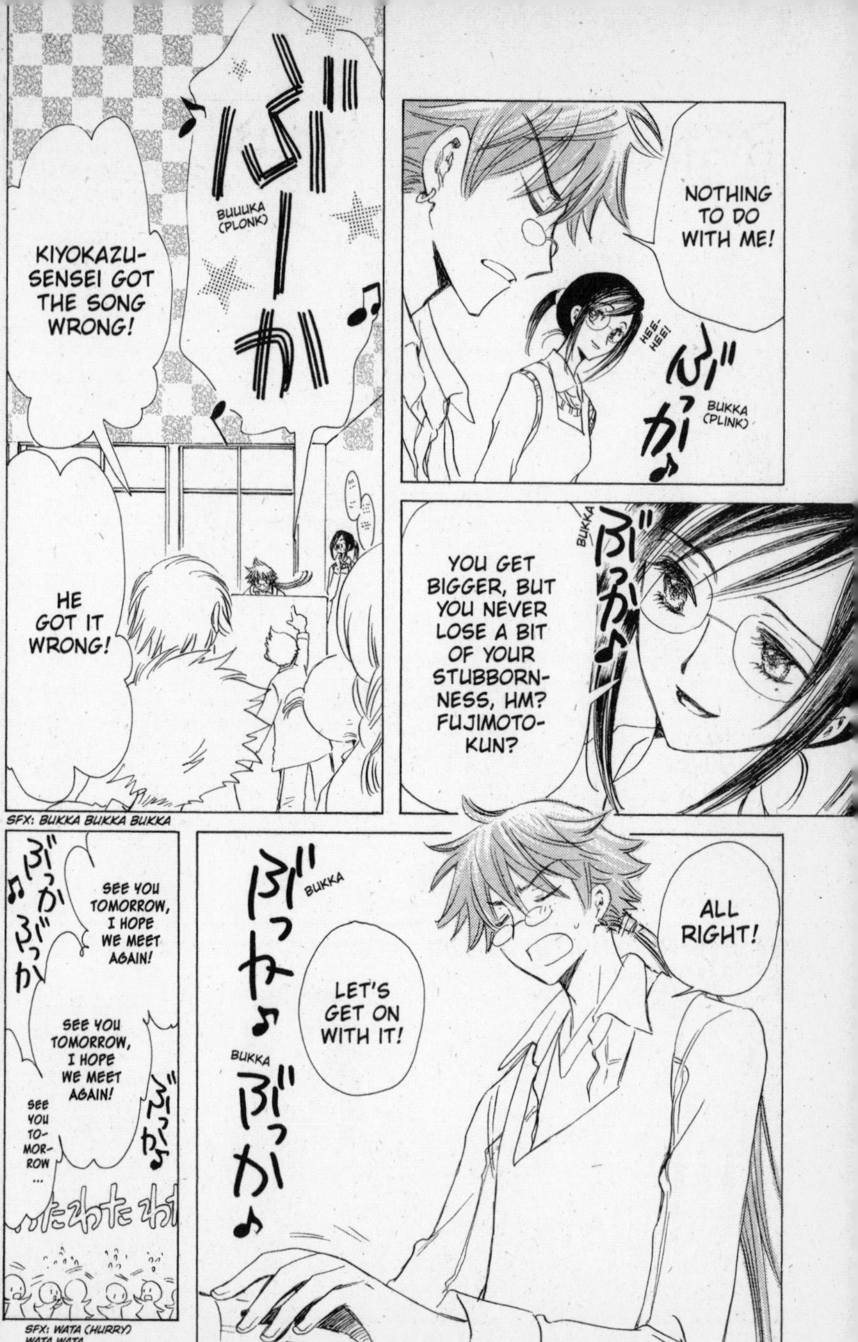
NOTHING TO DO WITH ME!
HEE-HEE!
BUKKA (PLINK)
BUKKA
YOU GET BIGGER, BUT YOU NEVER LOSE A BIT OF YOUR STUBBORN-NESS, HM? FUJIMOTO-KUN?
BUUUKA (PLONK)
KIYOKAZU-SENSEI GOT THE SONG WRONG!
HE GOT IT WRONG!
SFX: BUKKA BUKKA BUKKA
ALL RIGHT!
LET'S GET ON WITH IT!
BUKKA
BUKKA
SEE YOU TOMORROW, I HOPE WE MEET AGAIN!
SEE YOU TOMORROW, I HOPE WE MEET AGAIN!
SEE YOU TO-MOR-ROW ...
SFX: WATA (HURRY) WATA WATA

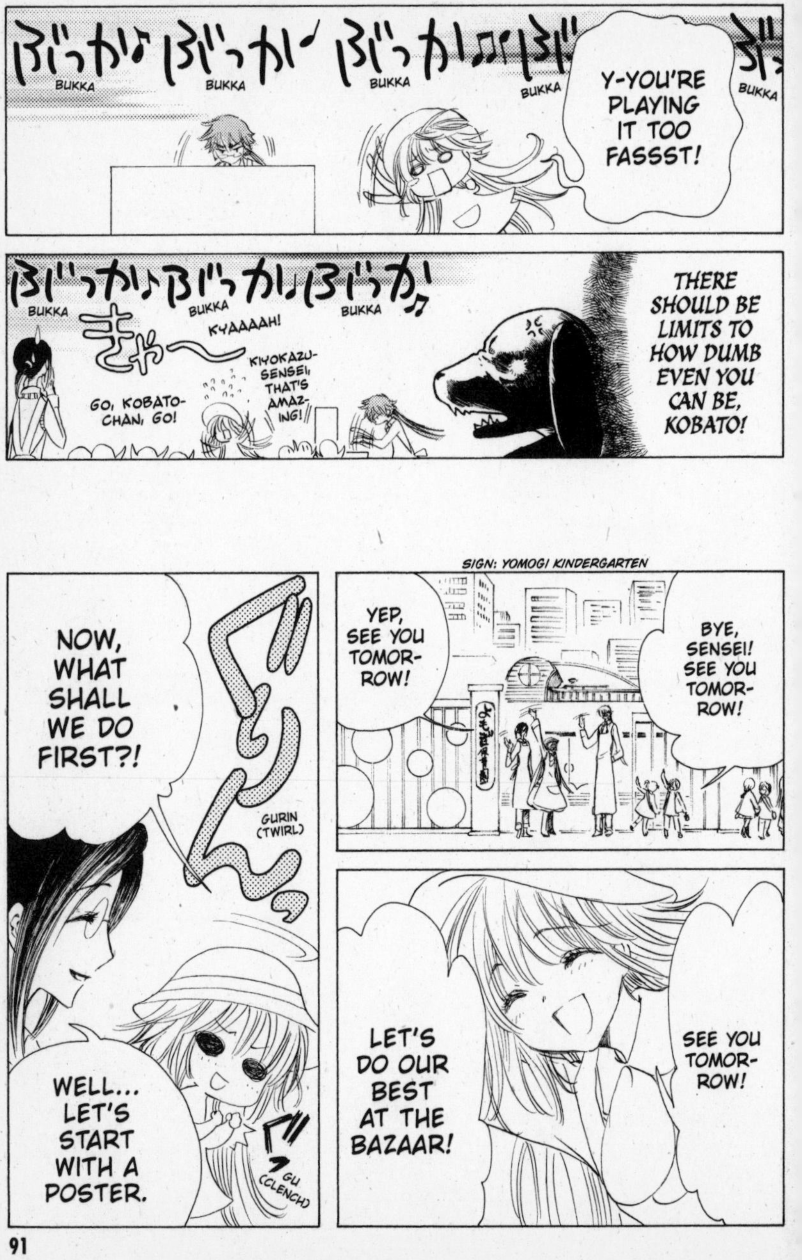

ぶ
BUKKA
Y-YOU'RE PLAYING IT TOO FASSST!
ぶっか
BUKKA
ぶっか
BUKKA
ぶっか
BUKKA
ぶっか
BUKKA
THERE SHOULD BE LIMITS TO HOW DUMB EVEN YOU CAN BE, KOBATO!
ぶっか
BUKKA
ぶっか
BUKKA
ぶっか
BUKKA
KIYOKAZU-SENSEI, THAT'S AMAZING!
きゃ〜
KYAAAAH!
GO, KOBATO-CHAN, GO!
SIGN: YOMOGI KINDERGARTEN
BYE, SENSEI! SEE YOU TOMORROW!
YEP, SEE YOU TOMORROW!
SEE YOU TOMORROW!
LET'S DO OUR BEST AT THE BAZAAR!
NOW, WHAT SHALL WE DO FIRST?!
GURIN (TWIRL)
WELL... LET'S START WITH A POSTER.
GU (CLENCH)

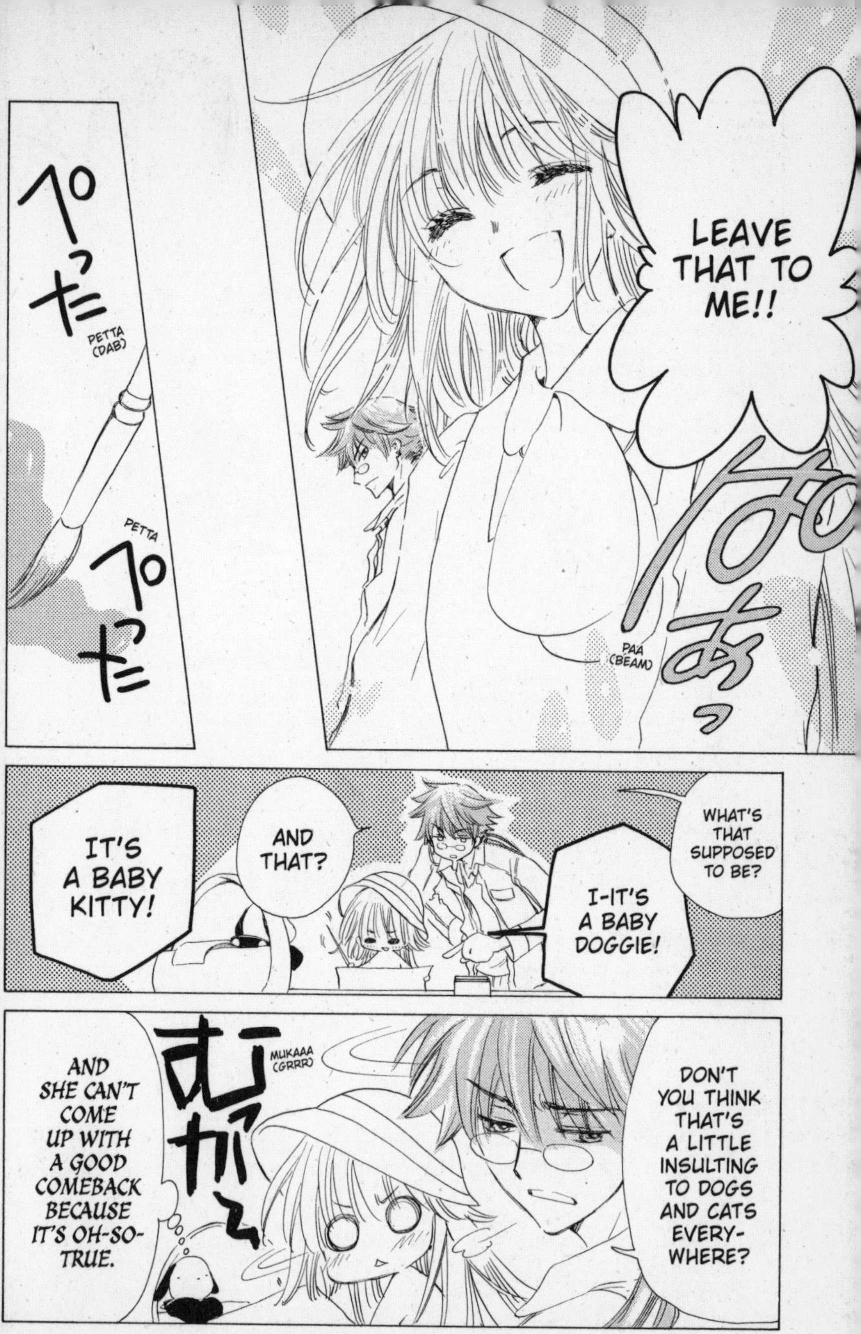
LEAVE THAT TO ME!!
ぱあっ
PAA (BEAM)
ぺった
PETTA (DAB)
ぺった
PETTA
WHAT'S THAT SUPPOSED TO BE?
I-IT'S A BABY DOGGIE!
AND THAT?
IT'S A BABY KITTY!
DON'T YOU THINK THAT'S A LITTLE INSULTING TO DOGS AND CATS EVERY-WHERE?
むかーっ
MUKAAA (GRRR)
AND SHE CAN'T COME UP WITH A GOOD COMEBACK BECAUSE IT'S OH-SO-TRUE.

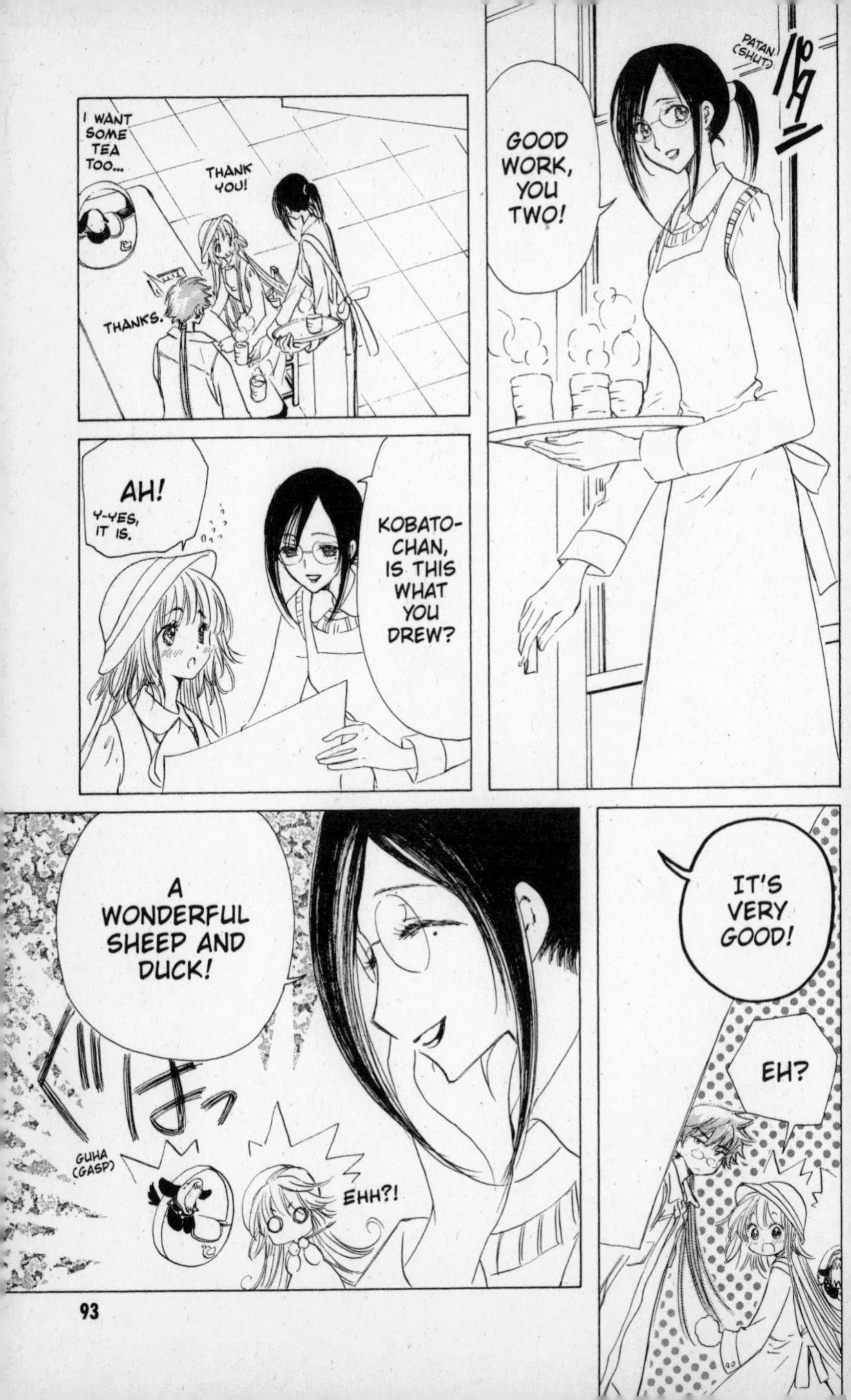
PATAN (SHUT)
GOOD WORK, YOU TWO!
THANK YOU!
I WANT SOME TEA TOO...
THANKS.
KOBATO-CHAN, IS THIS WHAT YOU DREW?
AH!
Y-YES, IT IS.
IT'S VERY GOOD!
EH?
A WONDERFUL SHEEP AND DUCK!
GUHA (GASP)
EHH?!

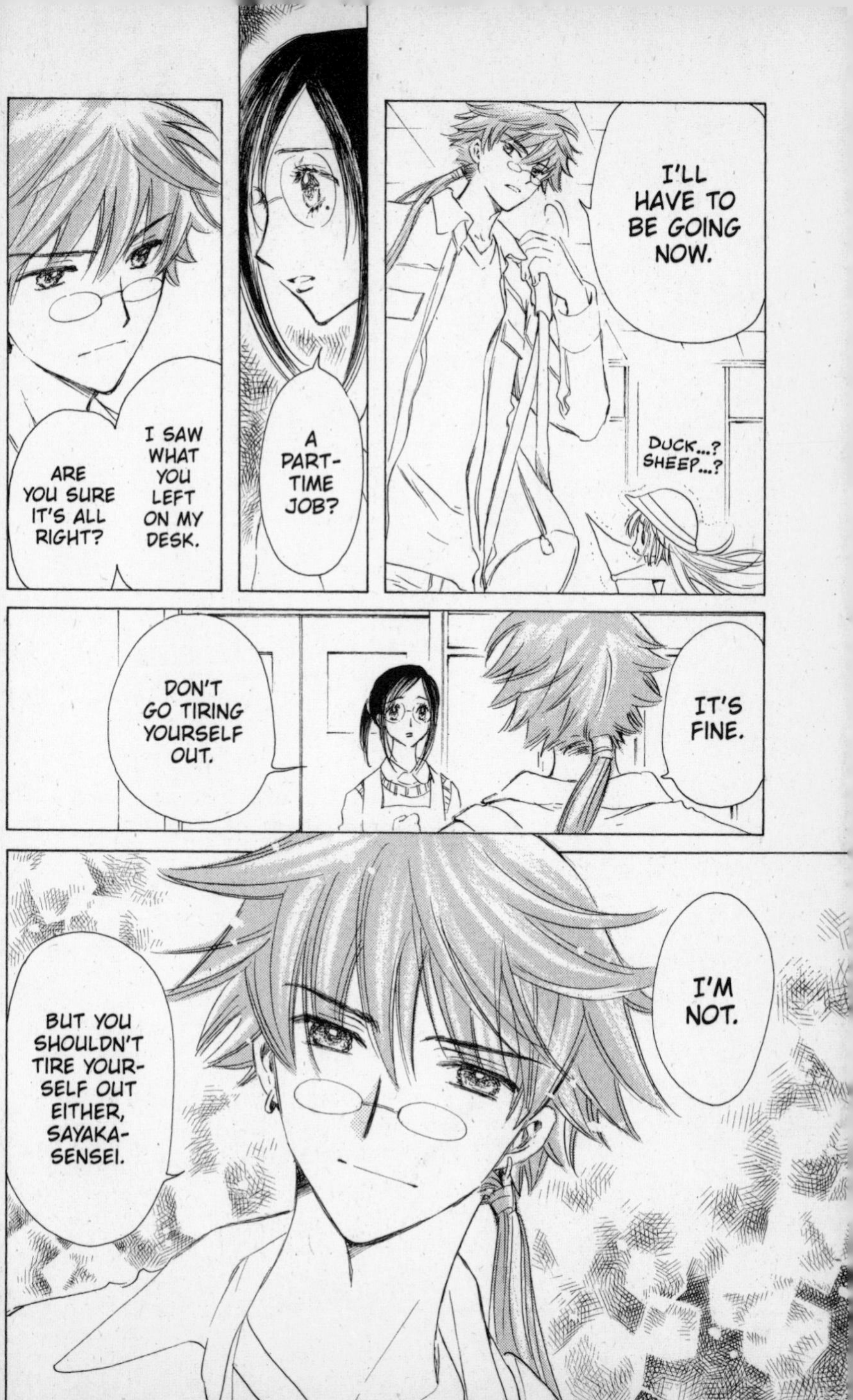
I'LL HAVE TO BE GOING NOW.
DUCK...? SHEEP...?
A PART-TIME JOB?
I SAW WHAT YOU LEFT ON MY DESK.
ARE YOU SURE IT'S ALL RIGHT?
IT'S FINE.
DON'T GO TIRING YOURSELF OUT.
I'M NOT.
BUT YOU SHOULDN'T TIRE YOUR-SELF OUT EITHER, SAYAKA-SENSEI.

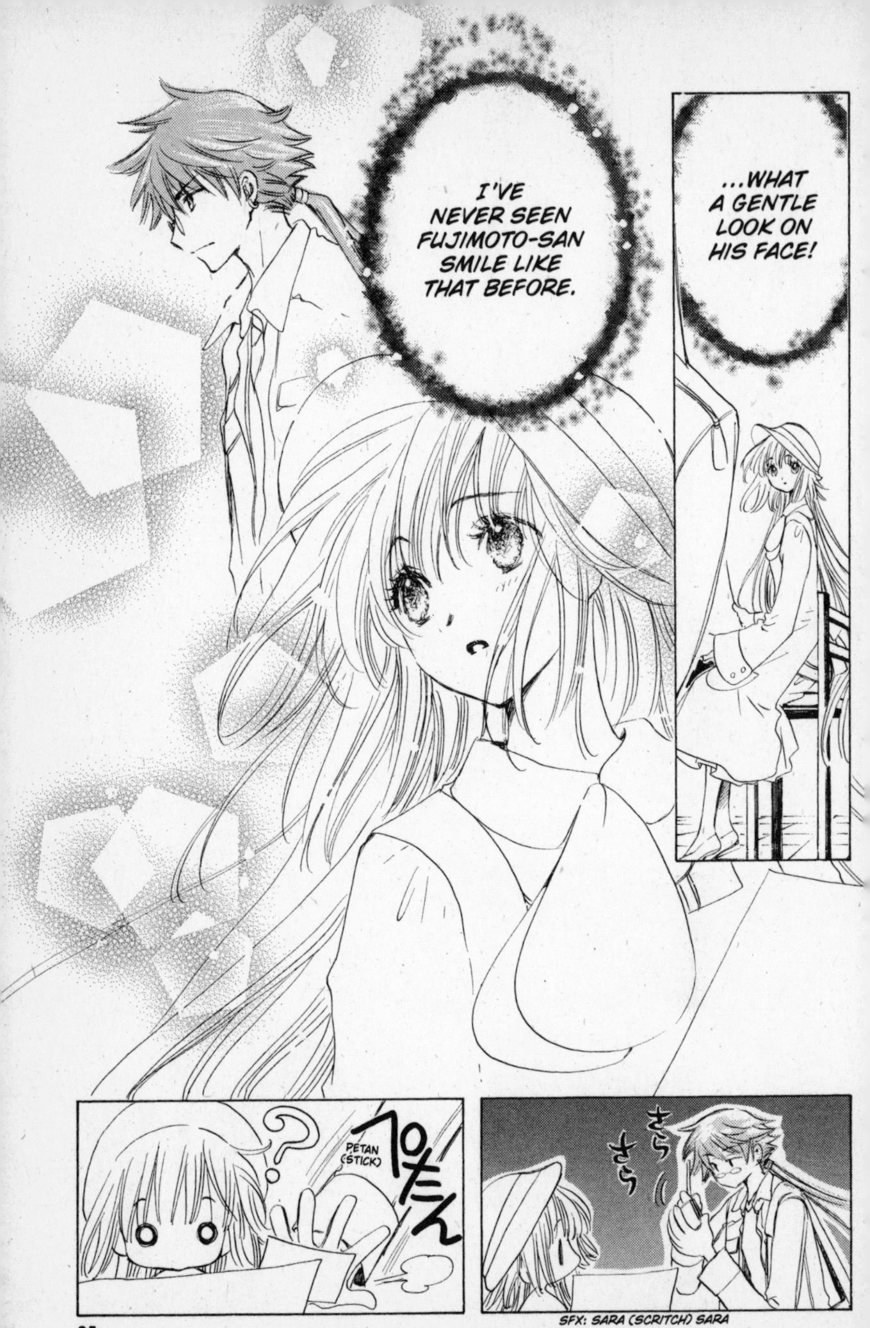
...WHAT A GENTLE LOOK ON HIS FACE!
I'VE NEVER SEEN FUJIMOTO-SAN SMILE LIKE THAT BEFORE.
さら さら
ぺたん
PETAN (STICK)
?

SFX: SARA (SCRITCH) SARA

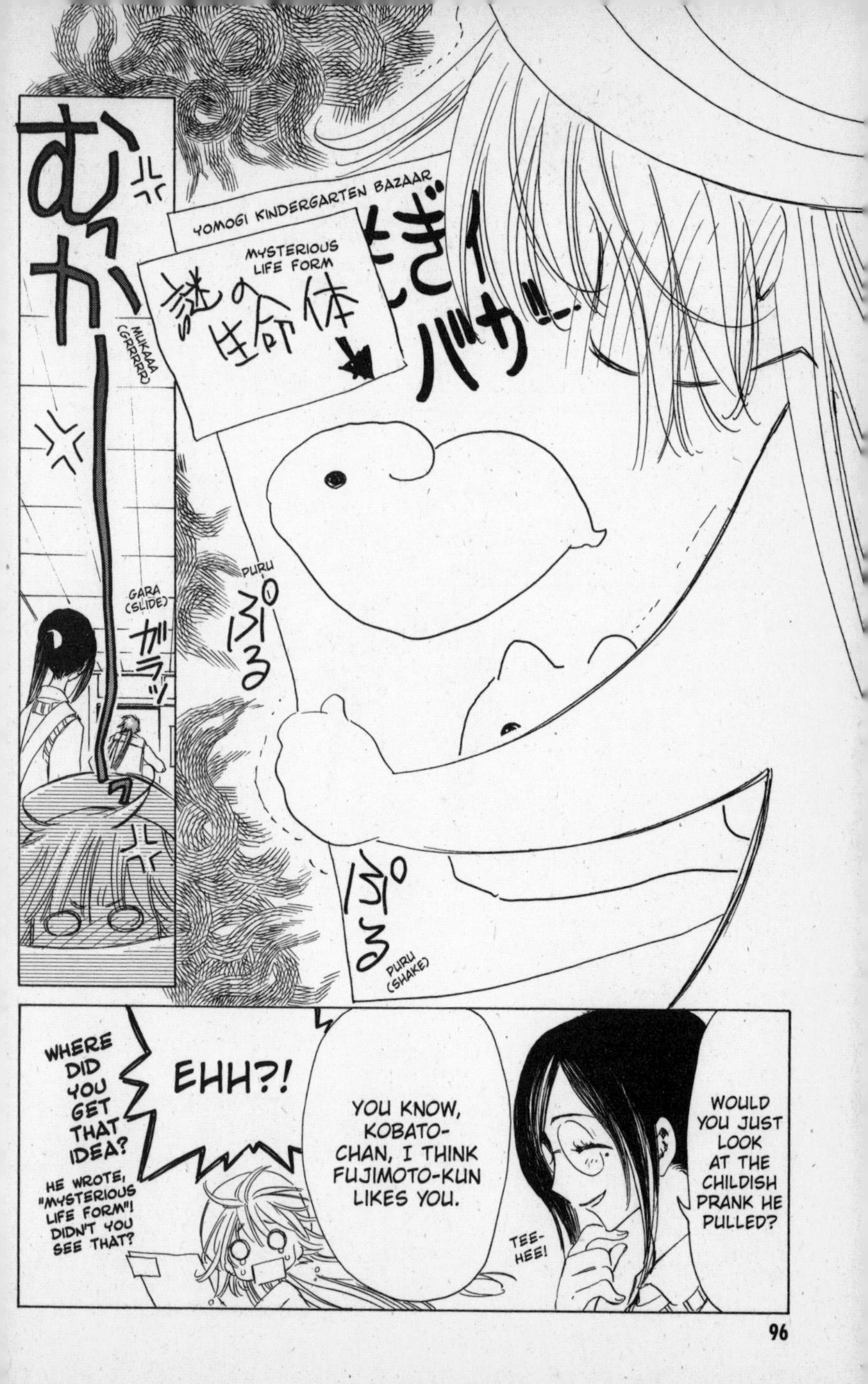
YOMOGI KINDERGARTEN BAZAAR
MYSTERIOUS LIFE FORM
謎の生命体
PURU
ぷる
ぷる
PURU (SHAKE)
むかーーっ
MUKAAA (GRRRR)
ガラッ
GARA (SLIDE)
WOULD YOU JUST LOOK AT THE CHILDISH PRANK HE PULLED?
TEE-HEE!
YOU KNOW, KOBATO-CHAN, I THINK FUJIMOTO-KUN LIKES YOU.
EHH?!
WHERE DID YOU GET THAT IDEA?
HE WROTE, "MYSTERIOUS LIFE FORM"! DIDN'T YOU SEE THAT?

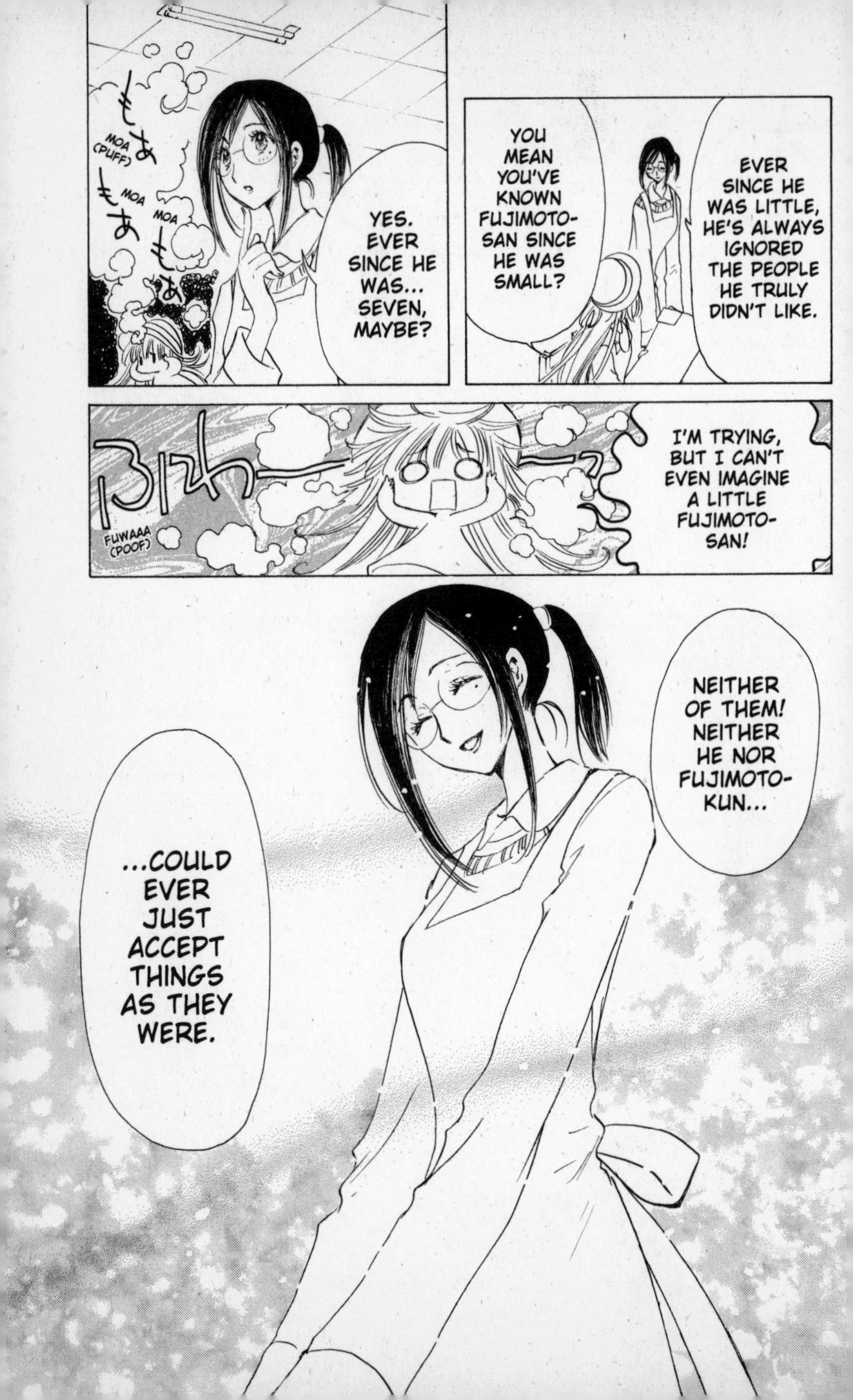
EVER SINCE HE WAS LITTLE, HE'S ALWAYS IGNORED THE PEOPLE HE TRULY DIDN'T LIKE.
YOU MEAN YOU'VE KNOWN FUJIMOTO-SAN SINCE HE WAS SMALL?
YES. EVER SINCE HE WAS... SEVEN, MAYBE?
もあ もあ もあ
MOA (PUFF)
MOA
MOA
I'M TRYING, BUT I CAN'T EVEN IMAGINE A LITTLE FUJIMOTO-SAN!
ふわ～～っ
FUWAAA (POOF)
NEITHER OF THEM! NEITHER HE NOR FUJIMOTO-KUN...
...COULD EVER JUST ACCEPT THINGS AS THEY WERE.

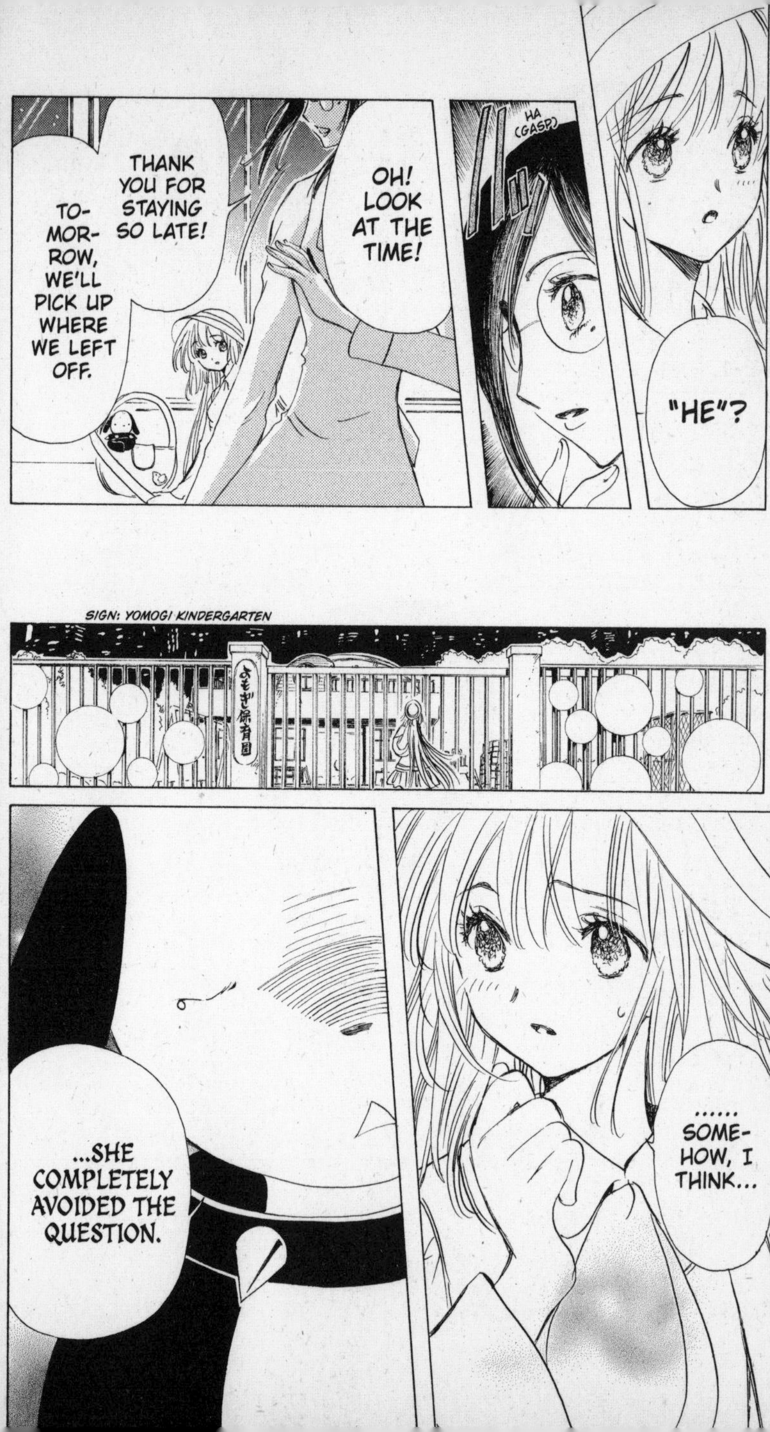
"HE"?
HA (GASP)
OH! LOOK AT THE TIME!
THANK YOU FOR STAYING SO LATE!
TO-MOR-ROW, WE'LL PICK UP WHERE WE LEFT OFF.
SIGN: YOMOGI KINDERGARTEN
...... SOME-HOW, I THINK...
...SHE COMPLETELY AVOIDED THE QUESTION.

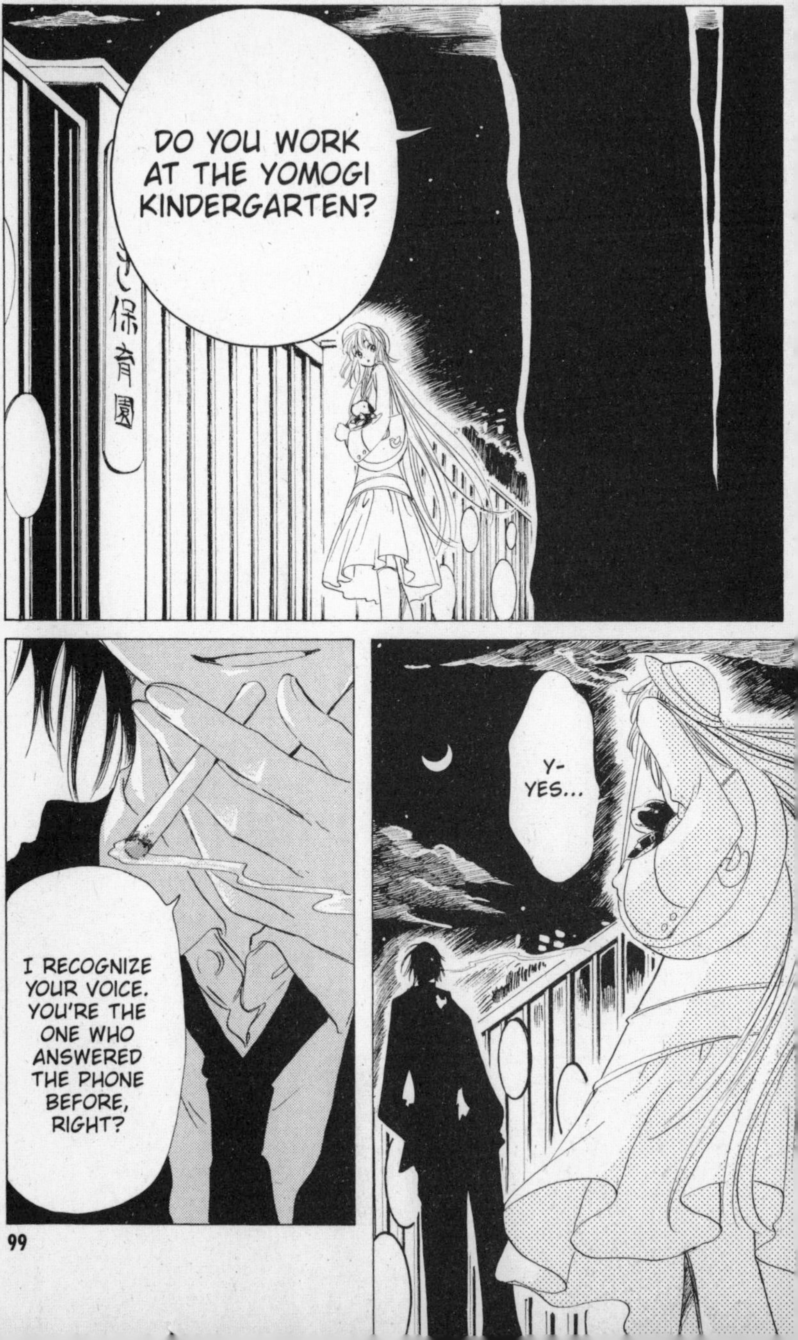
DO YOU WORK AT THE YOMOGI KINDERGARTEN?
Y- YES...
I RECOGNIZE YOUR VOICE. YOU'RE THE ONE WHO ANSWERED THE PHONE BEFORE, RIGHT?

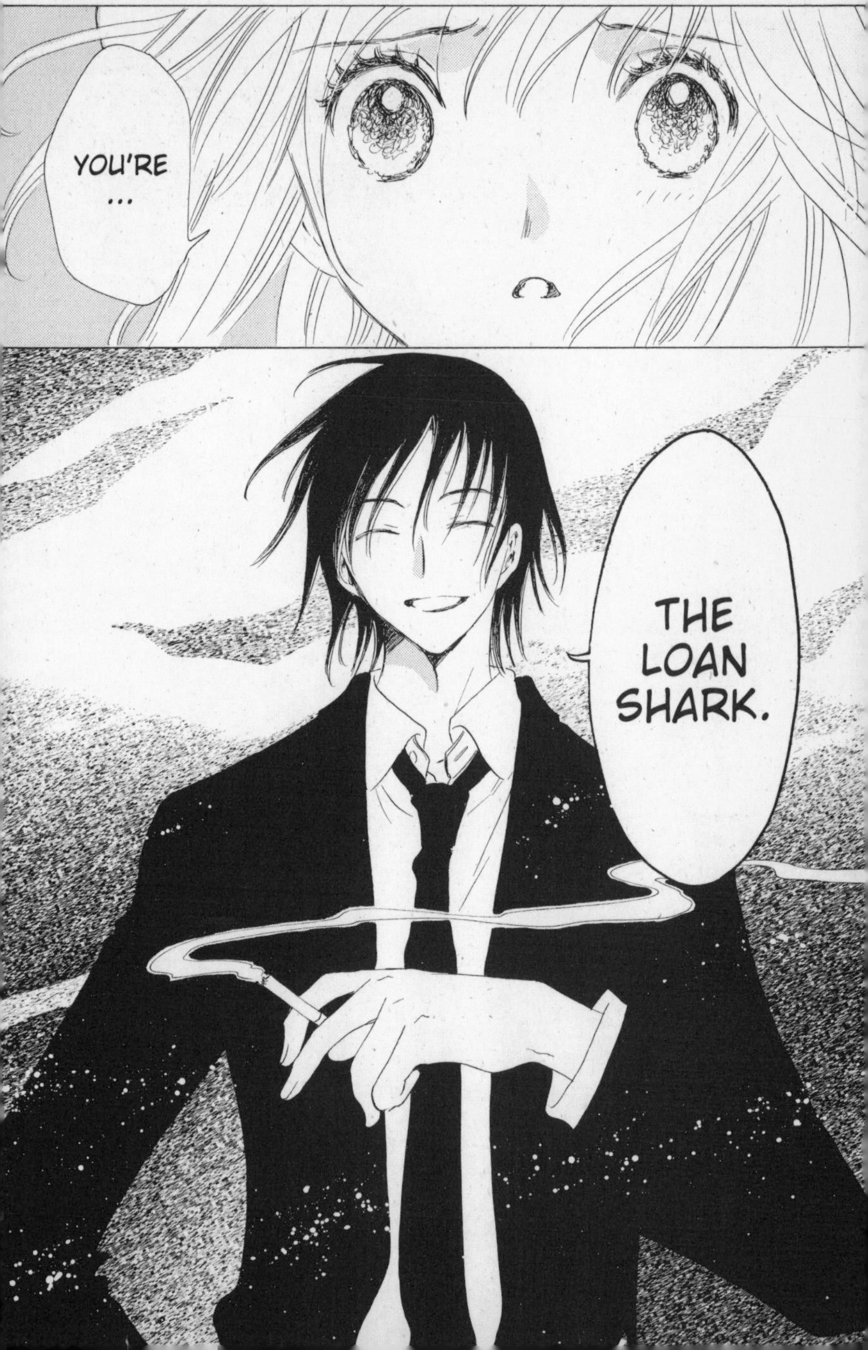
YOU'RE ...
THE LOAN SHARK.

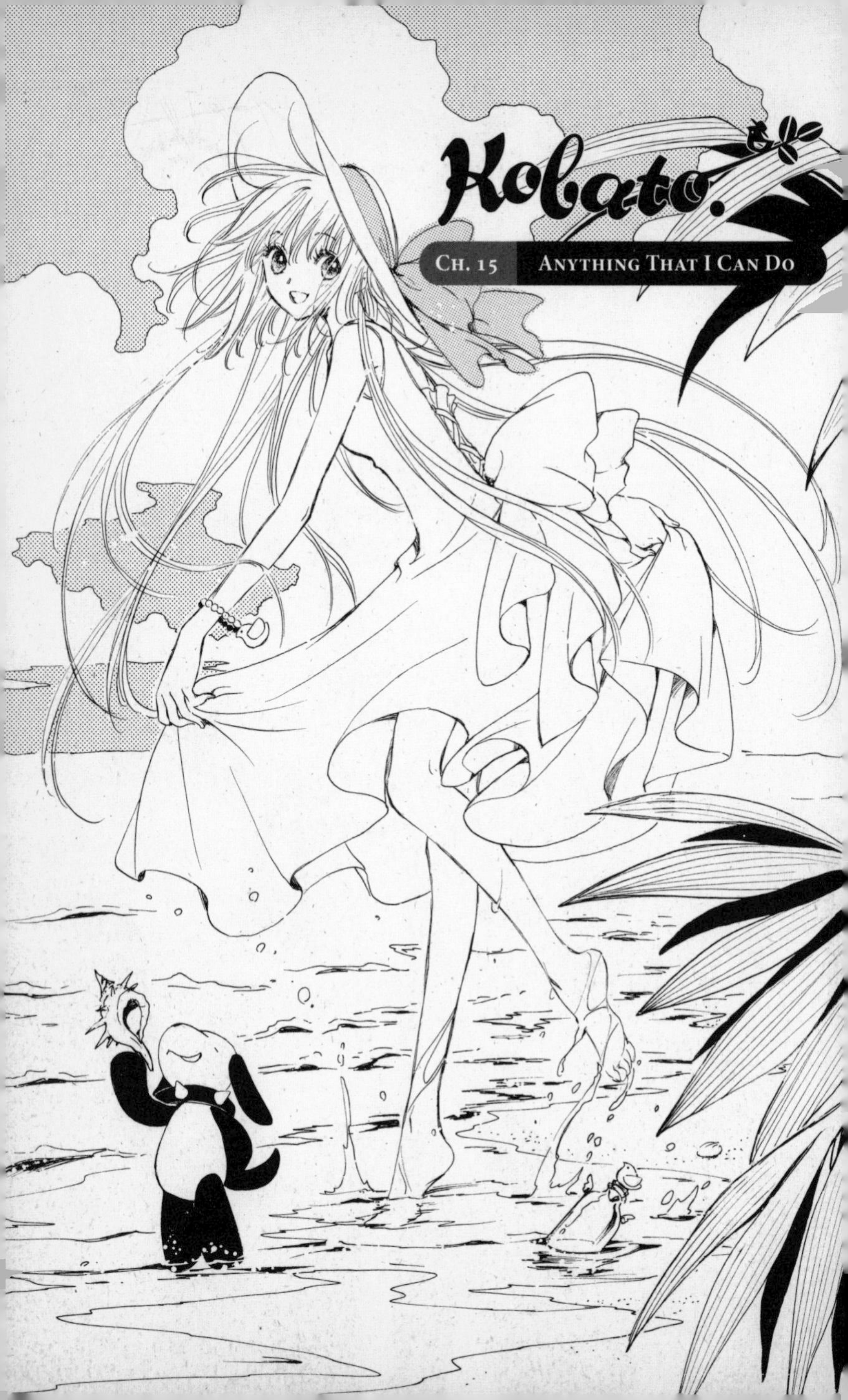
Kobato.
Ch. 15
Anything That I Can Do

SIGN: YOMOGI KINDERGARTEN

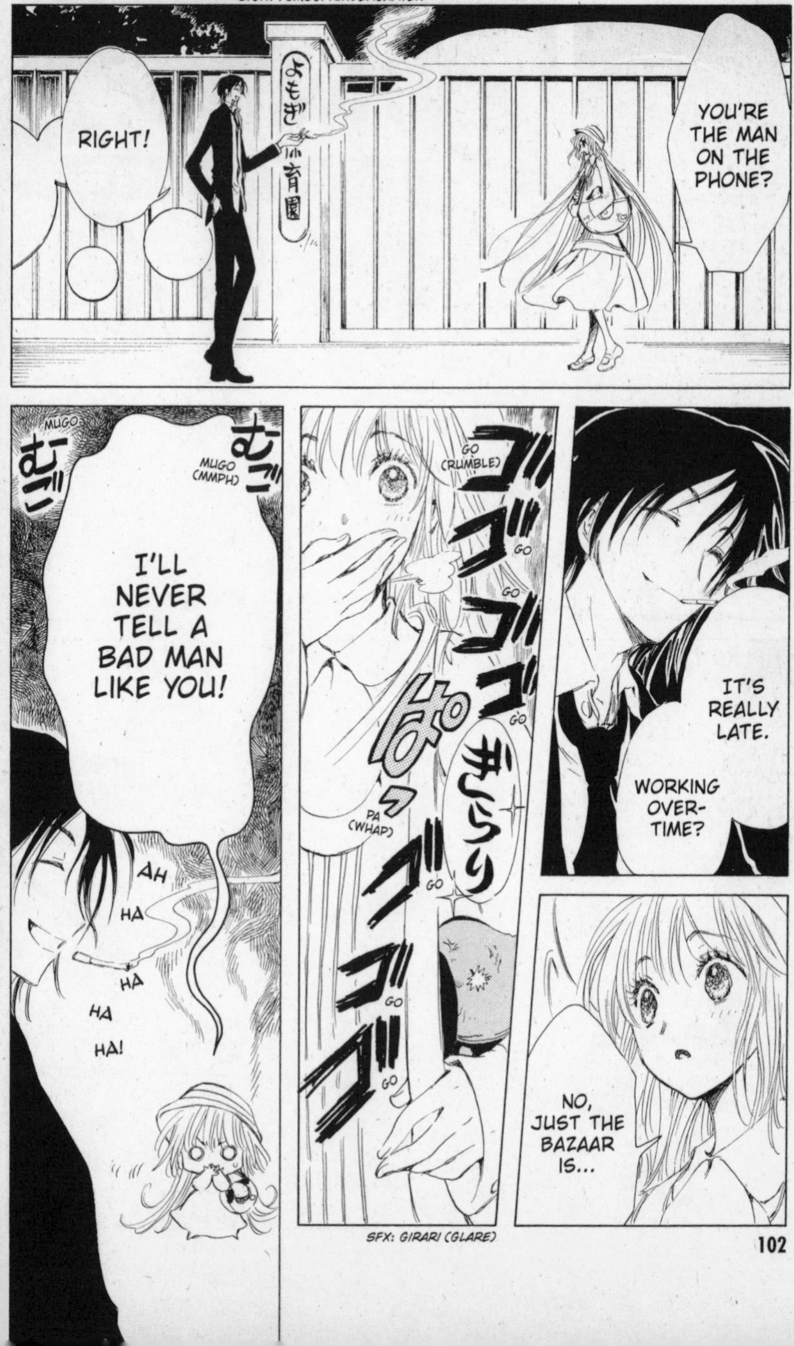

よもぎ保育園
YOU'RE THE MAN ON THE PHONE?
RIGHT!
IT'S REALLY LATE.
WORKING OVER-TIME?
NO, JUST THE BAZAAR IS...
ゴゴゴゴゴゴ
GO (RUMBLE)
GO
GO
GO
GO
GO
GO
ぱっ
PA (WHAP)
ぎらり
むご
MUGO (MMPH)
むご
MUGO
I'LL NEVER TELL A BAD MAN LIKE YOU!
AH HA HA HA HA!

SFX: GIRARI (GLARE)

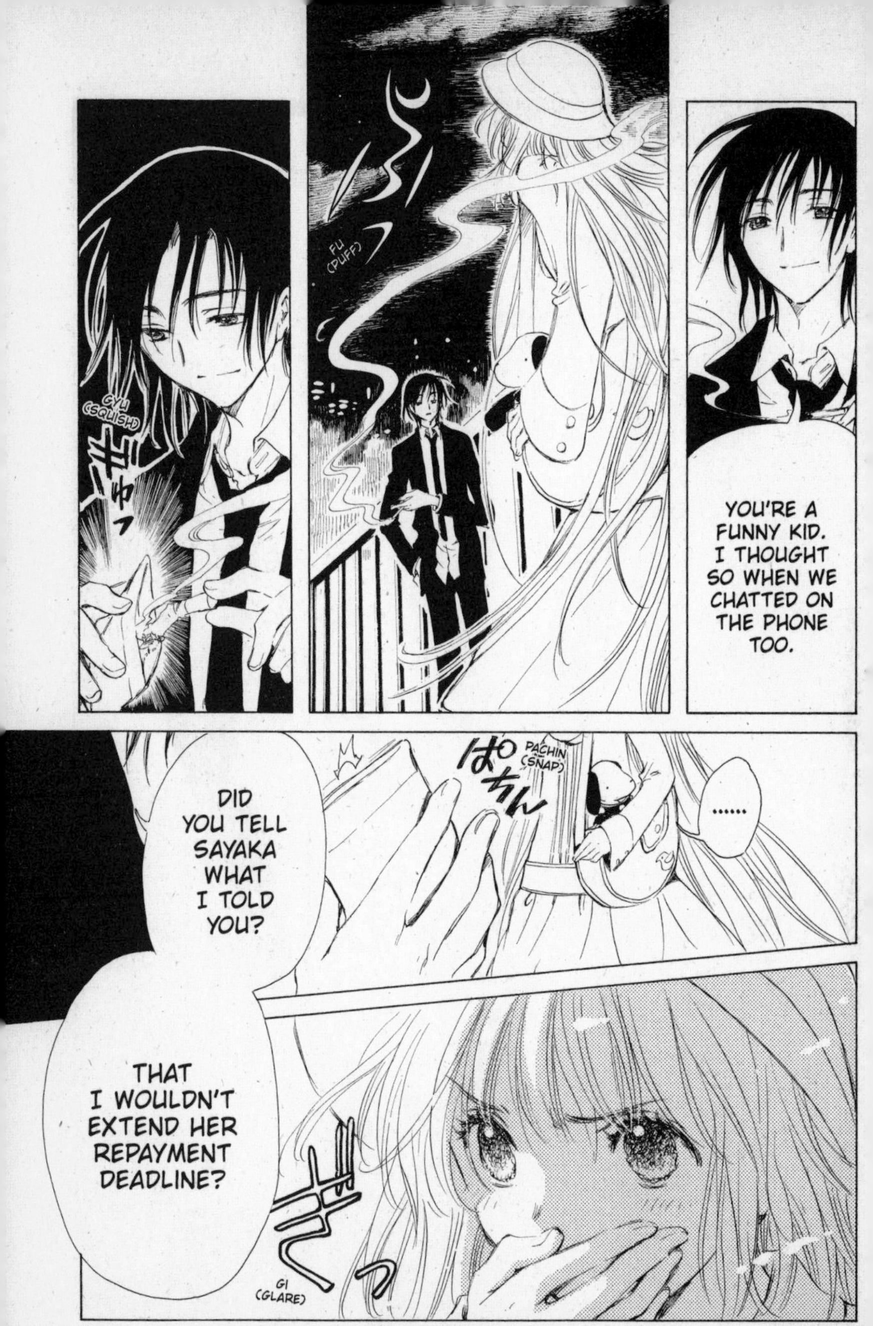
YOU'RE A FUNNY KID. I THOUGHT SO WHEN WE CHATTED ON THE PHONE TOO.
FU (PUFF)
GYU (SQUISH)
PACHIN (SNAP)
......
DID YOU TELL SAYAKA WHAT I TOLD YOU?
THAT I WOULDN'T EXTEND HER REPAYMENT DEADLINE?
GI (GLARE)

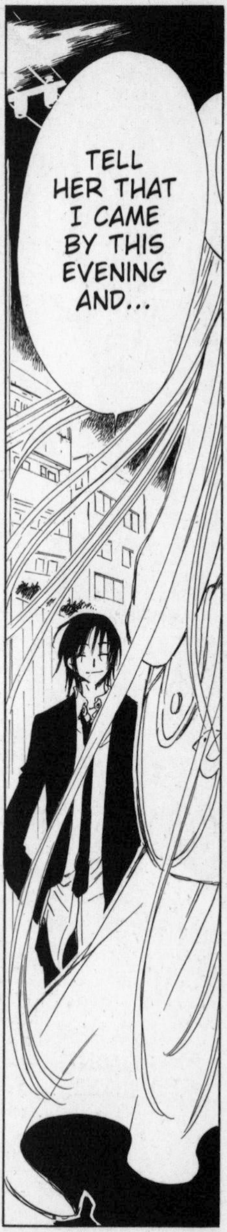
TELL HER THAT I CAME BY THIS EVENING AND...

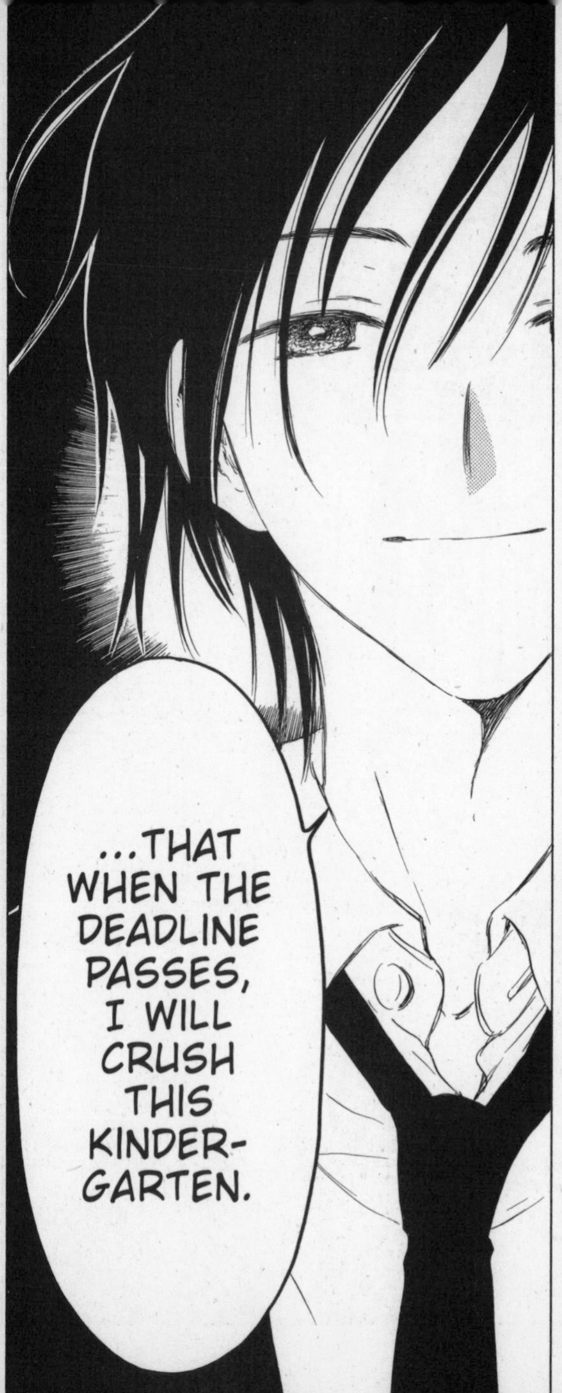
...THAT WHEN THE DEADLINE PASSES, I WILL CRUSH THIS KINDER-GARTEN.

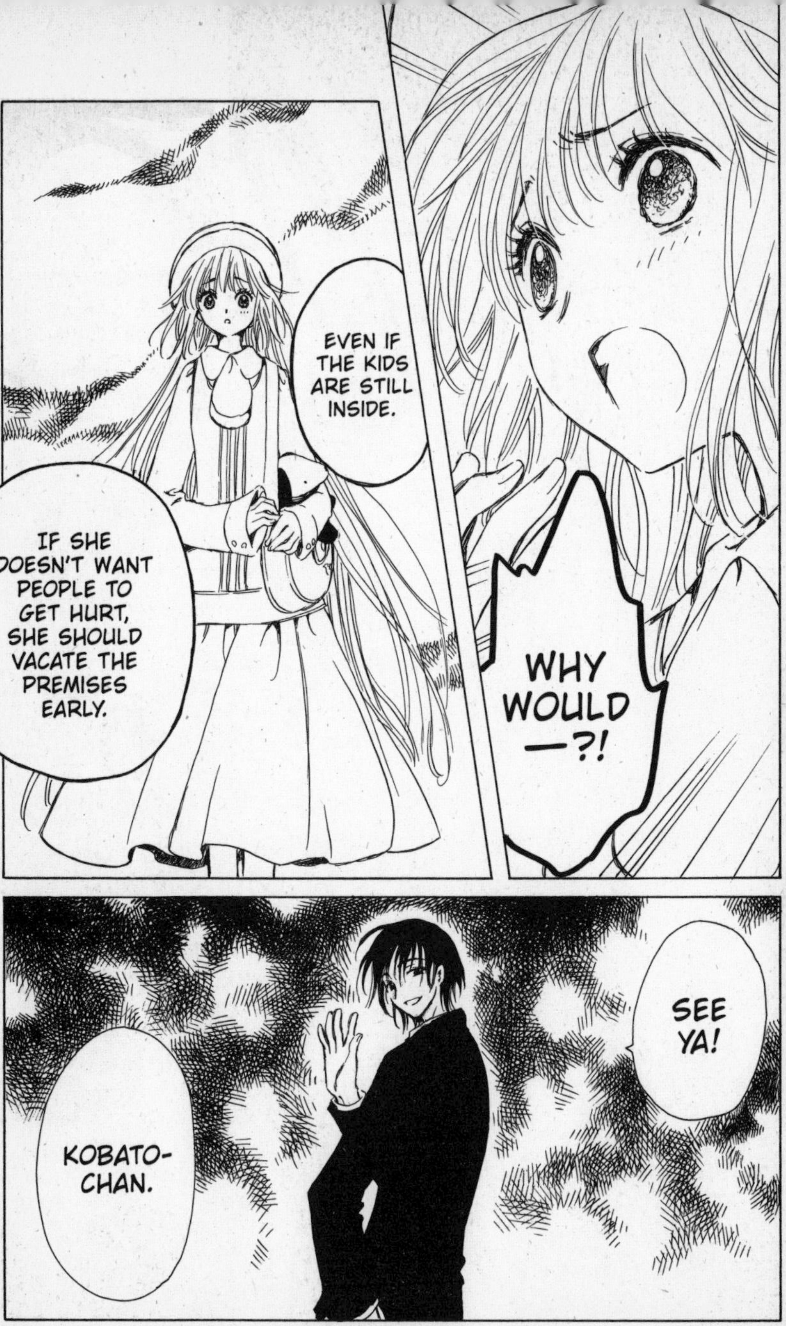
WHY WOULD—?!
EVEN IF THE KIDS ARE STILL INSIDE.
IF SHE DOESN'T WANT PEOPLE TO GET HURT, SHE SHOULD VACATE THE PREMISES EARLY.
SEE YA!
KOBATO-CHAN.

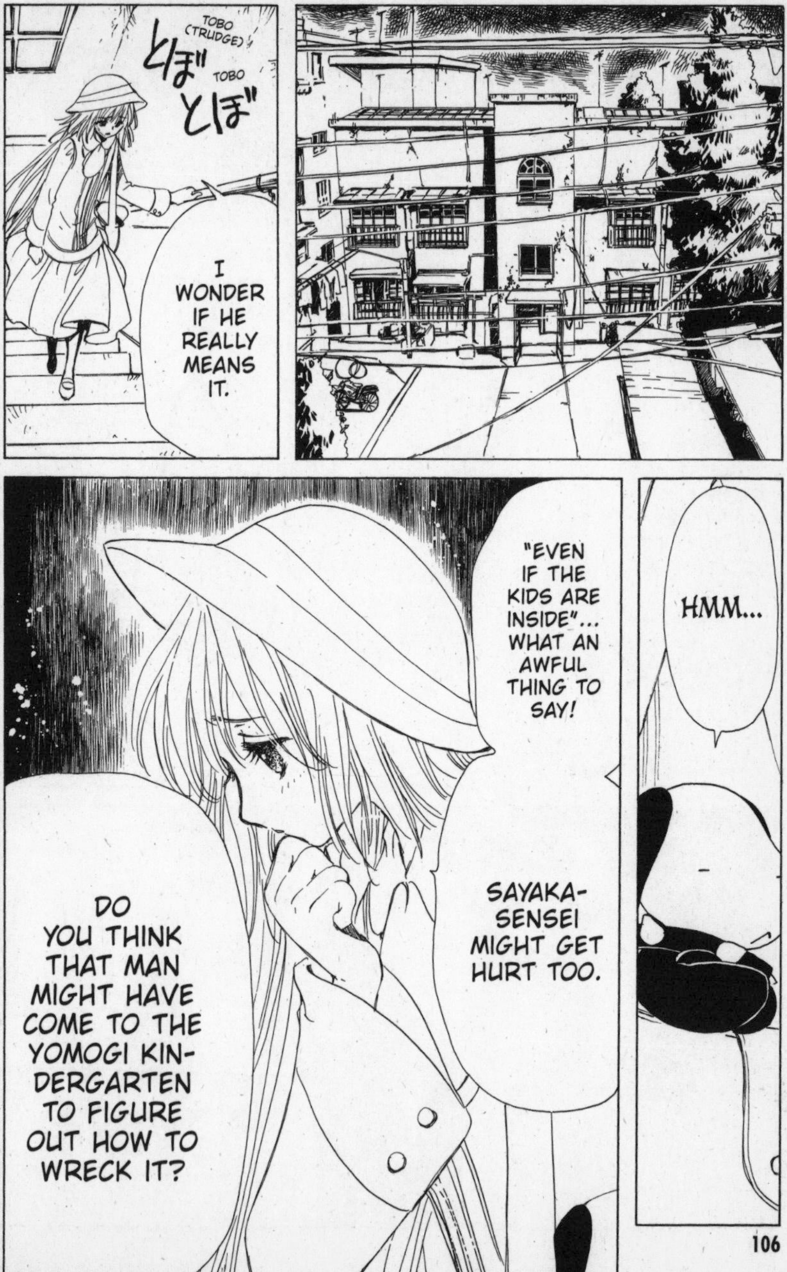
とぼとぼ
TOBO (TRUDGE) TOBO
I WONDER IF HE REALLY MEANS IT.
HMM...
"EVEN IF THE KIDS ARE INSIDE"... WHAT AN AWFUL THING TO SAY!
SAYAKA-SENSEI MIGHT GET HURT TOO.
DO YOU THINK THAT MAN MIGHT HAVE COME TO THE YOMOGI KIN-DERGARTEN TO FIGURE OUT HOW TO WRECK IT?

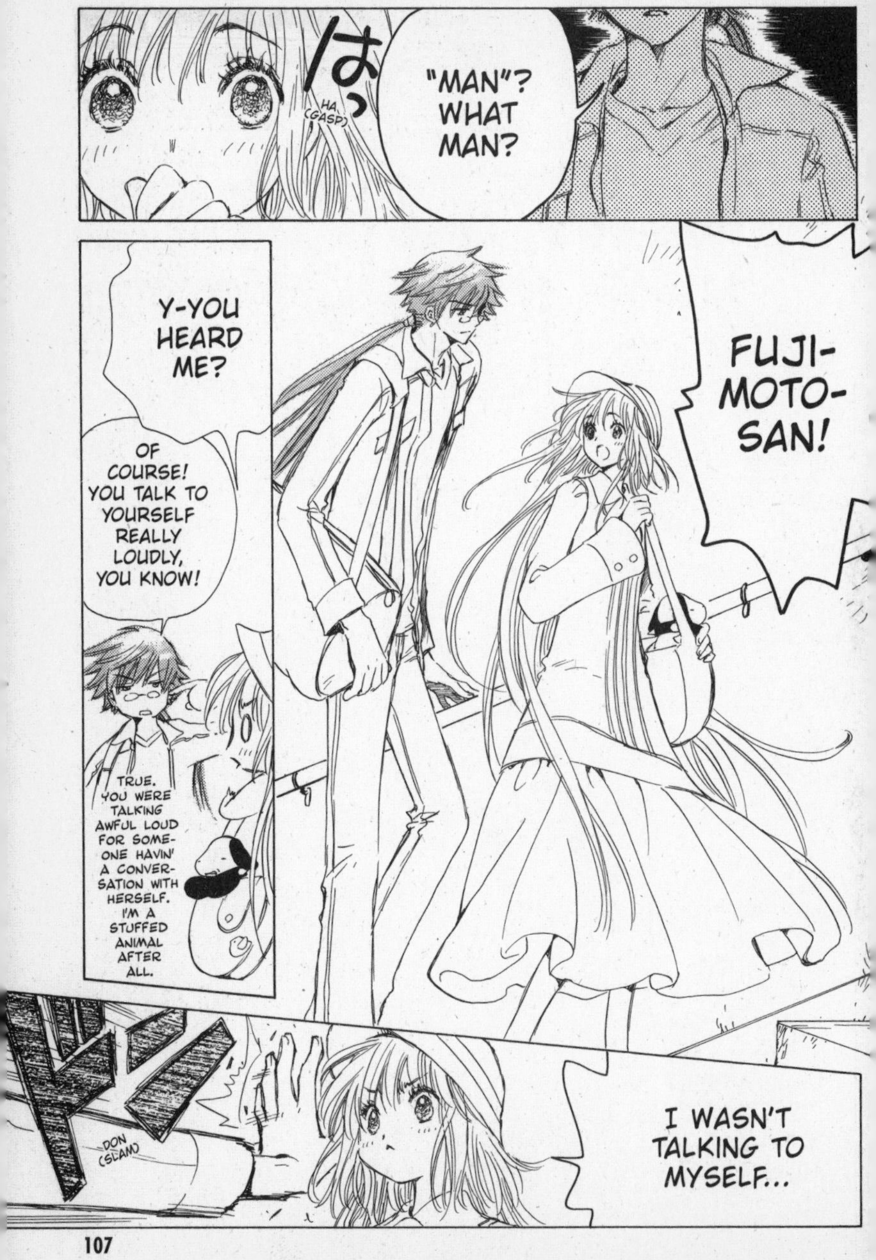
"MAN"? WHAT MAN?
は
HA (GASP)
FUJI-MOTO-SAN!
Y-YOU HEARD ME?
OF COURSE! YOU TALK TO YOURSELF REALLY LOUDLY, YOU KNOW!
TRUE. YOU WERE TALKING AWFUL LOUD FOR SOME-ONE HAVIN' A CONVER-SATION WITH HERSELF. I'M A STUFFED ANIMAL AFTER ALL.
I WASN'T TALKING TO MYSELF...
DON (SLAM)

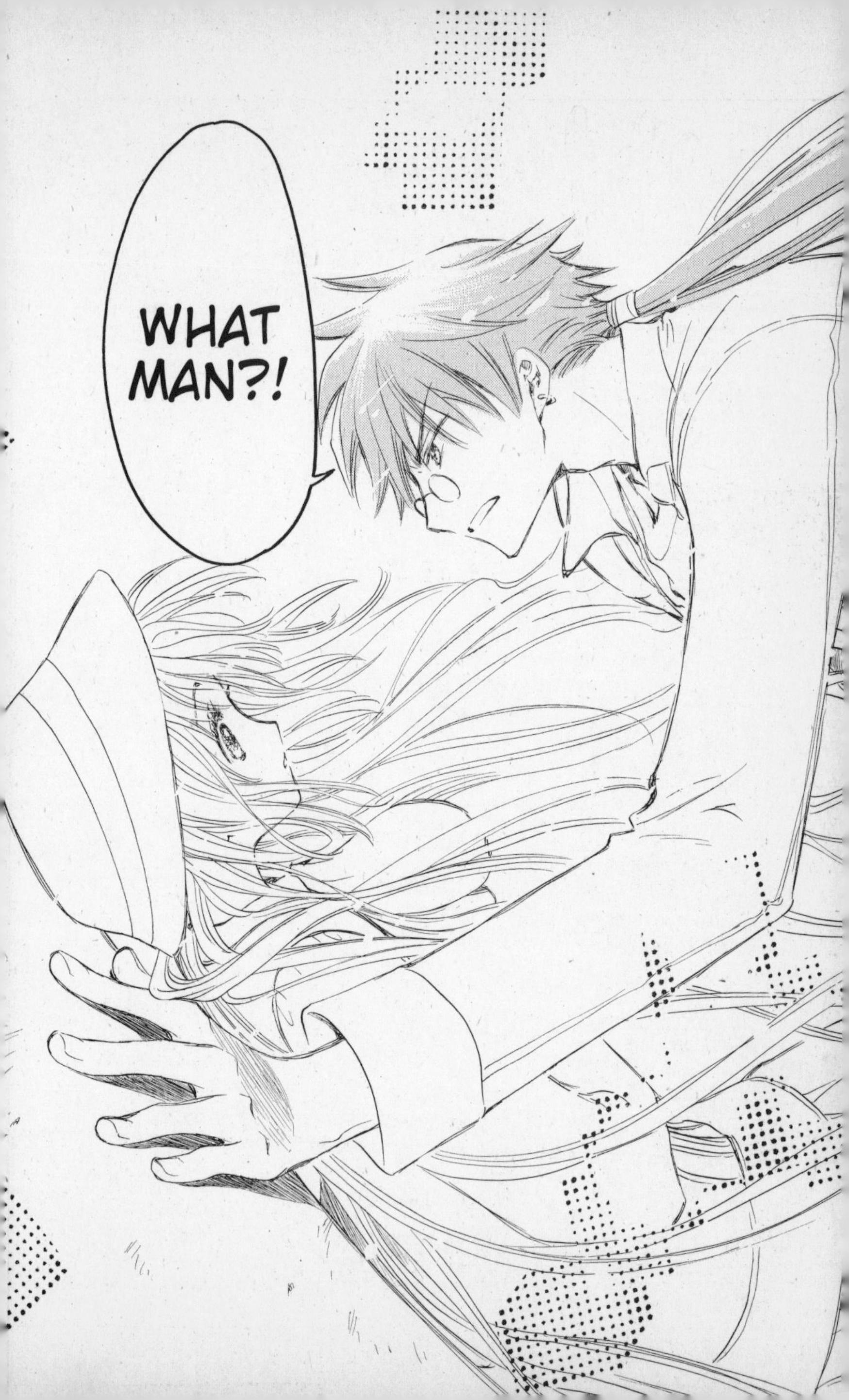
WHAT MAN?!

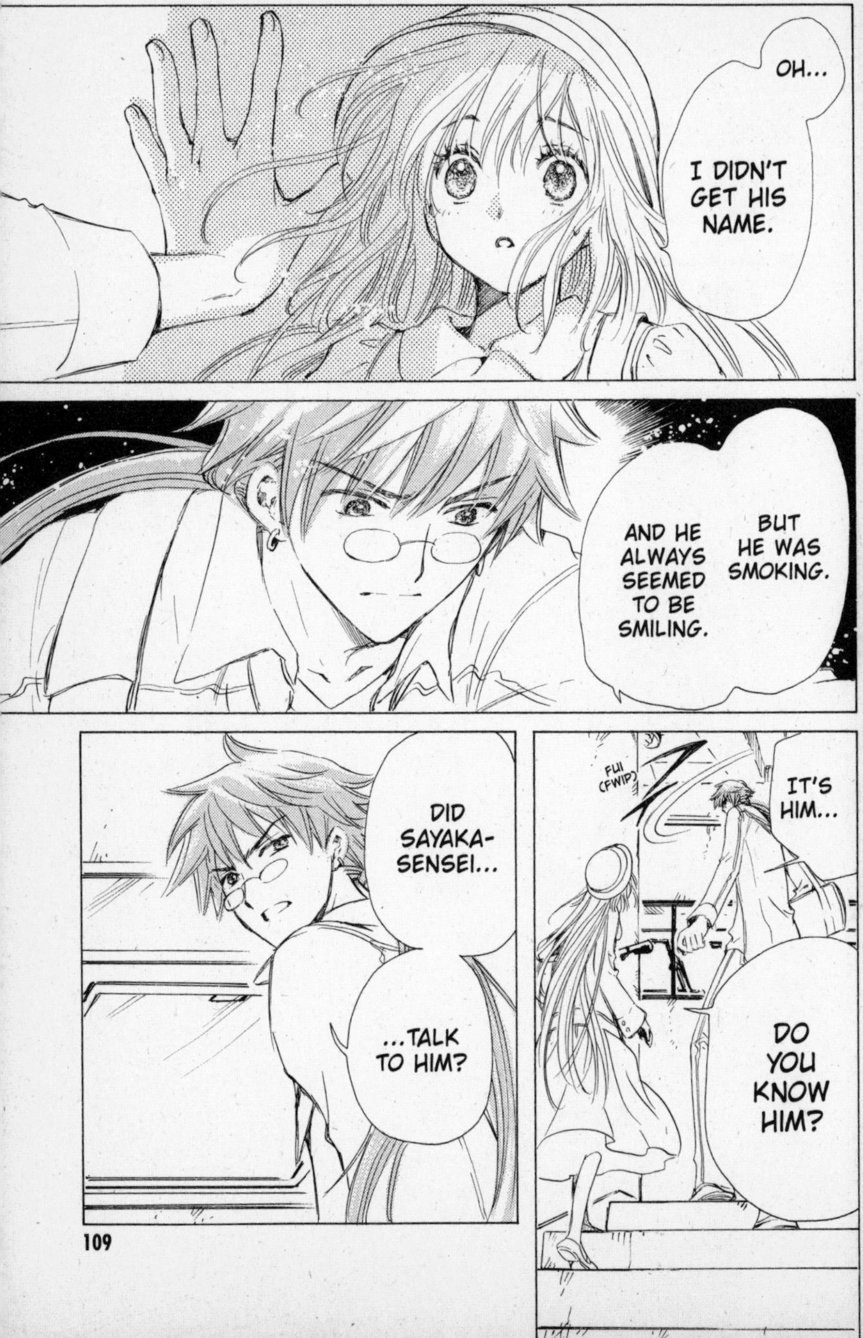
OH...
I DIDN'T GET HIS NAME.
BUT HE WAS SMOKING.
AND HE ALWAYS SEEMED TO BE SMILING.
FUI (FWIP)
IT'S HIM...
DO YOU KNOW HIM?
DID SAYAKA-SENSEI...
...TALK TO HIM?

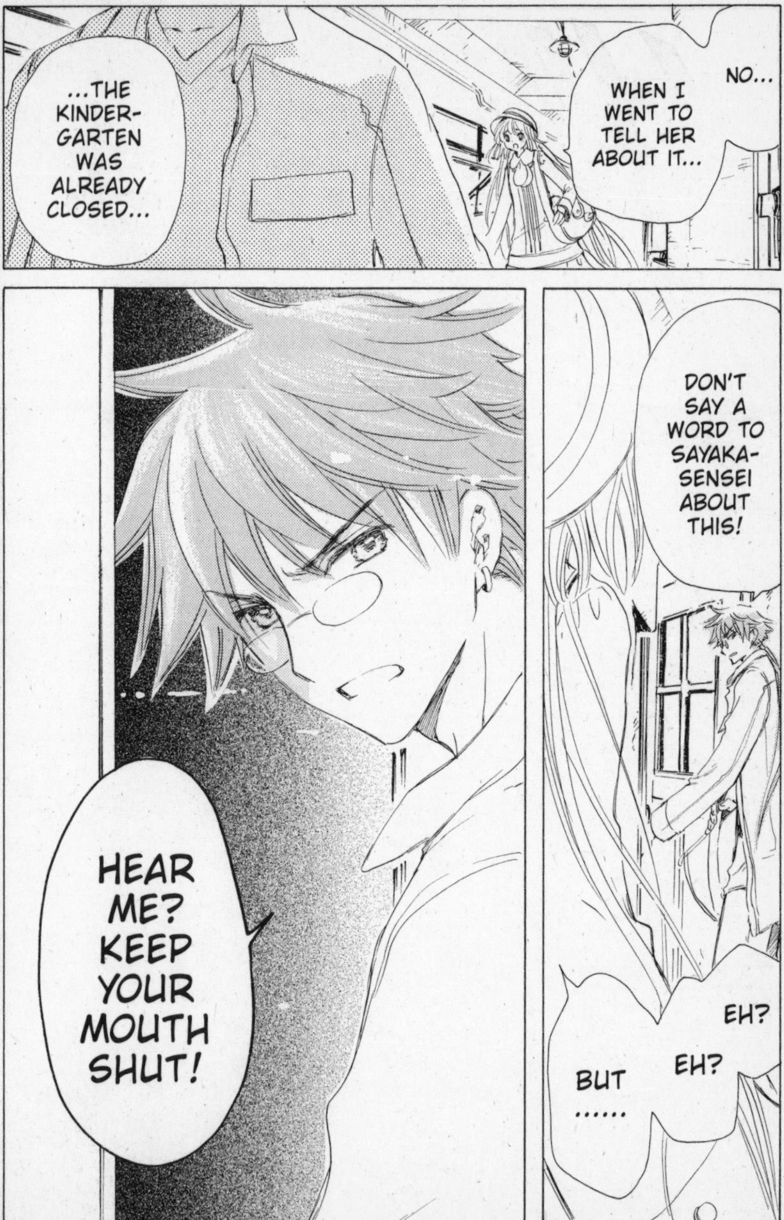
NO...
WHEN I WENT TO TELL HER ABOUT IT...
...THE KINDER-GARTEN WAS ALREADY CLOSED...
DON'T SAY A WORD TO SAYAKA-SENSEI ABOUT THIS!
EH?
EH?
BUT ......
...
HEAR ME? KEEP YOUR MOUTH SHUT!

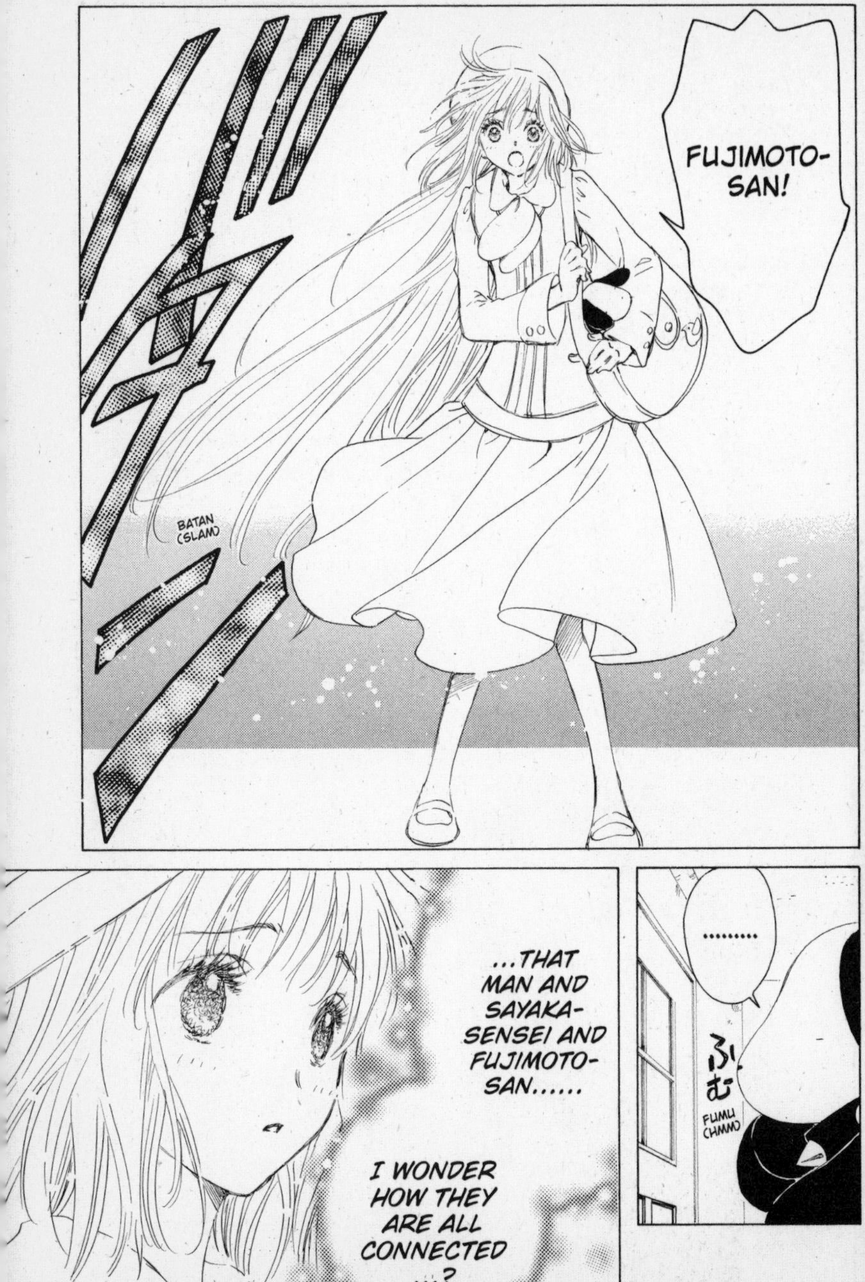
FUJIMOTO-SAN!
BATAN (SLAM)
....
ふむ
FUMU (HMM)
...THAT MAN AND SAYAKA-SENSEI AND FUJIMOTO-SAN......
I WONDER HOW THEY ARE ALL CONNECTED ...?

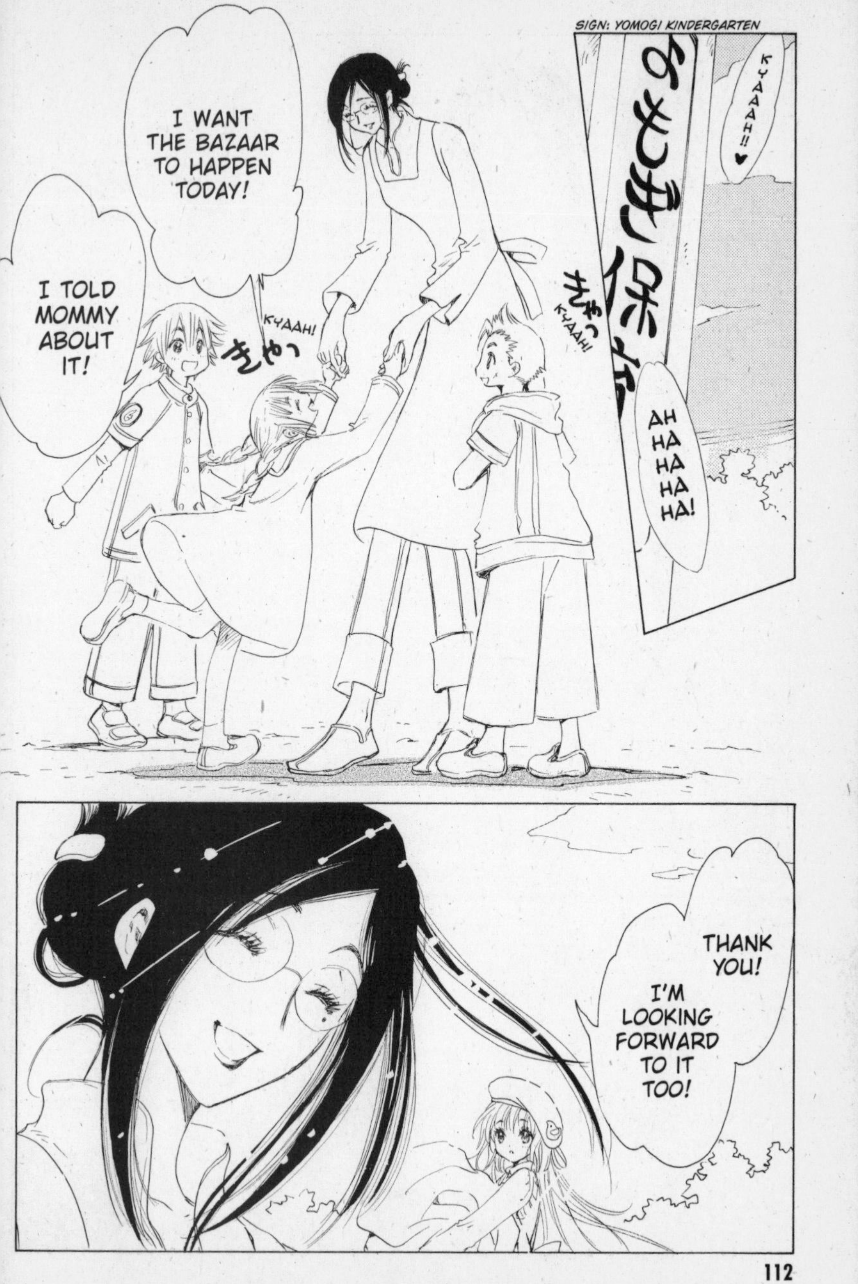
SIGN: YOMOGI KINDERGARTEN
KYAAAAH!! ♥
よもぎ保育
きゃっ KYAAH!
AH HA HA HA HA!
I WANT THE BAZAAR TO HAPPEN TODAY!
KYAAH! きゃっ
I TOLD MOMMY ABOUT IT!
THANK YOU! I'M LOOKING FORWARD TO IT TOO!

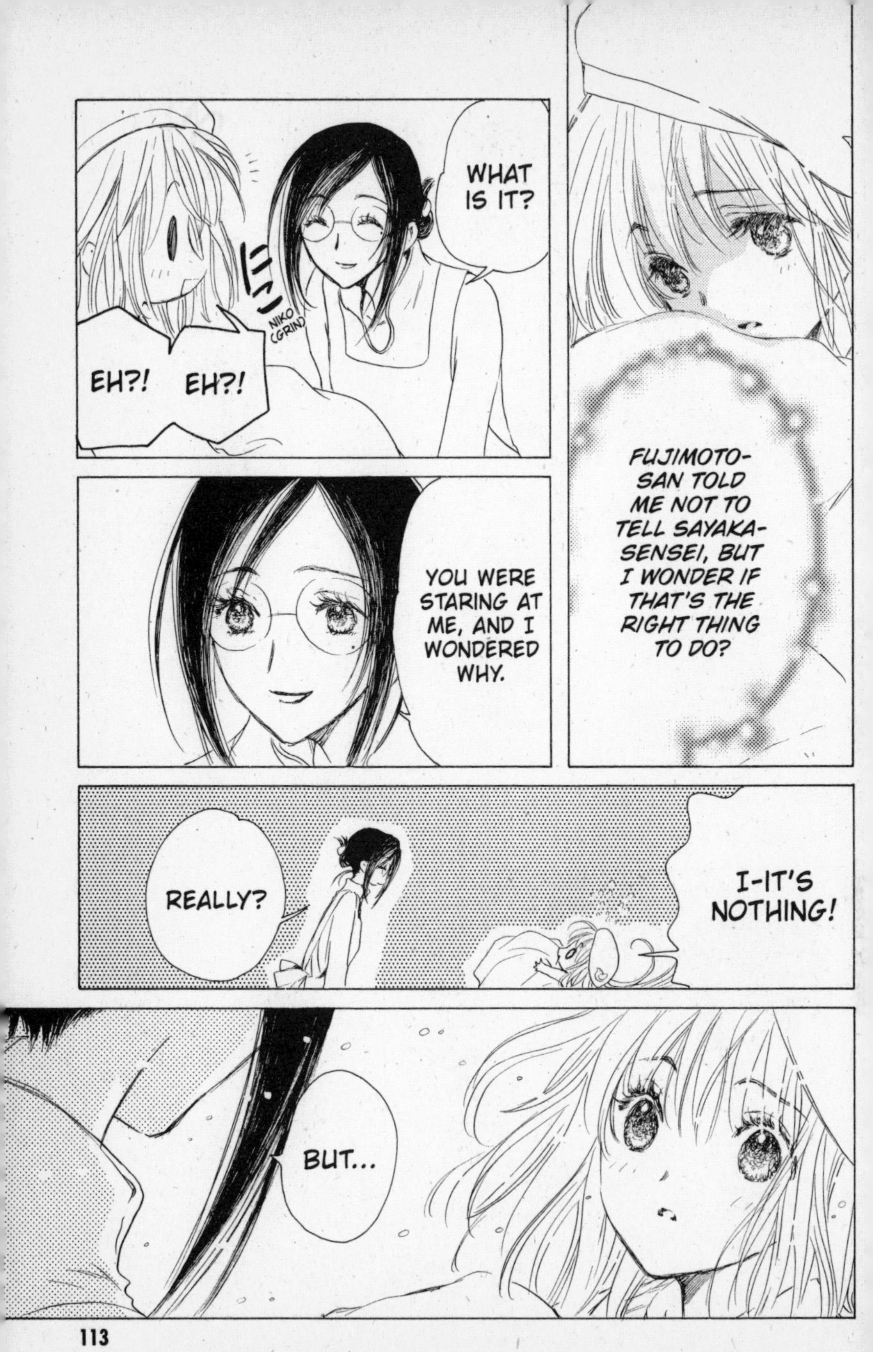
FUJIMOTO-SAN TOLD ME NOT TO TELL SAYAKA-SENSEI, BUT I WONDER IF THAT'S THE RIGHT THING TO DO?
WHAT IS IT?
NIKO (GRIN)
EH?! EH?!
YOU WERE STARING AT ME, AND I WONDERED WHY.
I-IT'S NOTHING!
REALLY?
BUT...

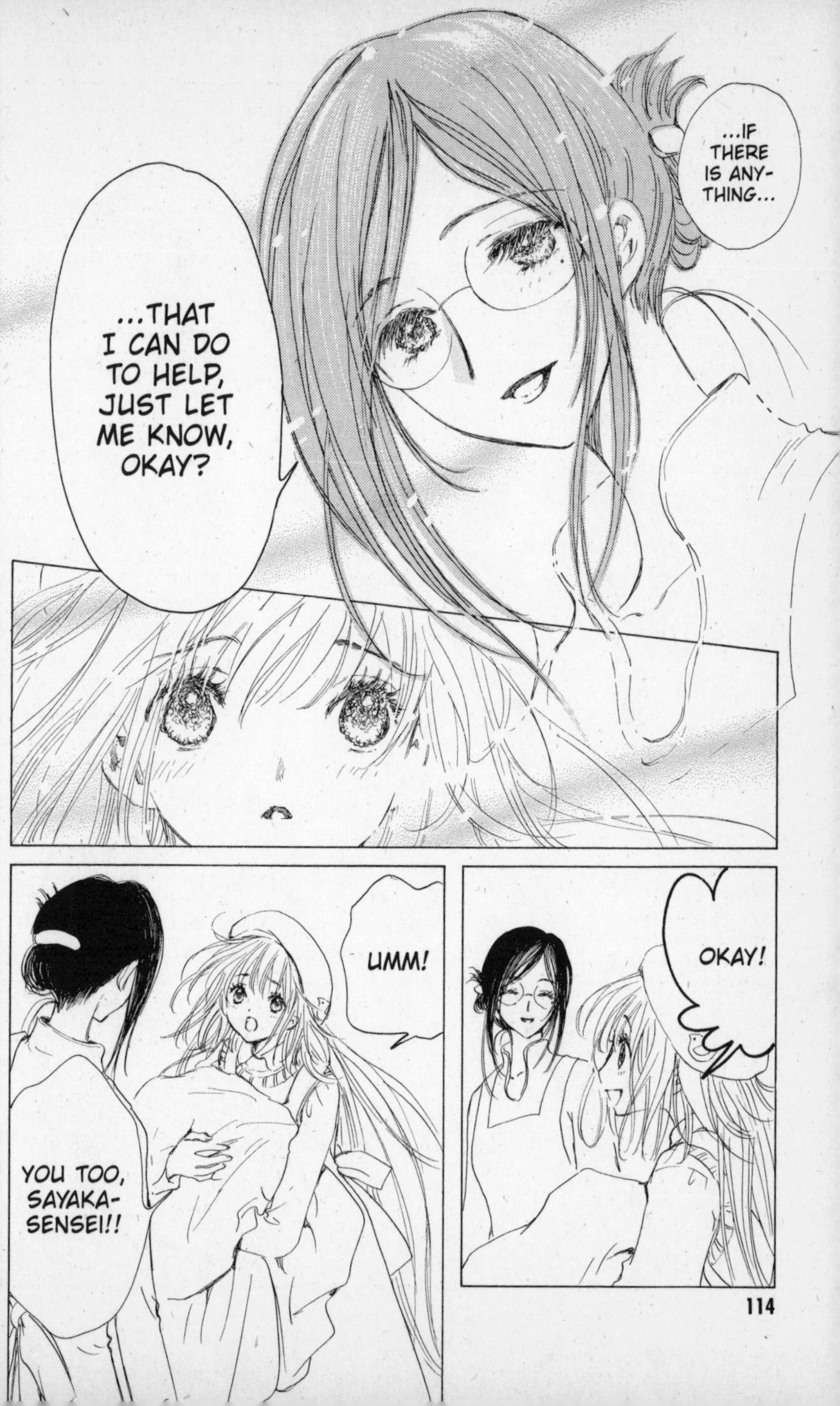
...IF THERE IS ANY-THING...
...THAT I CAN DO TO HELP, JUST LET ME KNOW, OKAY?
OKAY!
UMM!
YOU TOO, SAYAKA-SENSEI!!

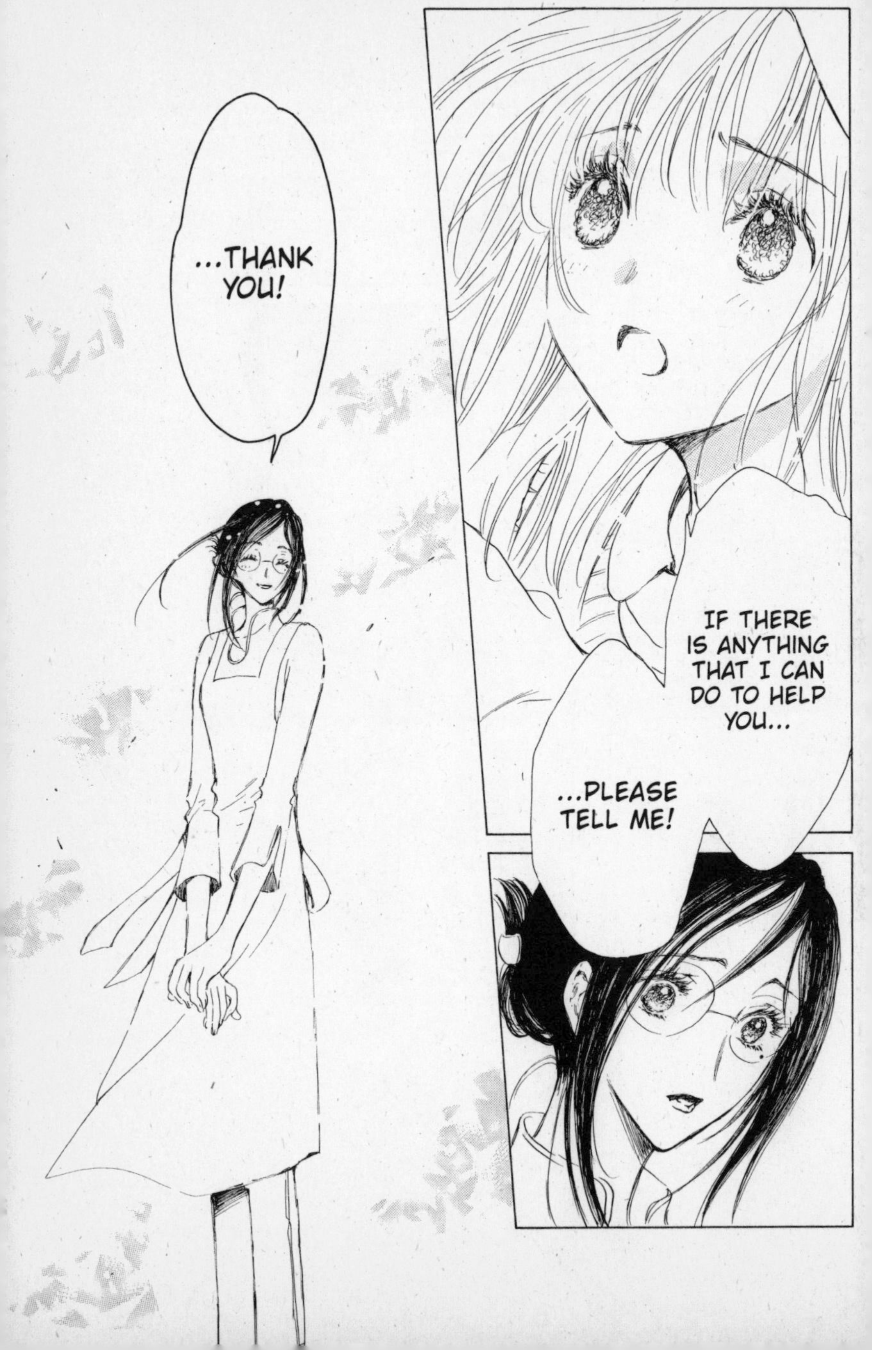
IF THERE IS ANYTHING THAT I CAN DO TO HELP YOU...
...PLEASE TELL ME!
...THANK YOU!

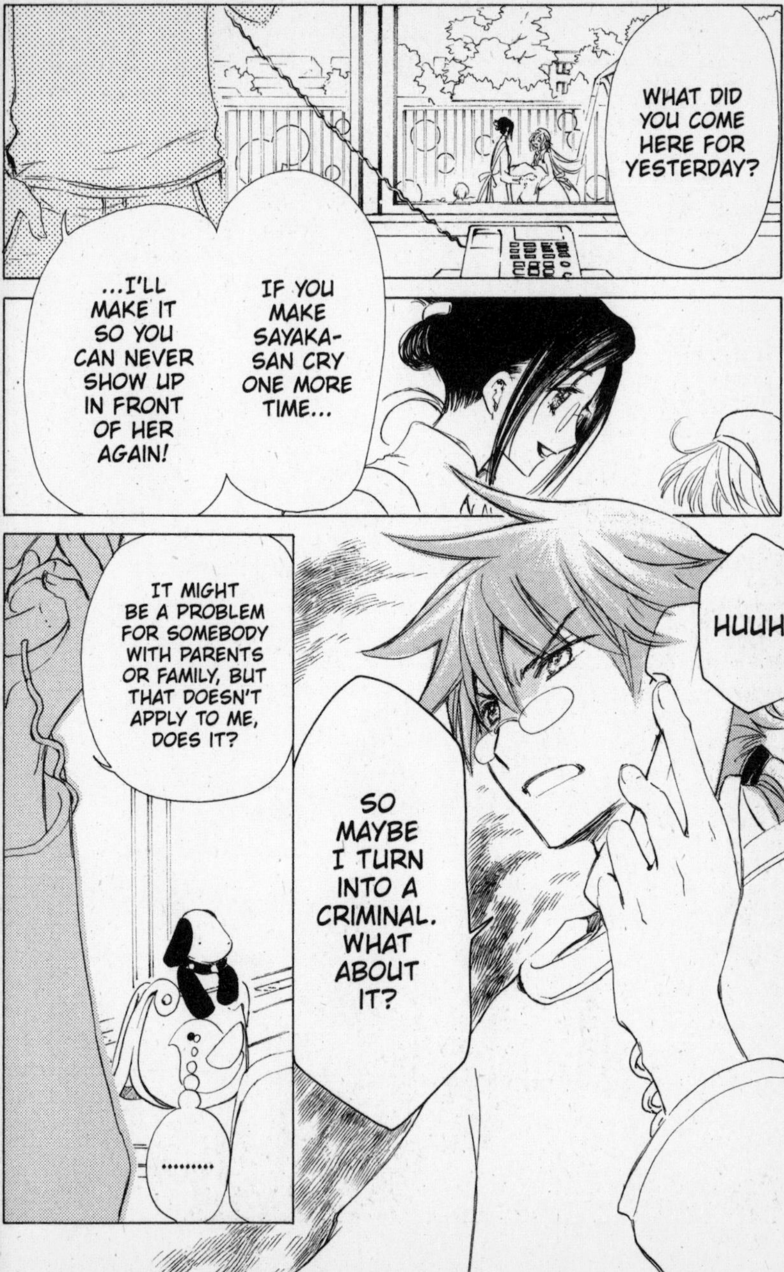
WHAT DID YOU COME HERE FOR YESTERDAY?
IF YOU MAKE SAYAKA-SAN CRY ONE MORE TIME...
...I'LL MAKE IT SO YOU CAN NEVER SHOW UP IN FRONT OF HER AGAIN!
HUUH?
SO MAYBE I TURN INTO A CRIMINAL. WHAT ABOUT IT?
IT MIGHT BE A PROBLEM FOR SOMEBODY WITH PARENTS OR FAMILY, BUT THAT DOESN'T APPLY TO ME, DOES IT?
....

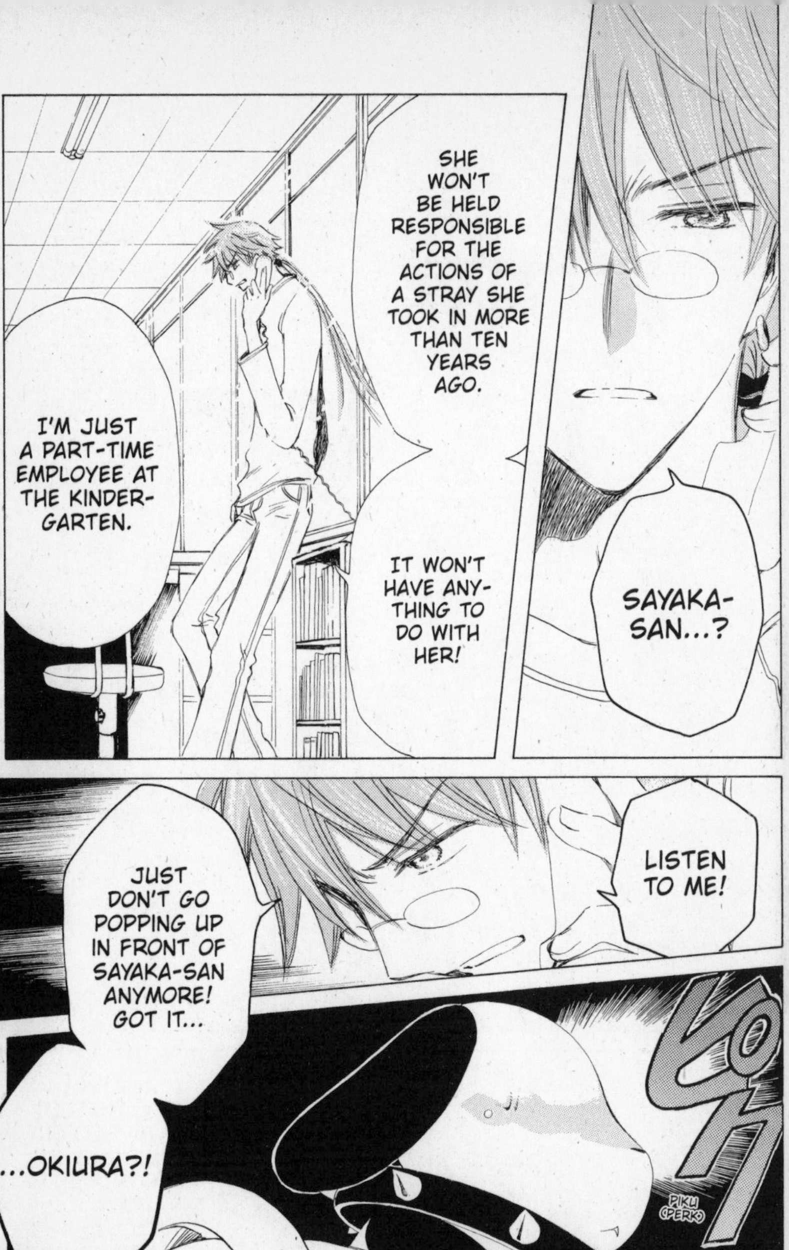
SAYAKA-SAN...?
SHE WON'T BE HELD RESPONSIBLE FOR THE ACTIONS OF A STRAY SHE TOOK IN MORE THAN TEN YEARS AGO.
IT WON'T HAVE ANYTHING TO DO WITH HER!
I'M JUST A PART-TIME EMPLOYEE AT THE KINDER-GARTEN.
LISTEN TO ME!
JUST DON'T GO POPPING UP IN FRONT OF SAYAKA-SAN ANYMORE! GOT IT...
...OKIURA?!
PIKU (PERK)

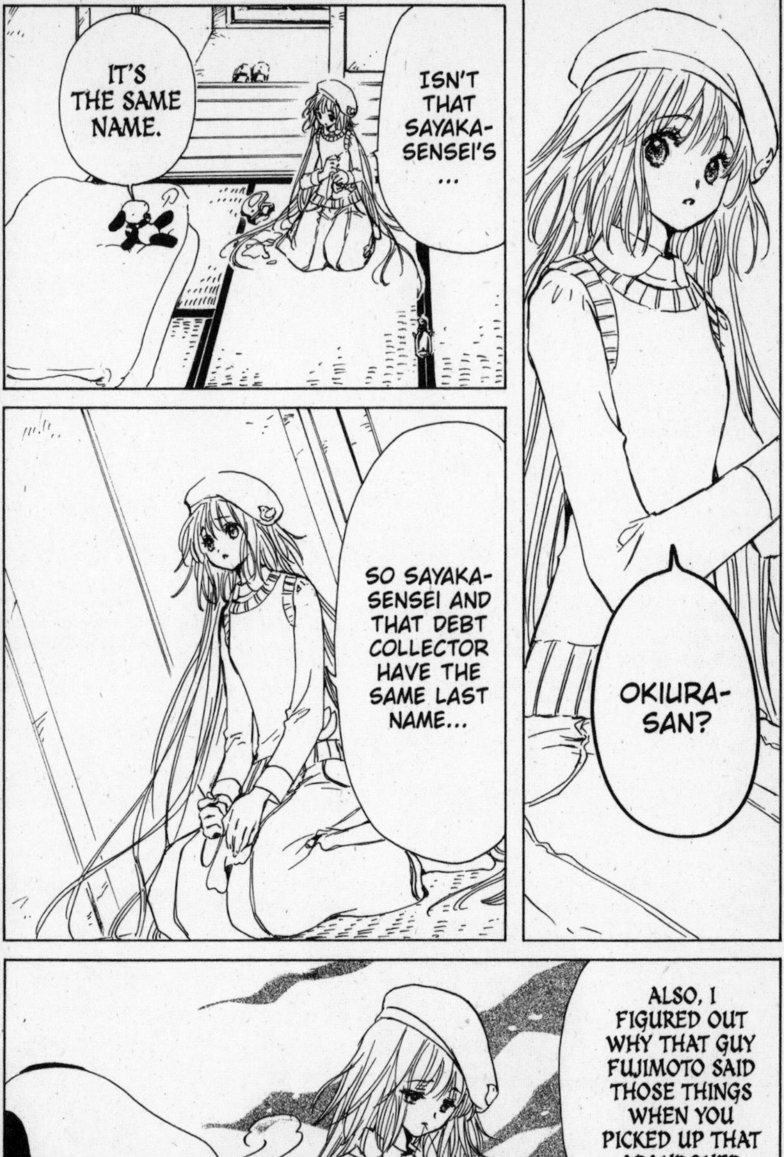
OKIURA-SAN?
ISN'T THAT SAYAKA-SENSEI'S ...
IT'S THE SAME NAME.
SO SAYAKA-SENSEI AND THAT DEBT COLLECTOR HAVE THE SAME LAST NAME...
ALSO, I FIGURED OUT WHY THAT GUY FUJIMOTO SAID THOSE THINGS WHEN YOU PICKED UP THAT ABANDONED CAT.

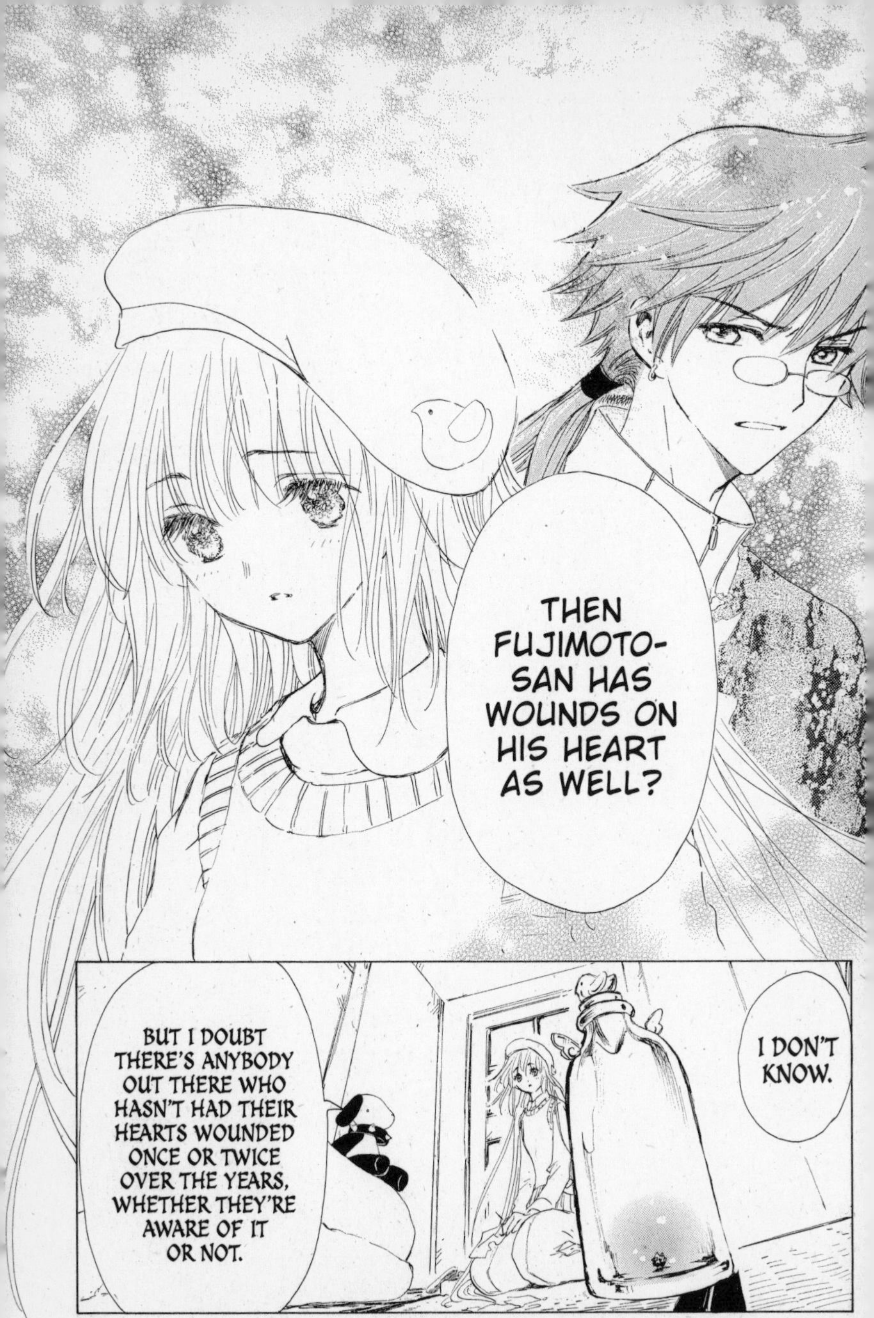
THEN FUJIMOTO-SAN HAS WOUNDS ON HIS HEART AS WELL?
I DON'T KNOW.
BUT I DOUBT THERE'S ANYBODY OUT THERE WHO HASN'T HAD THEIR HEARTS WOUNDED ONCE OR TWICE OVER THE YEARS, WHETHER THEY'RE AWARE OF IT OR NOT.

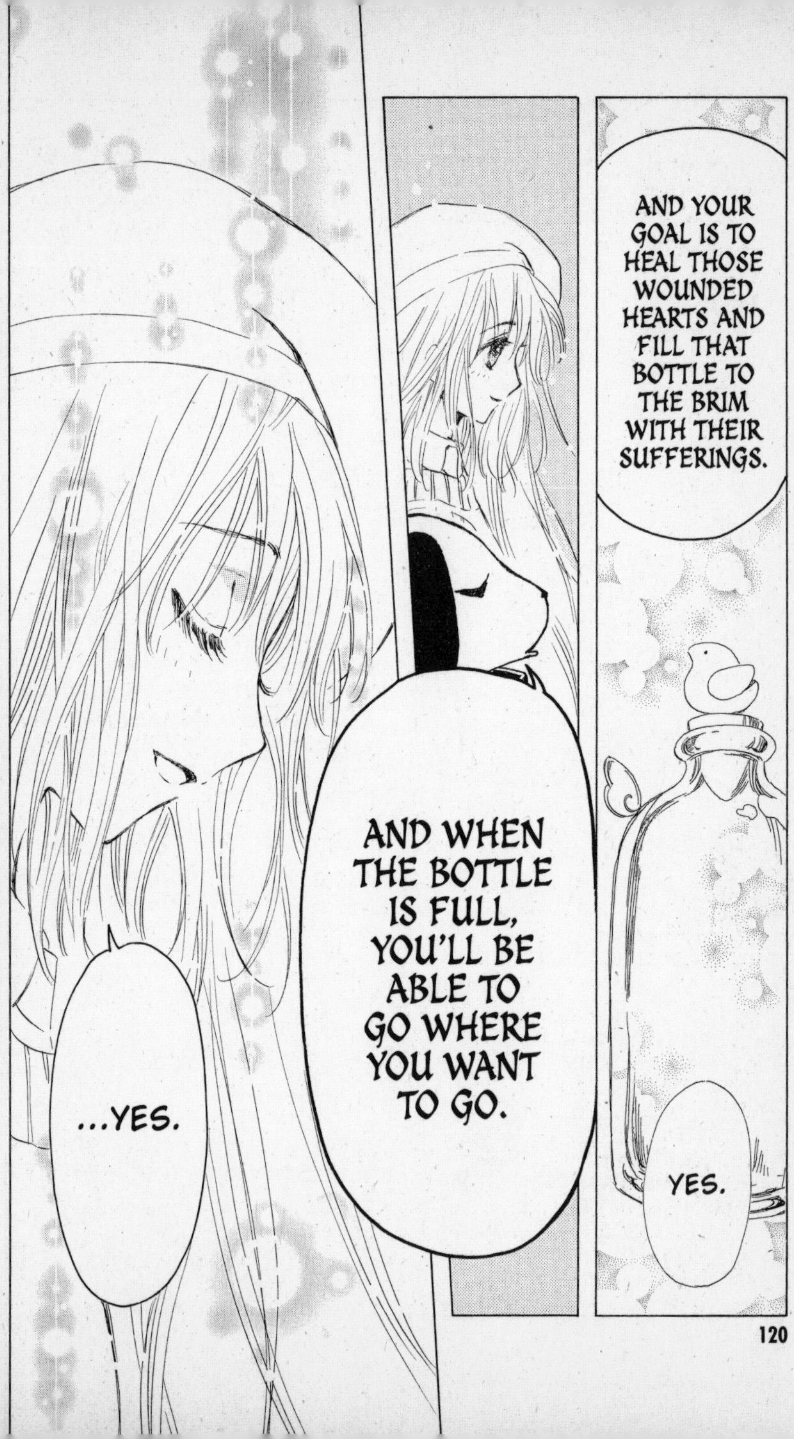
AND YOUR GOAL IS TO HEAL THOSE WOUNDED HEARTS AND FILL THAT BOTTLE TO THE BRIM WITH THEIR SUFFERINGS.
YES.
AND WHEN THE BOTTLE IS FULL, YOU'LL BE ABLE TO GO WHERE YOU WANT TO GO.
...YES.

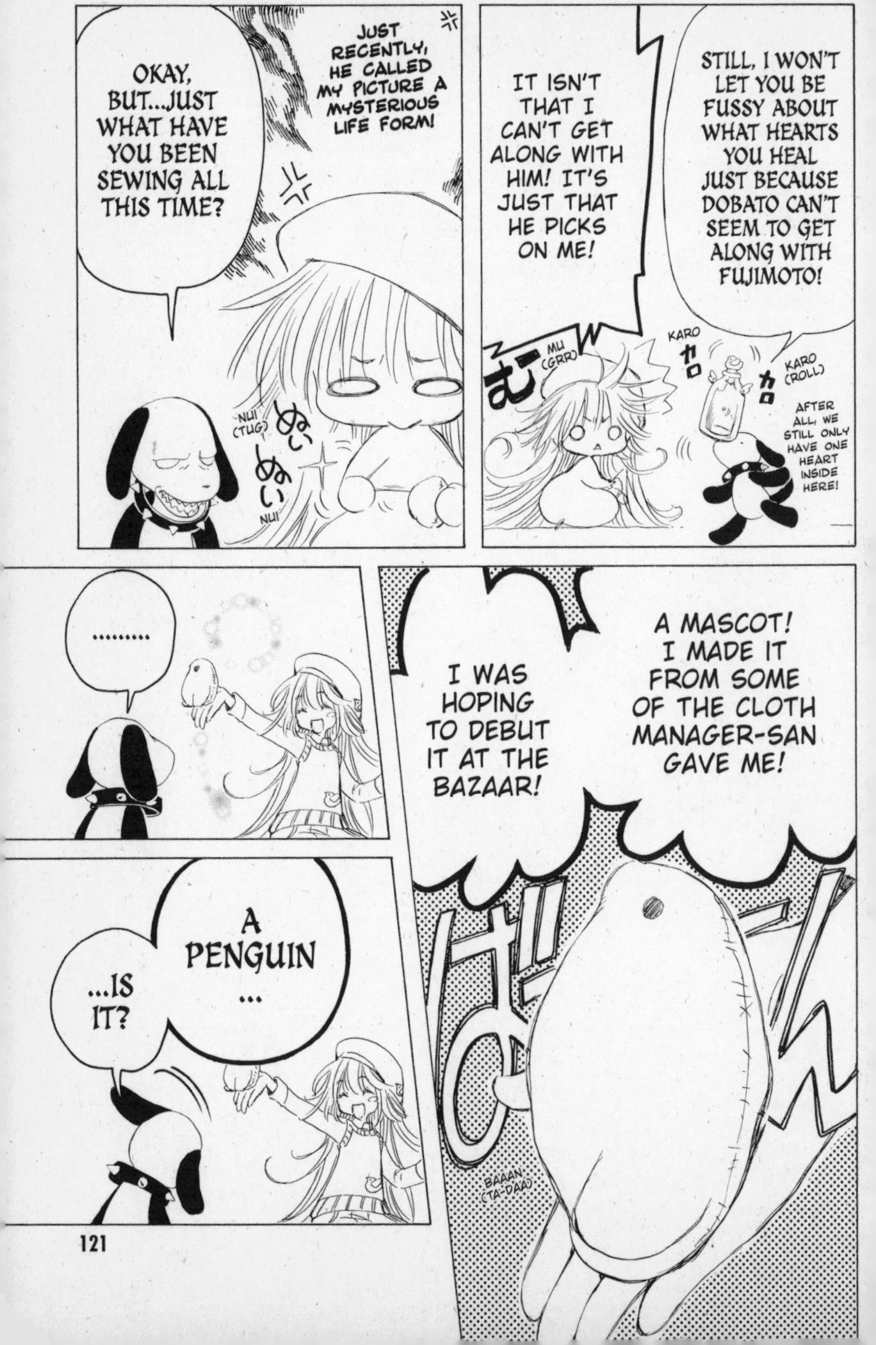
STILL, I WON'T LET YOU BE FUSSY ABOUT WHAT HEARTS YOU HEAL JUST BECAUSE DOBATO CAN'T SEEM TO GET ALONG WITH FUJIMOTO!
IT ISN'T THAT I CAN'T GET ALONG WITH HIM! IT'S JUST THAT HE PICKS ON ME!
KARO
カロ
KARO (ROLL)
カロ
MU (GRR)
む
AFTER ALL, WE STILL ONLY HAVE ONE HEART INSIDE HERE!
JUST RECENTLY, HE CALLED MY PICTURE A MYSTERIOUS LIFE FORM!
OKAY, BUT...JUST WHAT HAVE YOU BEEN SEWING ALL THIS TIME?
NUI (TUG)
ぬい
ぬい
NUI
A MASCOT! I MADE IT FROM SOME OF THE CLOTH MANAGER-SAN GAVE ME!
I WAS HOPING TO DEBUT IT AT THE BAZAAR!
ばーん
BAAAN (TA-DAA)
....
A PENGUIN ...
...IS IT?

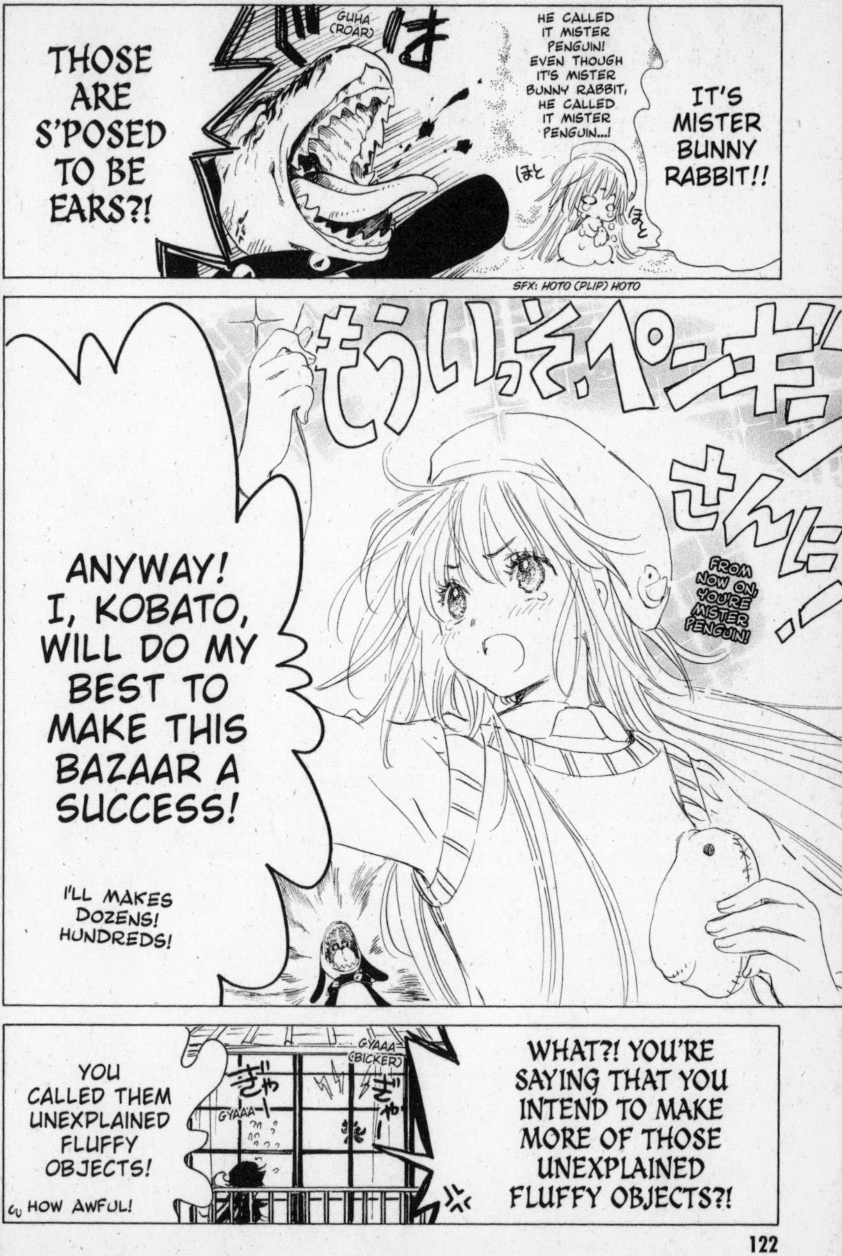

IT'S MISTER BUNNY RABBIT!!
HE CALLED IT MISTER PENGUIN! EVEN THOUGH IT'S MISTER BUNNY RABBIT, HE CALLED IT MISTER PENGUIN...!
ほと
ほと
GUHA (ROAR)
THOSE ARE S'POSED TO BE EARS?!
SFX: HOTO (PLIP) HOTO
もういっそ、ペンギンさんに！
FROM NOW ON, YOU'RE MISTER PENGUIN!
ANYWAY! I, KOBATO, WILL DO MY BEST TO MAKE THIS BAZAAR A SUCCESS!
I'LL MAKES DOZENS! HUNDREDS!
WHAT?! YOU'RE SAYING THAT YOU INTEND TO MAKE MORE OF THOSE UNEXPLAINED FLUFFY OBJECTS?!
GYAAA (BICKER)
ぎゃー
ぎゃー
GYAAA
YOU CALLED THEM UNEXPLAINED FLUFFY OBJECTS!
HOW AWFUL!

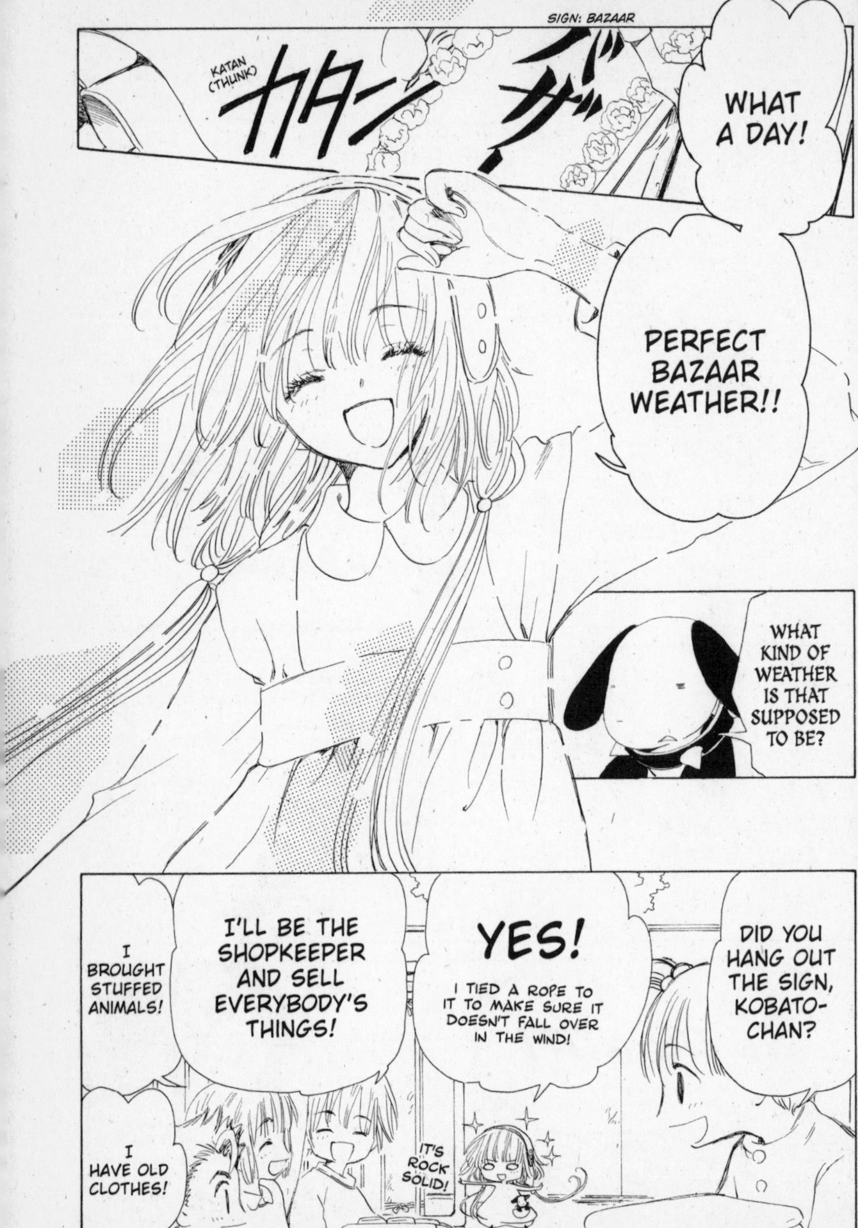
SIGN: BAZAAR
KATAN (THUNK)
WHAT A DAY!
PERFECT BAZAAR WEATHER!!
WHAT KIND OF WEATHER IS THAT SUPPOSED TO BE?
DID YOU HANG OUT THE SIGN, KOBATO-CHAN?
YES!
I TIED A ROPE TO IT TO MAKE SURE IT DOESN'T FALL OVER IN THE WIND!
IT'S ROCK SOLID!
I'LL BE THE SHOPKEEPER AND SELL EVERYBODY'S THINGS!
I BROUGHT STUFFED ANIMALS!
I HAVE OLD CLOTHES!

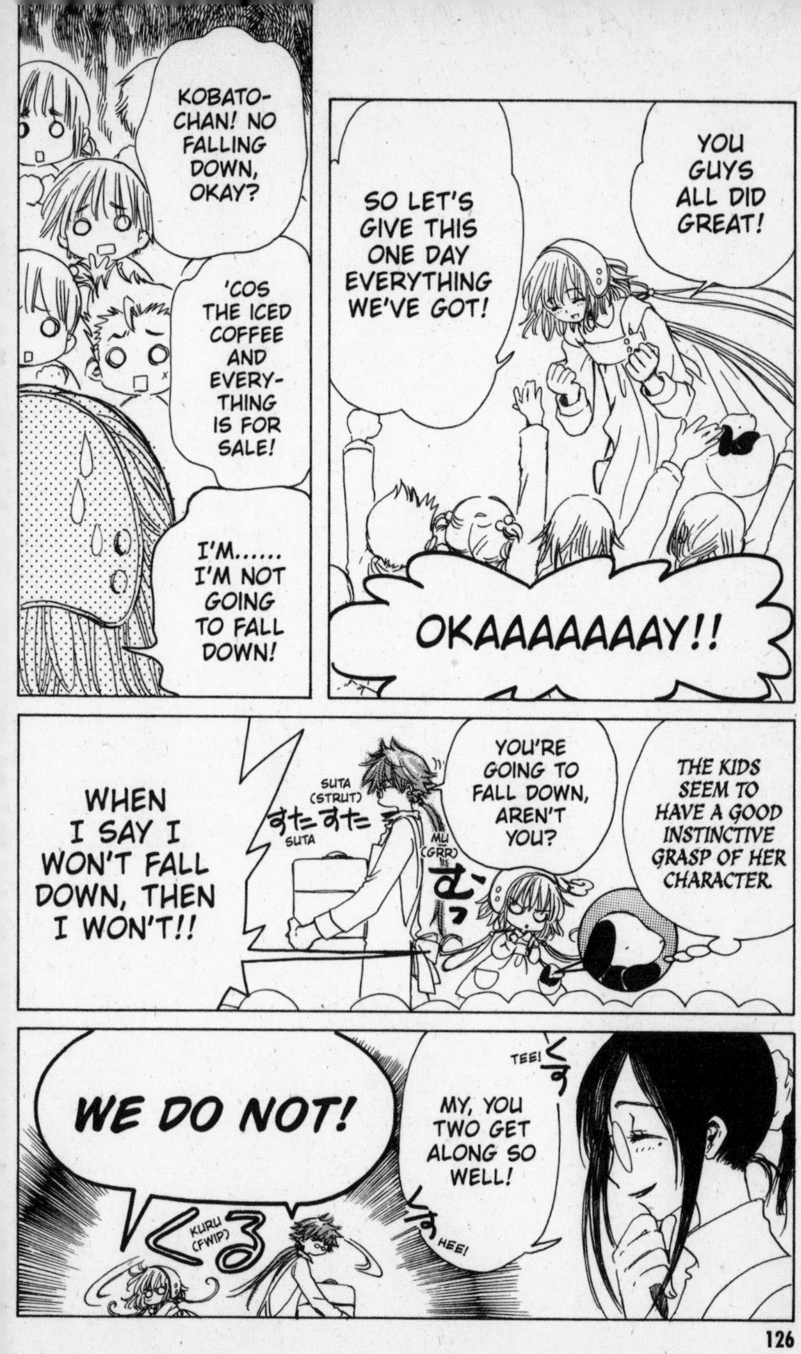
YOU GUYS ALL DID GREAT!
SO LET'S GIVE THIS ONE DAY EVERYTHING WE'VE GOT!
OKAAAAAAAY!!
KOBATO-CHAN! NO FALLING DOWN, OKAY?
'COS THE ICED COFFEE AND EVERY-THING IS FOR SALE!
I'M...... I'M NOT GOING TO FALL DOWN!
THE KIDS SEEM TO HAVE A GOOD INSTINCTIVE GRASP OF HER CHARACTER.
YOU'RE GOING TO FALL DOWN, AREN'T YOU?
MU (GRR)
SUTA (STRUT) SUTA
WHEN I SAY I WON'T FALL DOWN, THEN I WON'T!!
TEE!
MY, YOU TWO GET ALONG SO WELL!
HEE!
WE DO NOT!
KURU (FWIP)

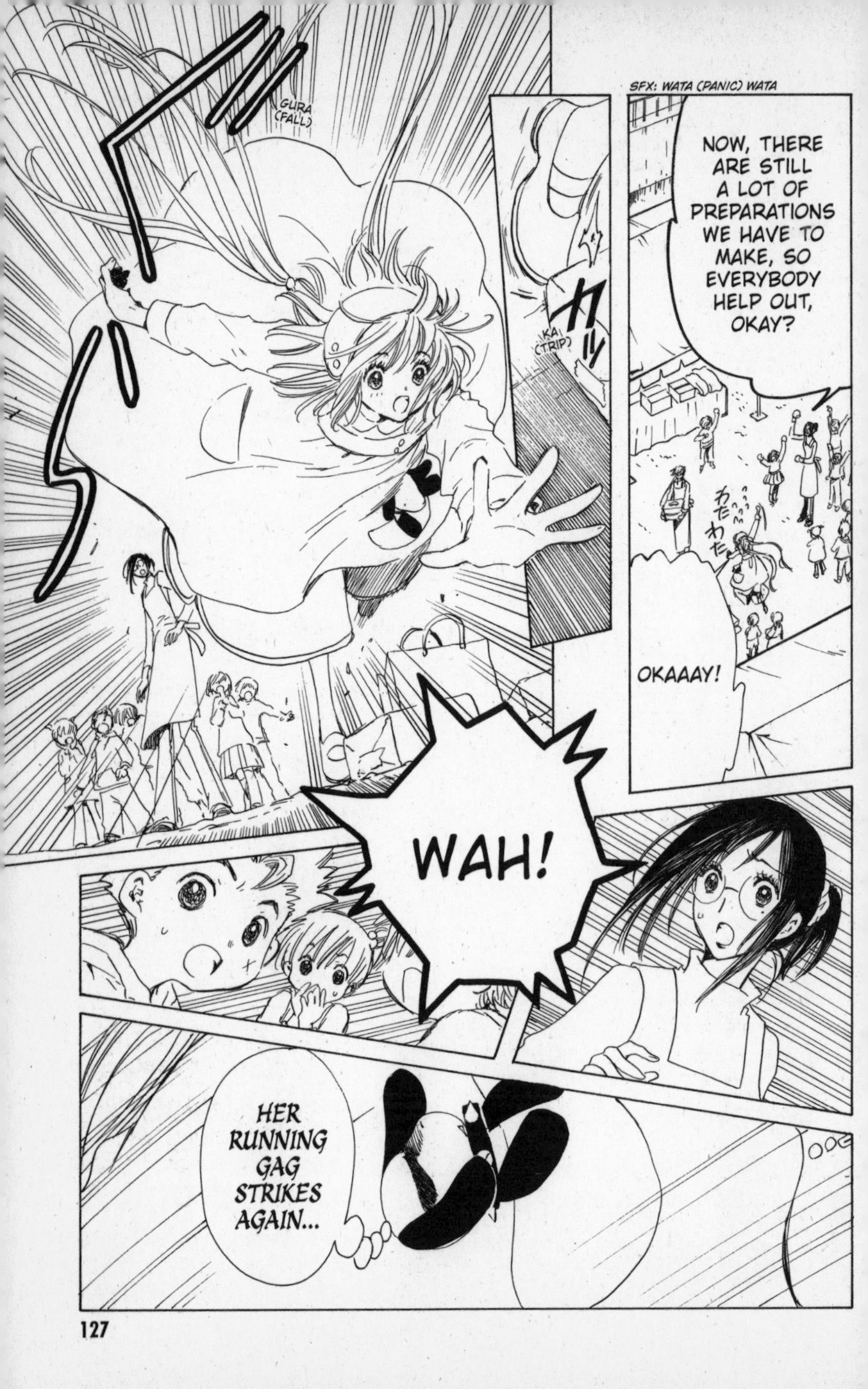
SFX: WATA (PANIC) WATA
NOW, THERE ARE STILL A LOT OF PREPARATIONS WE HAVE TO MAKE, SO EVERYBODY HELP OUT, OKAY?
わたわた
OKAAAY!
KA (TRIP)
GURA (FALL)
WAH!
HER RUNNING GAG STRIKES AGAIN...

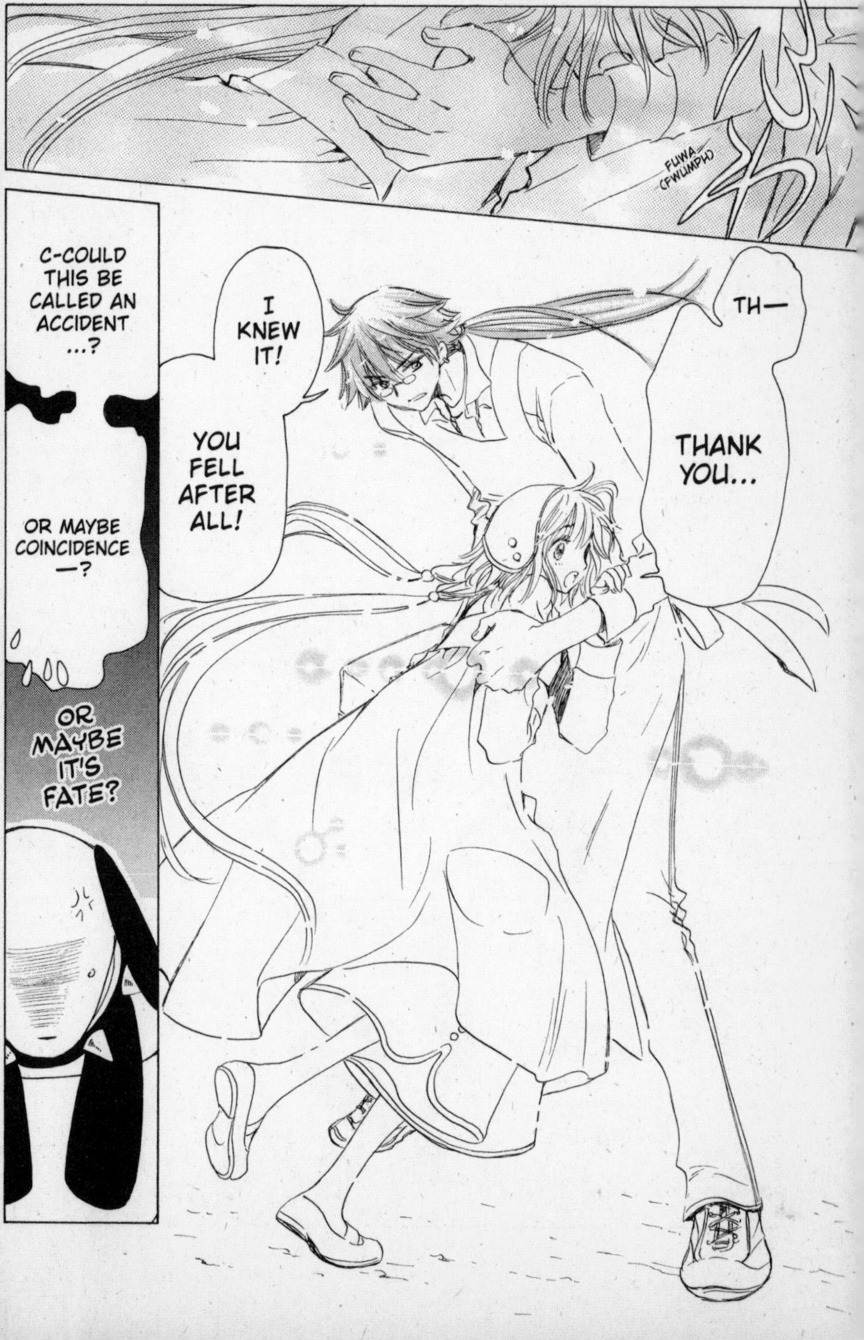
FUWA (FWUMPH)
TH—
THANK YOU...
I KNEW IT!
YOU FELL AFTER ALL!
C-COULD THIS BE CALLED AN ACCIDENT ...?
OR MAYBE COINCIDENCE —?
OR MAYBE IT'S FATE?

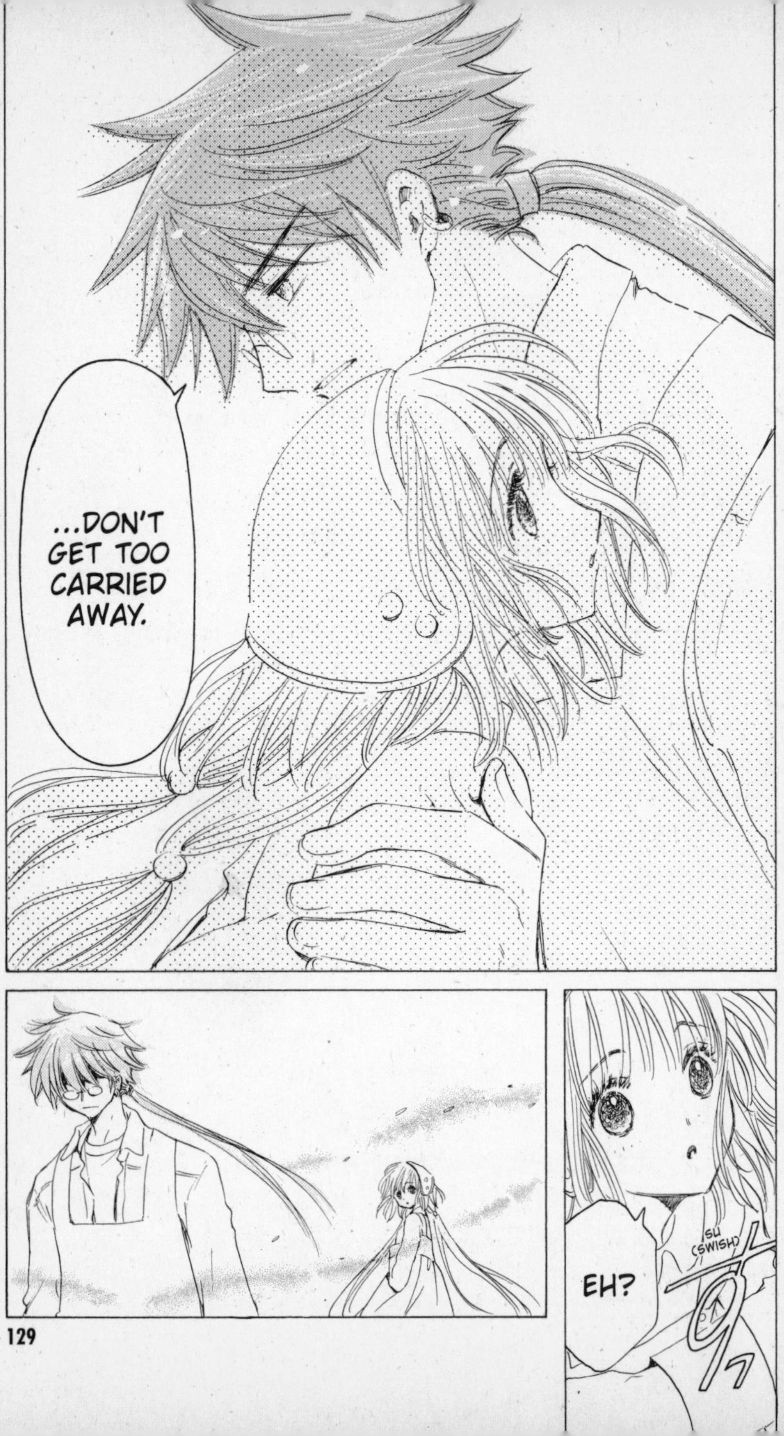
...DON'T GET TOO CARRIED AWAY.
SU (SWISH)
EH?

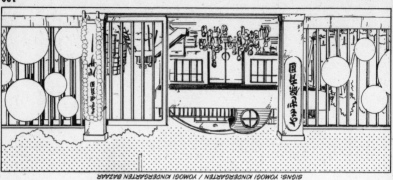

I-I THINK THAT HE WAS PICKING ON ME THEN...
...BUT HIS VOICE WAS SOMEHOW GENTLE...
HMMM ...
KOBATO-CHAAAN!
COMIIING!
WE HAVE TO HURRY!
ZUBE (TRIP)
KYAN!!
AND, OF COURSE, THE RUNNING GAG...
....
SIGNS: YOMOGI KINDERGARTEN / YOMOGI KINDERGARTEN BAZAAR
よもぎ保育園
よもぎ保育園バザー

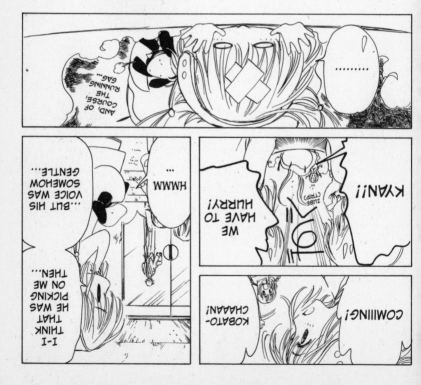

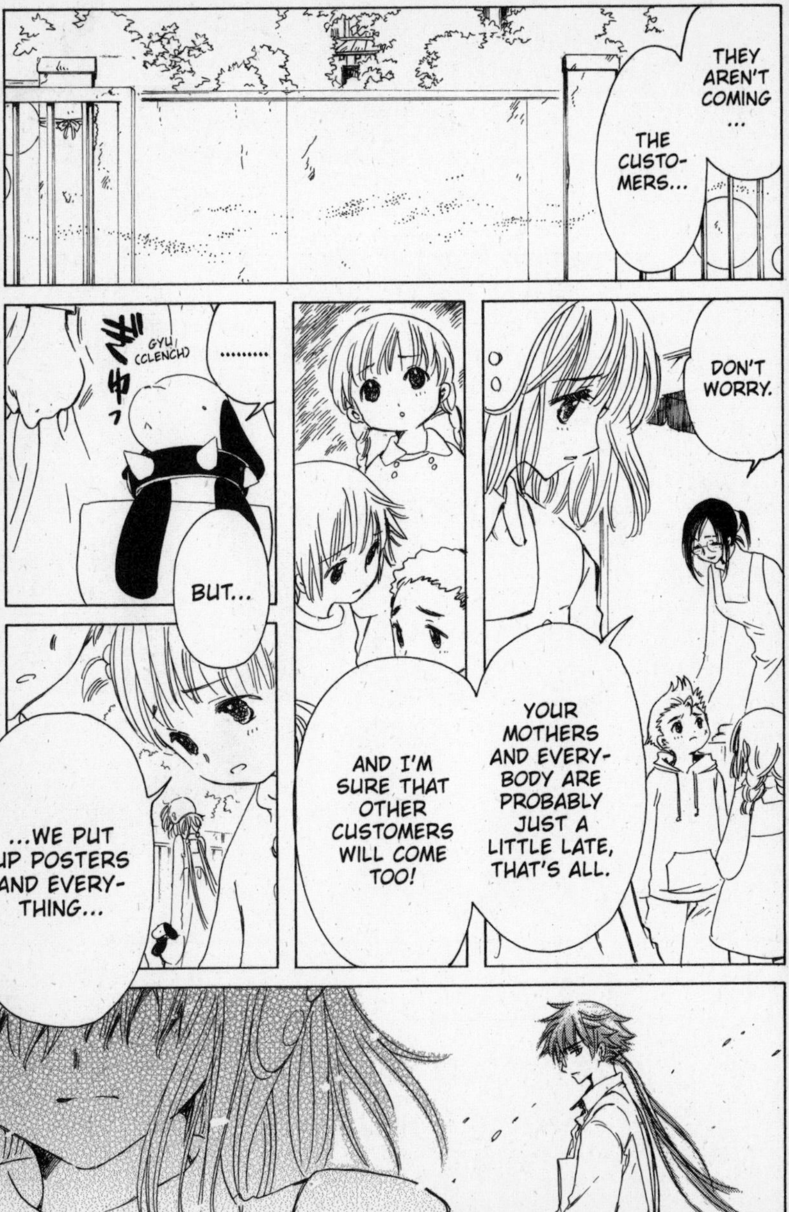
THEY AREN'T COMING...
THE CUSTOMERS...
DON'T WORRY.
YOUR MOTHERS AND EVERYBODY ARE PROBABLY JUST A LITTLE LATE, THAT'S ALL.
AND I'M SURE THAT OTHER CUSTOMERS WILL COME TOO!
....
ぎゅっ GYU (CLENCH)
BUT...
...WE PUT UP POSTERS AND EVERYTHING...

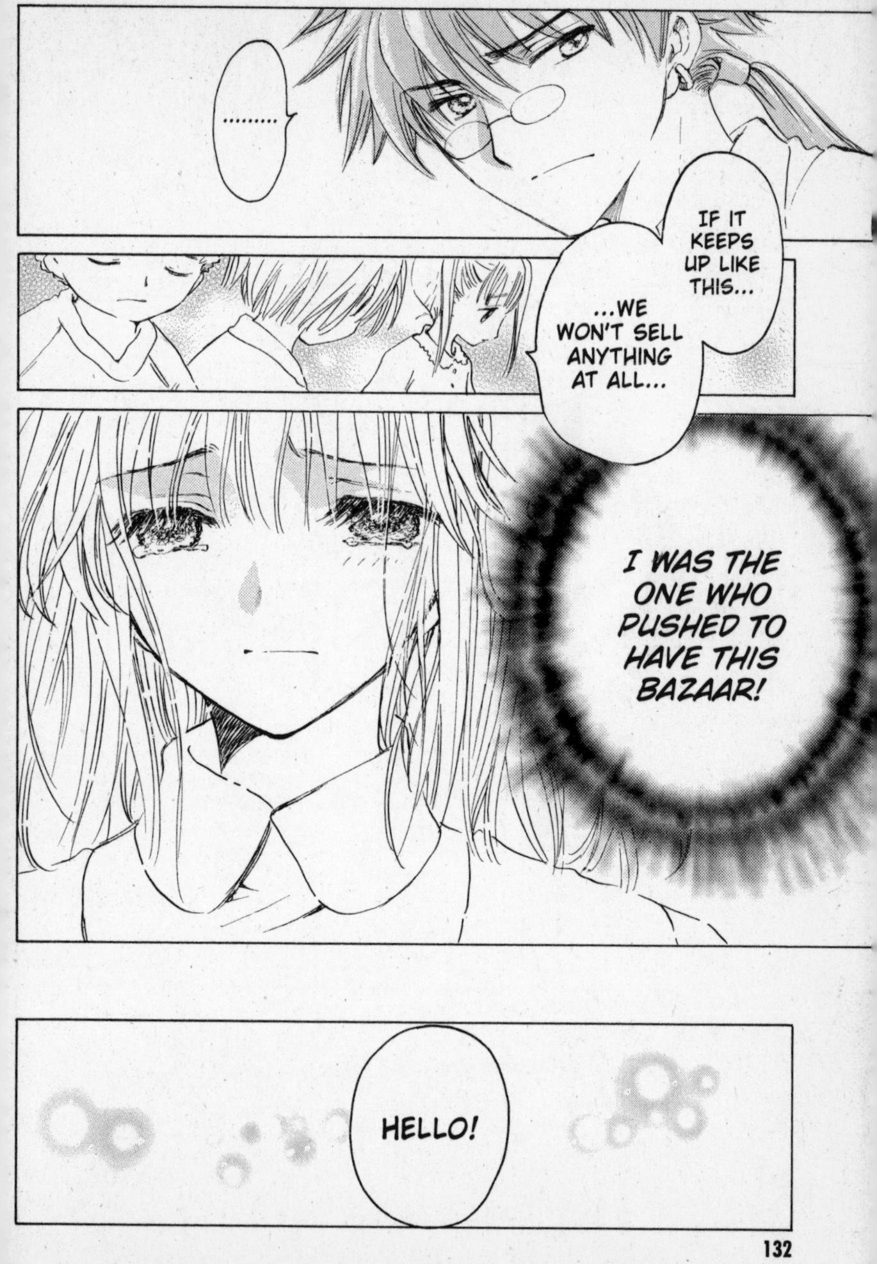
....
IF IT KEEPS UP LIKE THIS...
...WE WON'T SELL ANYTHING AT ALL...
I WAS THE ONE WHO PUSHED TO HAVE THIS BAZAAR!
HELLO!

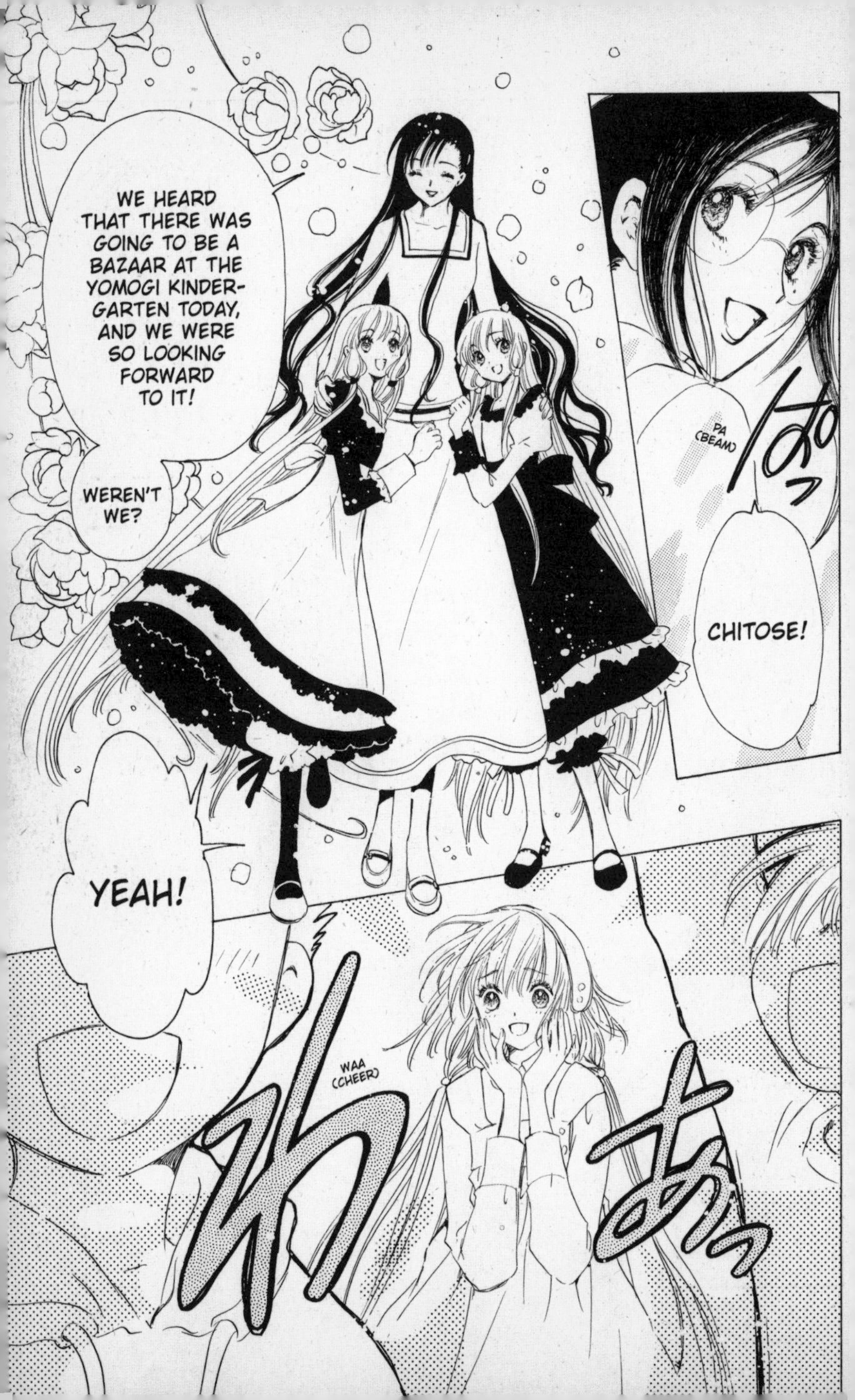
ぱっ
PA (BEAM)
CHITOSE!
WE HEARD THAT THERE WAS GOING TO BE A BAZAAR AT THE YOMOGI KINDER-GARTEN TODAY, AND WE WERE SO LOOKING FORWARD TO IT!
WEREN'T WE?
YEAH!
わあっ
WAA (CHEER)

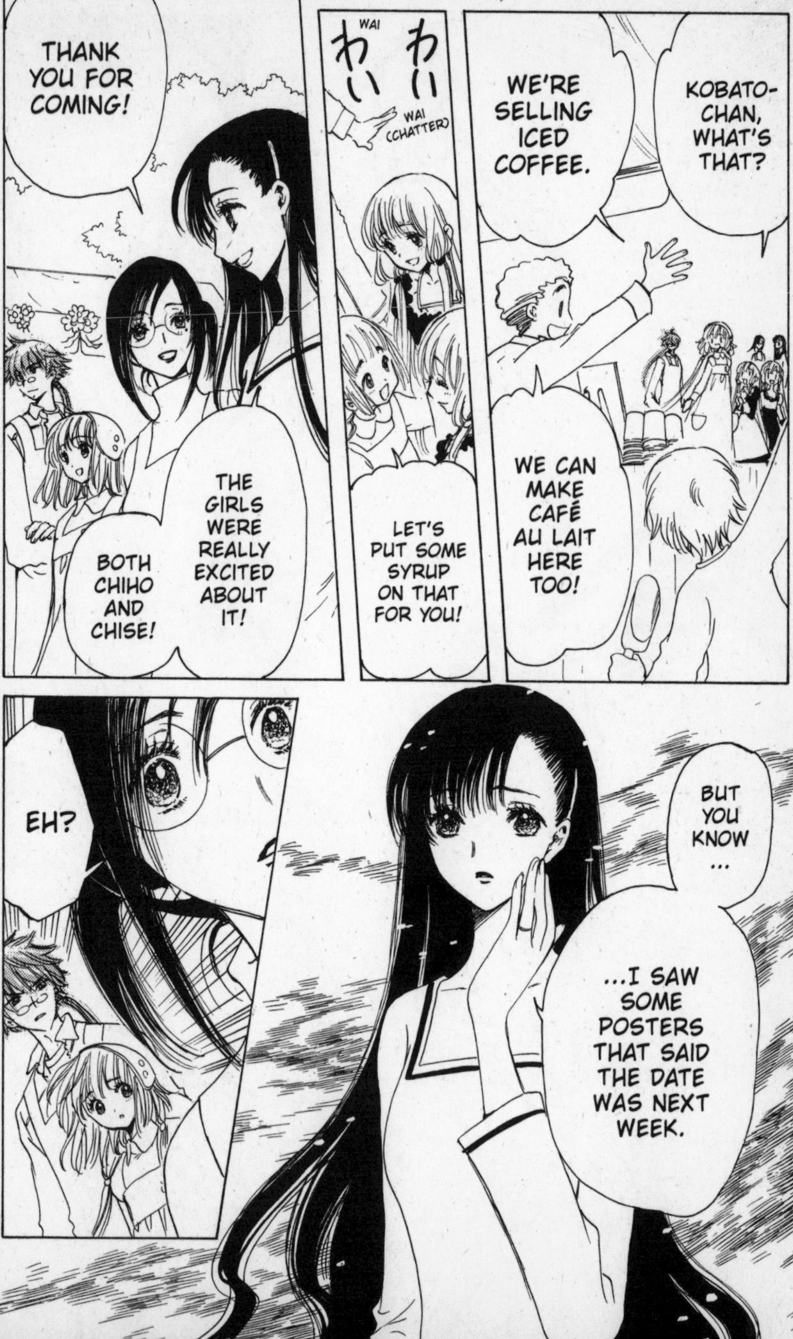
KOBATO-CHAN, WHAT'S THAT?
WE'RE SELLING ICED COFFEE.
WE CAN MAKE CAFÉ AU LAIT HERE TOO!
わいわい
WAI WAI (CHATTER)
LET'S PUT SOME SYRUP ON THAT FOR YOU!
THANK YOU FOR COMING!
THE GIRLS WERE REALLY EXCITED ABOUT IT!
BOTH CHIHO AND CHISE!
BUT YOU KNOW ...
...I SAW SOME POSTERS THAT SAID THE DATE WAS NEXT WEEK.
EH?

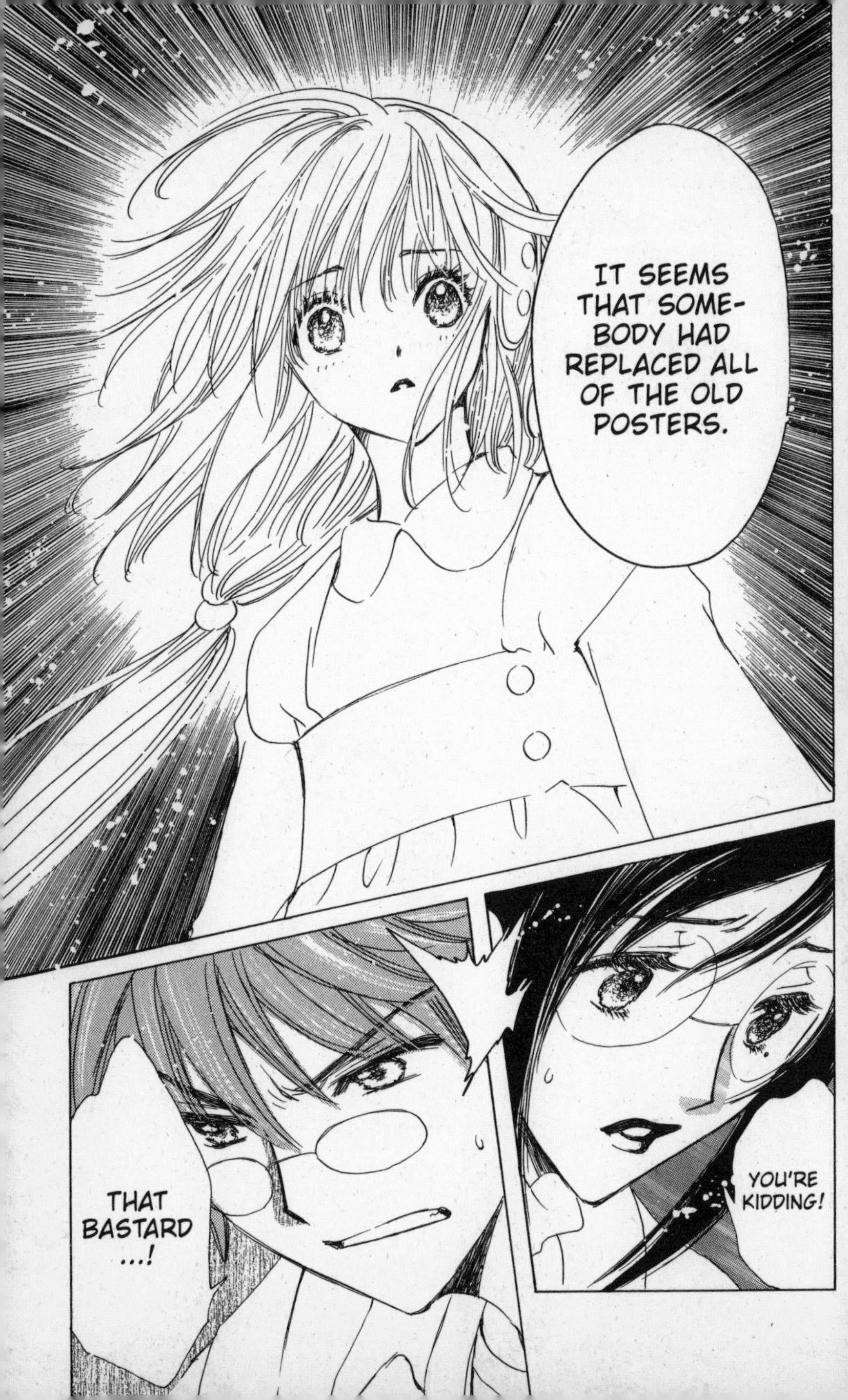
IT SEEMS THAT SOME-BODY HAD REPLACED ALL OF THE OLD POSTERS.
YOU'RE KIDDING!
THAT BASTARD ...!

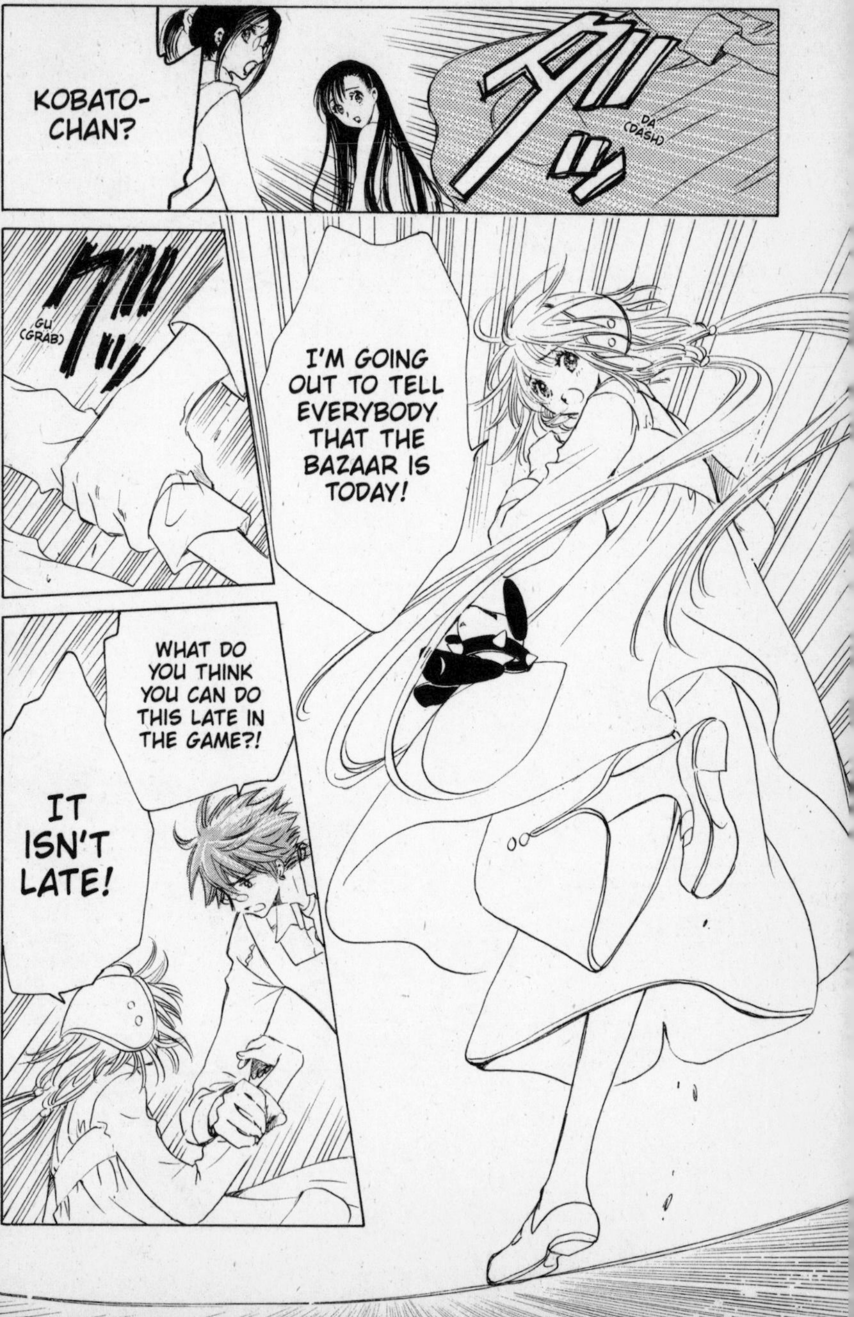
DA
(DASH)
KOBATO-CHAN?
I'M GOING OUT TO TELL EVERYBODY THAT THE BAZAAR IS TODAY!
GU
(GRAB)
WHAT DO YOU THINK YOU CAN DO THIS LATE IN THE GAME?!
IT ISN'T LATE!

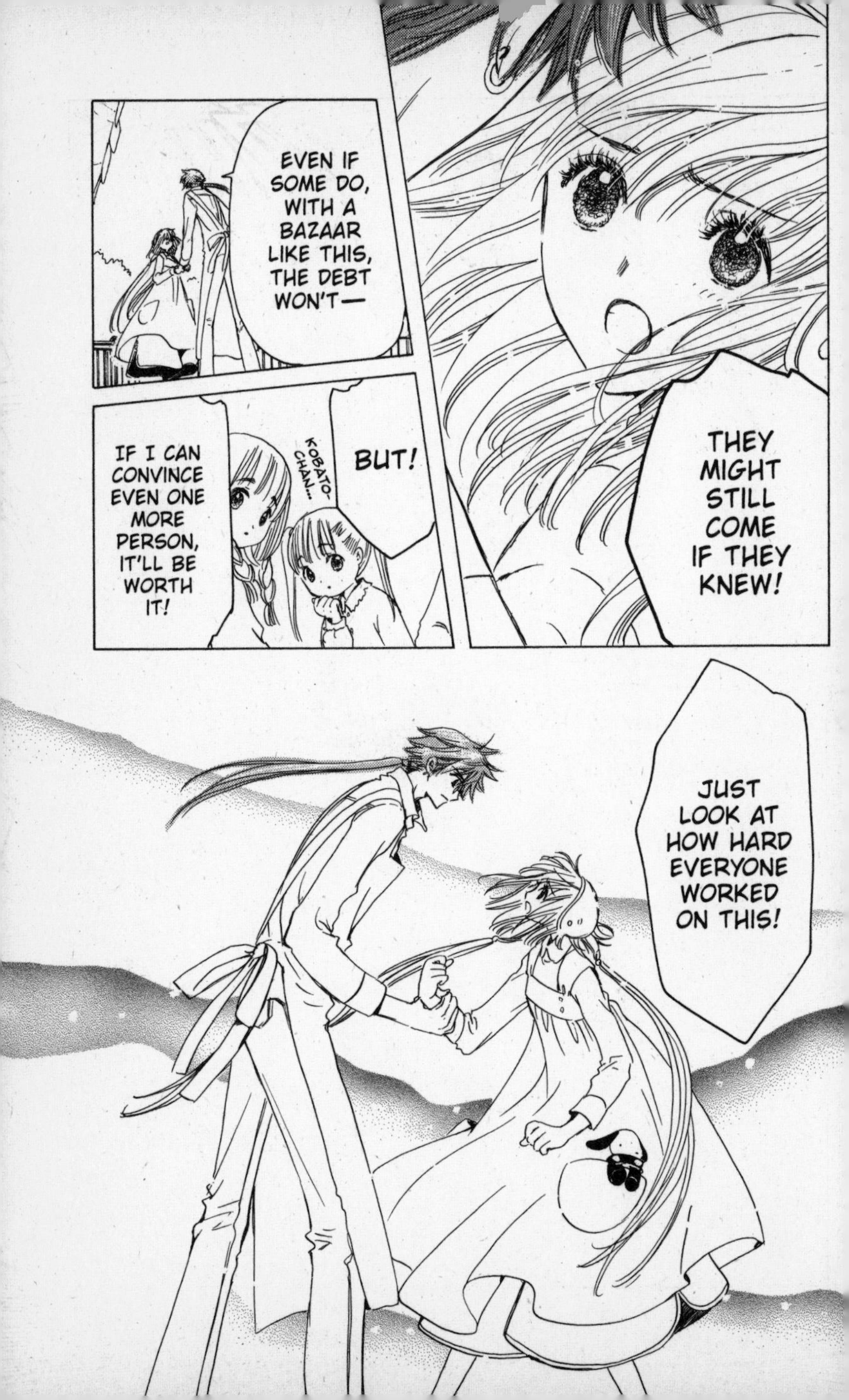
THEY MIGHT STILL COME IF THEY KNEW!
EVEN IF SOME DO, WITH A BAZAAR LIKE THIS, THE DEBT WON'T—
BUT!
KOBATO-CHAN...
IF I CAN CONVINCE EVEN ONE MORE PERSON, IT'LL BE WORTH IT!
JUST LOOK AT HOW HARD EVERYONE WORKED ON THIS!

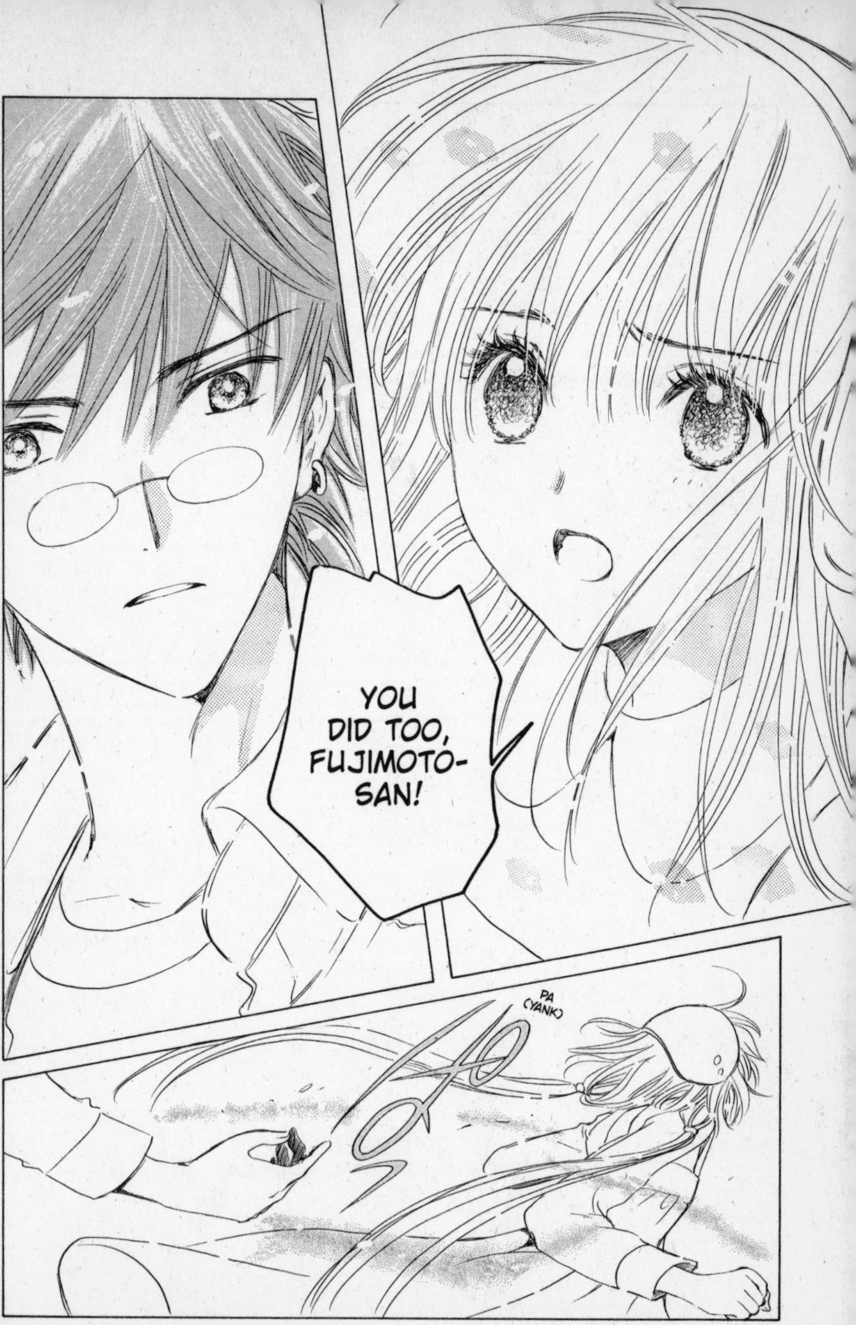
YOU DID TOO, FUJIMOTO-SAN!
PA (YANK)

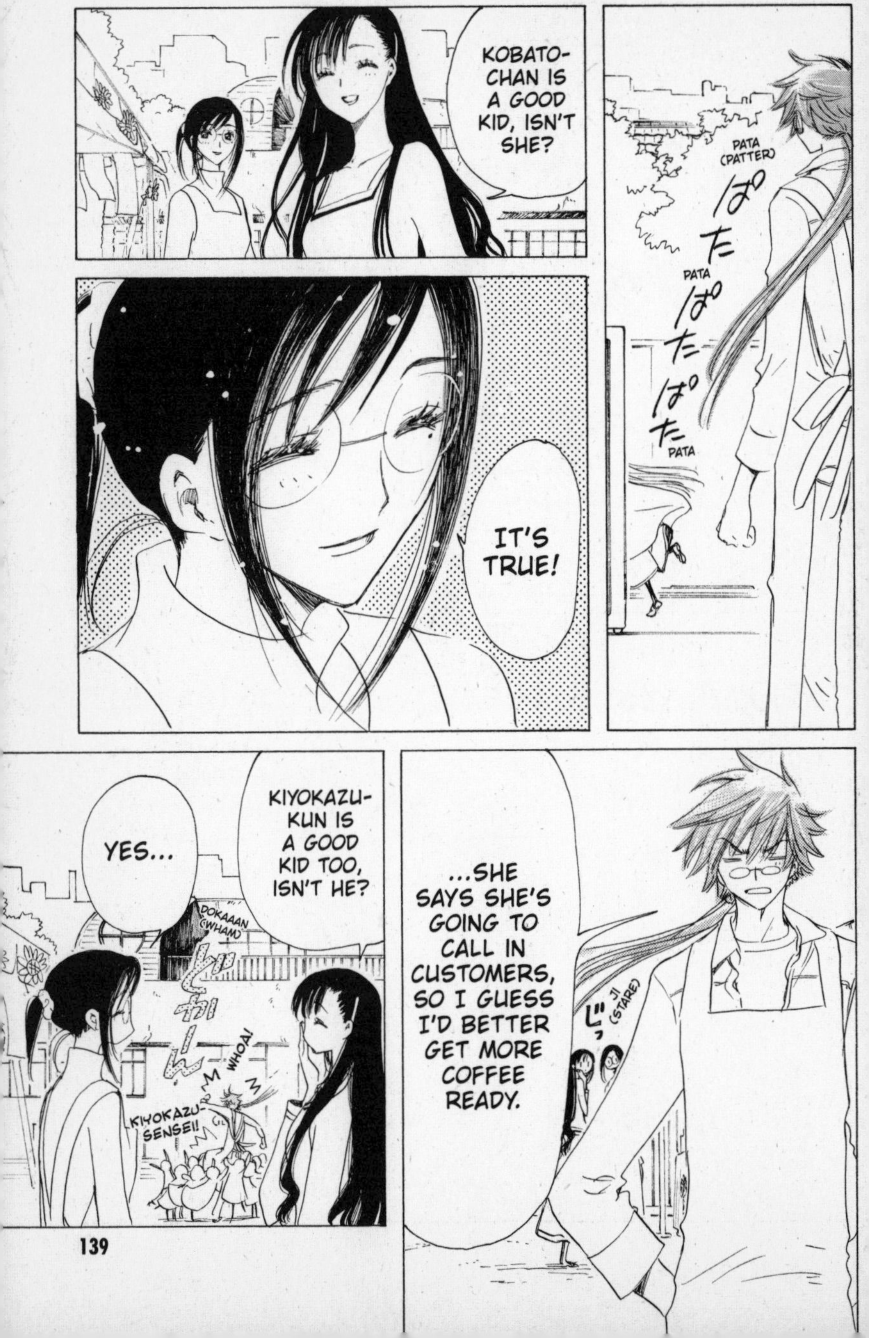
PATA (PATTER)
ぱた
PATA
ぱた
ぱた
PATA
KOBATO-CHAN IS A GOOD KID, ISN'T SHE?
IT'S TRUE!
...SHE SAYS SHE'S GOING TO CALL IN CUSTOMERS, SO I GUESS I'D BETTER GET MORE COFFEE READY.
じっ
JI (STARE)
KIYOKAZU-KUN IS A GOOD KID TOO, ISN'T HE?
YES...
DOKAAAN (WHAM)
どかーん
WHOA!
KIYOKAZU-SENSEI!

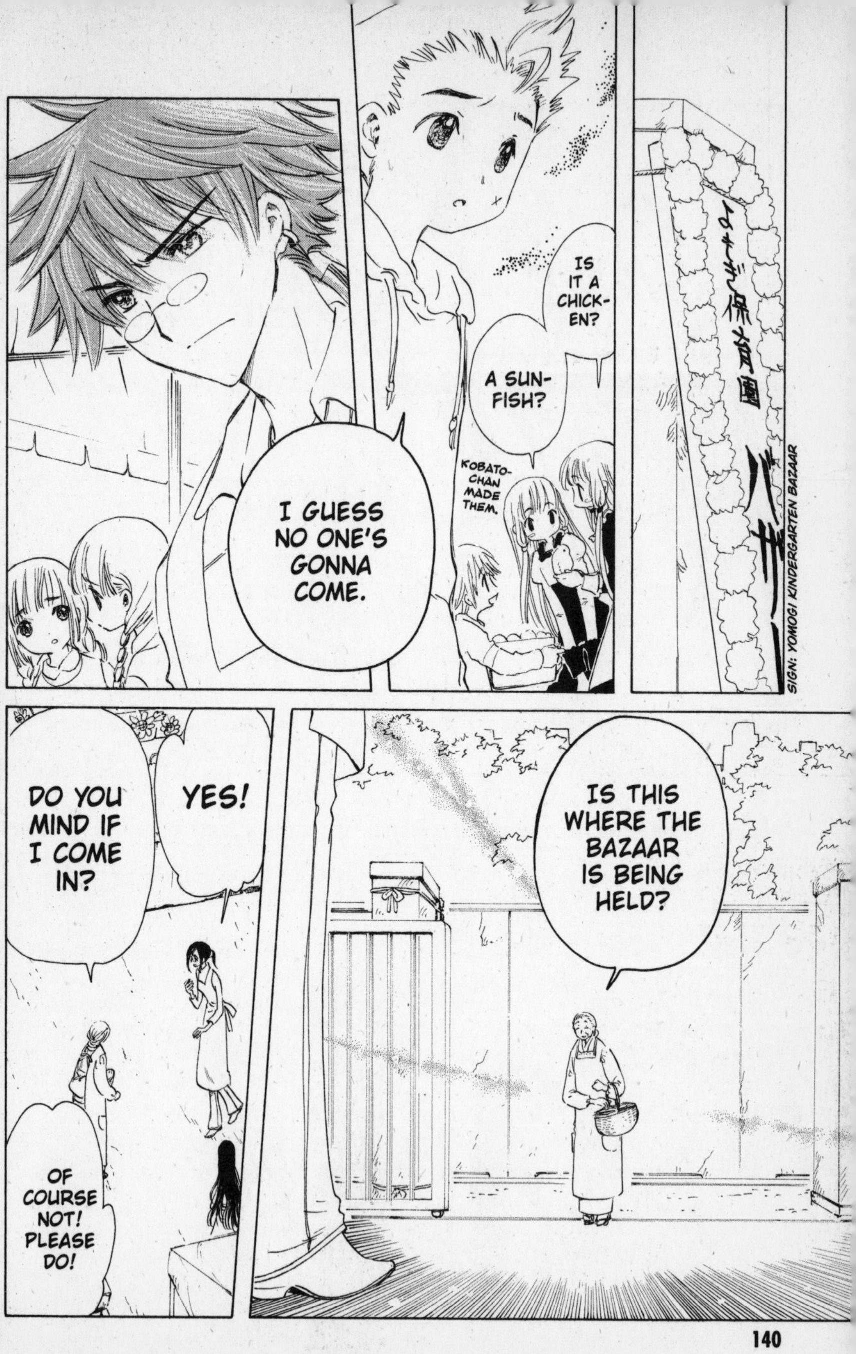
よもぎ保育園 バザー
SIGN: YOMOGI KINDERGARTEN BAZAAR
IS IT A CHICK-EN?
A SUN-FISH?
KOBATO-CHAN MADE THEM.
I GUESS NO ONE'S GONNA COME.
IS THIS WHERE THE BAZAAR IS BEING HELD?
YES!
DO YOU MIND IF I COME IN?
OF COURSE NOT! PLEASE DO!

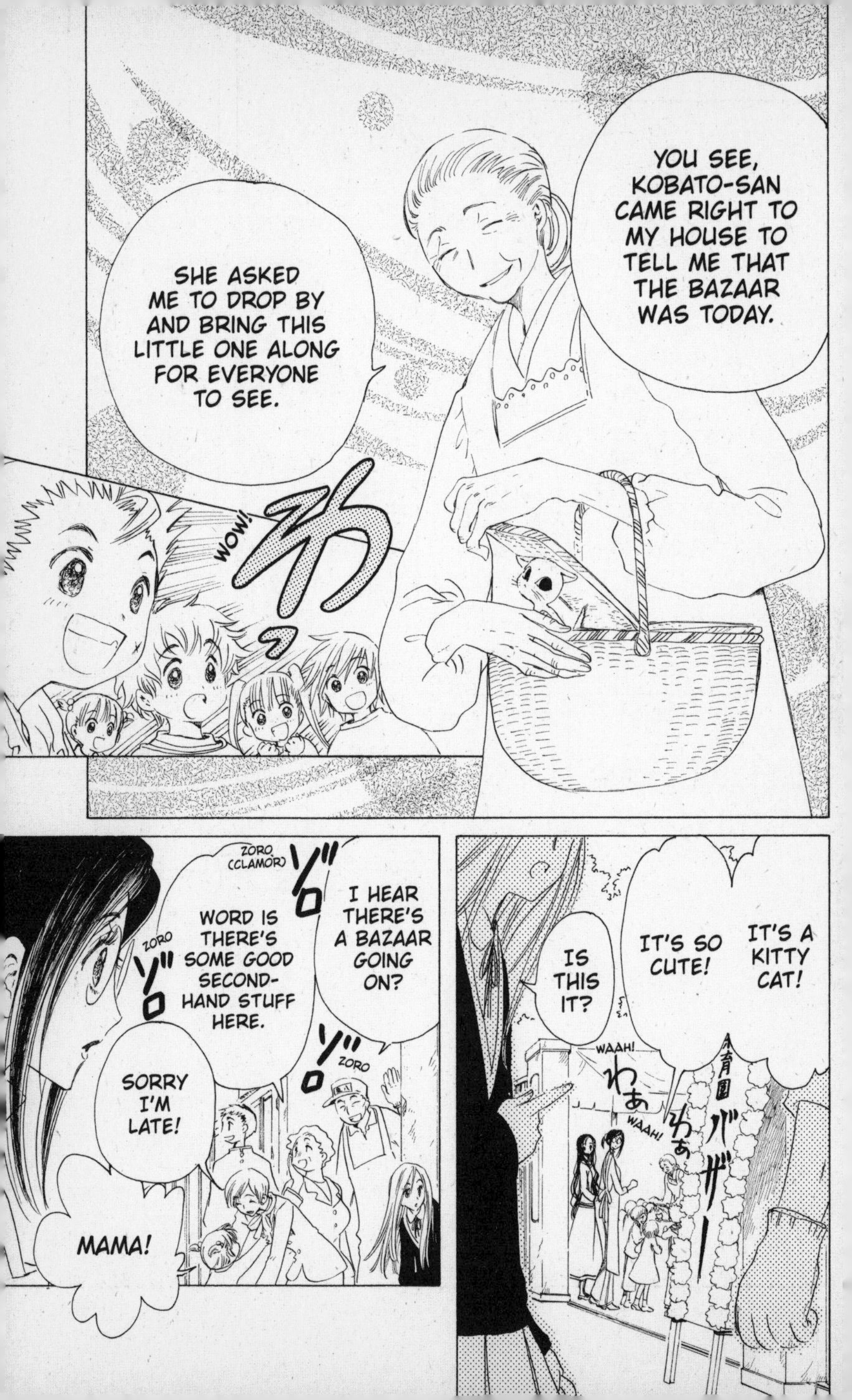
YOU SEE, KOBATO-SAN CAME RIGHT TO MY HOUSE TO TELL ME THAT THE BAZAAR WAS TODAY.
SHE ASKED ME TO DROP BY AND BRING THIS LITTLE ONE ALONG FOR EVERYONE TO SEE.
WOW!
IT'S A KITTY CAT!
IT'S SO CUTE!
IS THIS IT?
WAAH!
WAAH!
ZORO (CLAMOR)
I HEAR THERE'S A BAZAAR GOING ON?
WORD IS THERE'S SOME GOOD SECOND-HAND STUFF HERE.
ZORO
ZORO
SORRY I'M LATE!
MAMA!

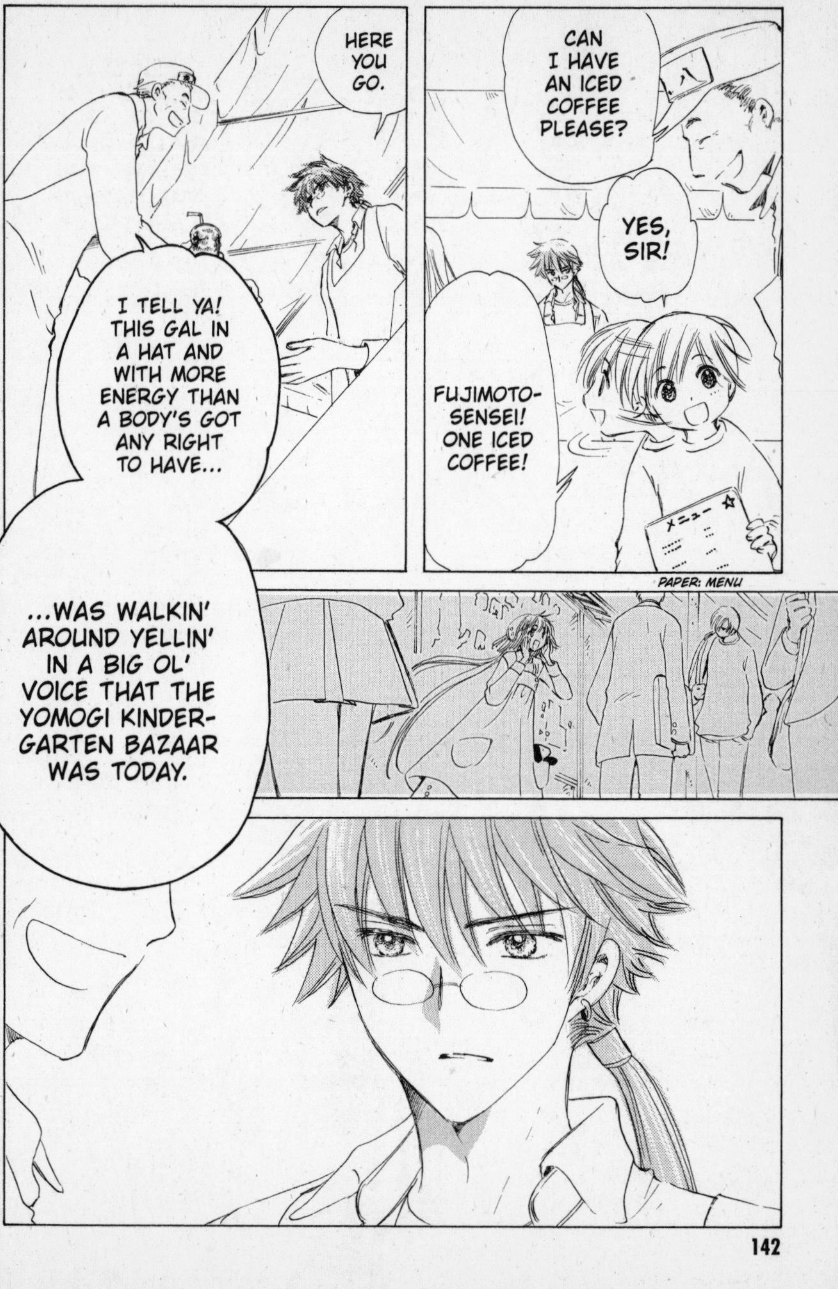
CAN I HAVE AN ICED COFFEE PLEASE?
YES, SIR!
FUJIMOTO-SENSEI! ONE ICED COFFEE!
PAPER: MENU
HERE YOU GO.
I TELL YA! THIS GAL IN A HAT AND WITH MORE ENERGY THAN A BODY'S GOT ANY RIGHT TO HAVE...
...WAS WALKIN' AROUND YELLIN' IN A BIG OL' VOICE THAT THE YOMOGI KINDER-GARTEN BAZAAR WAS TODAY.

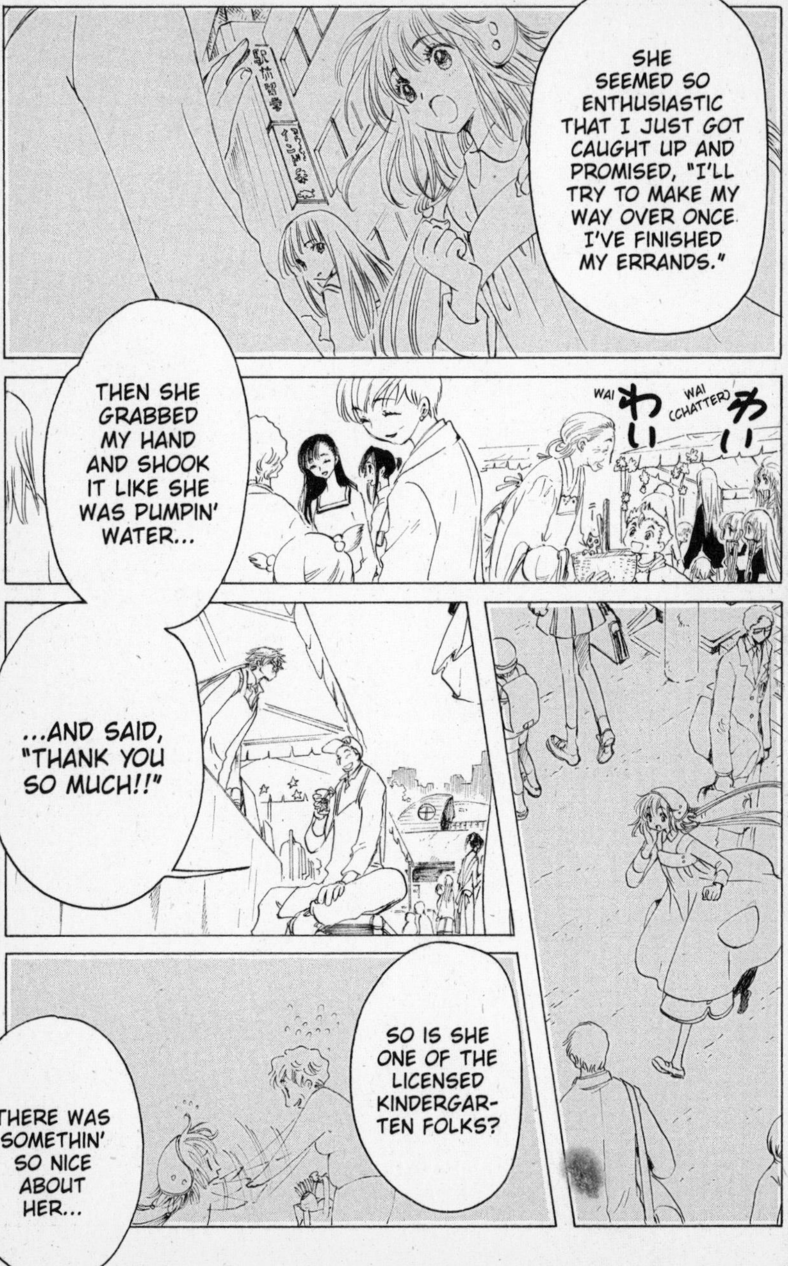
SHE SEEMED SO ENTHUSIASTIC THAT I JUST GOT CAUGHT UP AND PROMISED, "I'LL TRY TO MAKE MY WAY OVER ONCE I'VE FINISHED MY ERRANDS."
わい WAI (CHATTER)
わい WAI
THEN SHE GRABBED MY HAND AND SHOOK IT LIKE SHE WAS PUMPIN' WATER...
...AND SAID, "THANK YOU SO MUCH!!"
SO IS SHE ONE OF THE LICENSED KINDERGAR-TEN FOLKS?
THERE WAS SOMETHIN' SO NICE ABOUT HER...

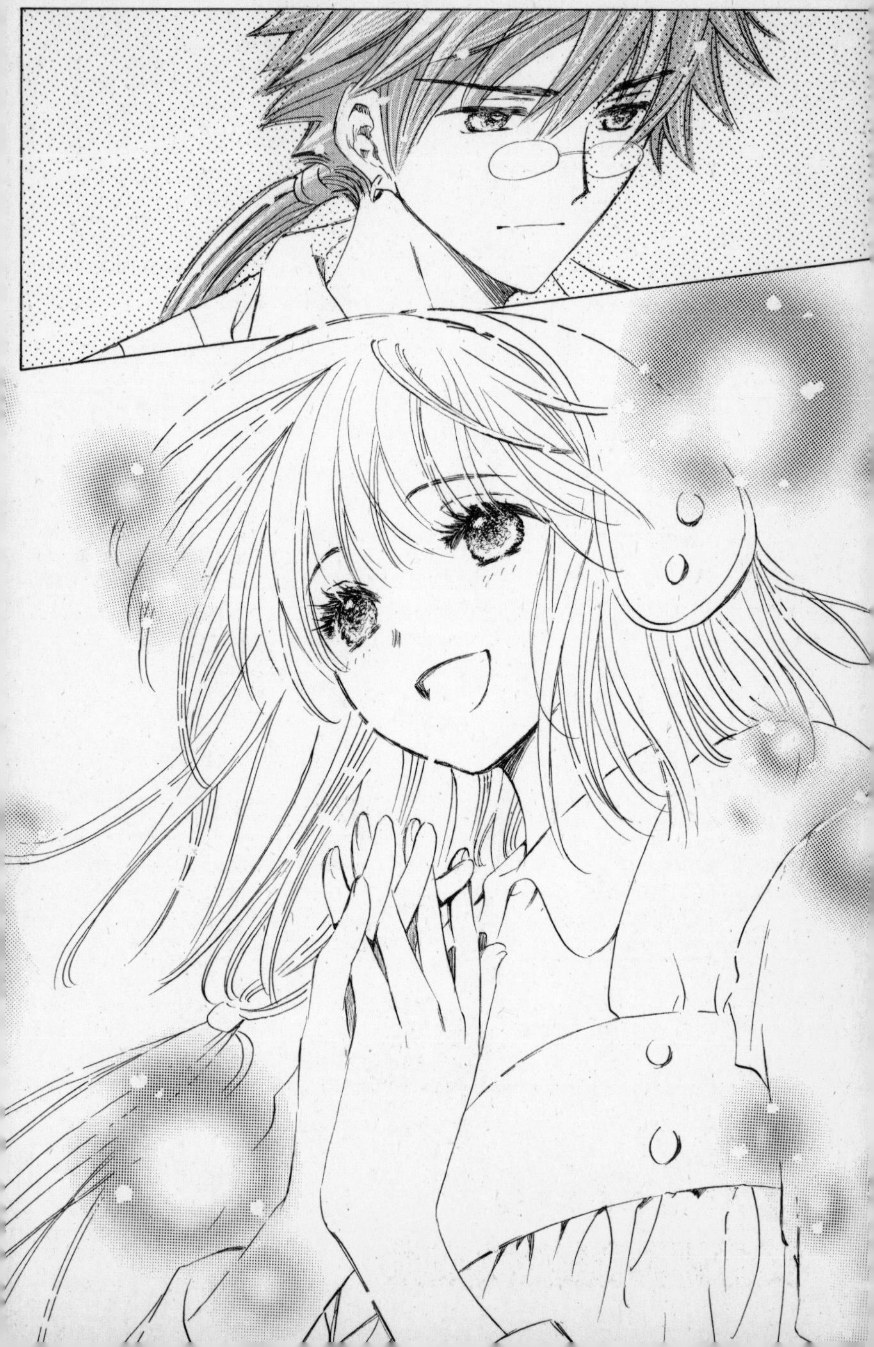

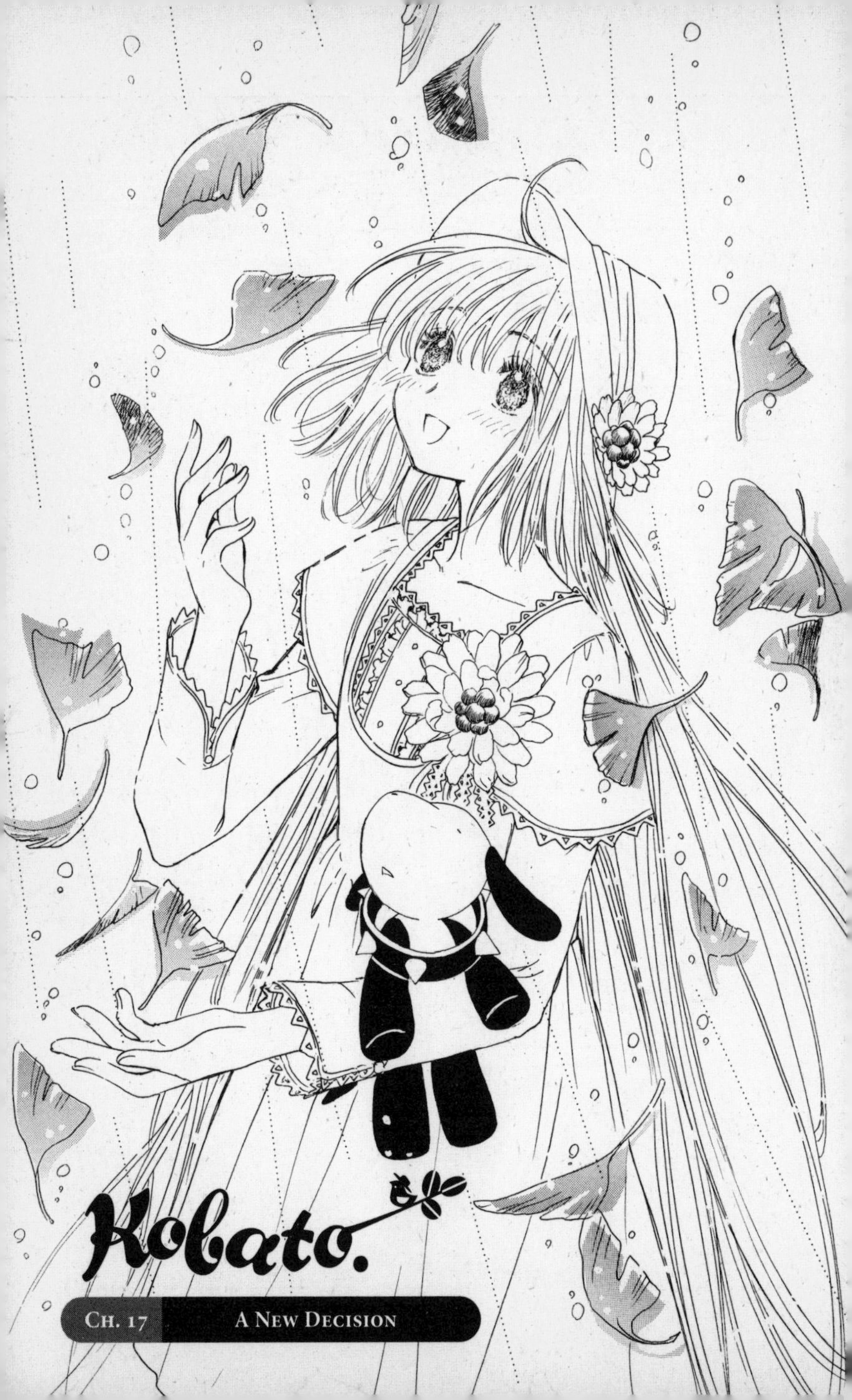
Kobato.
Ch. 17
A New Decision

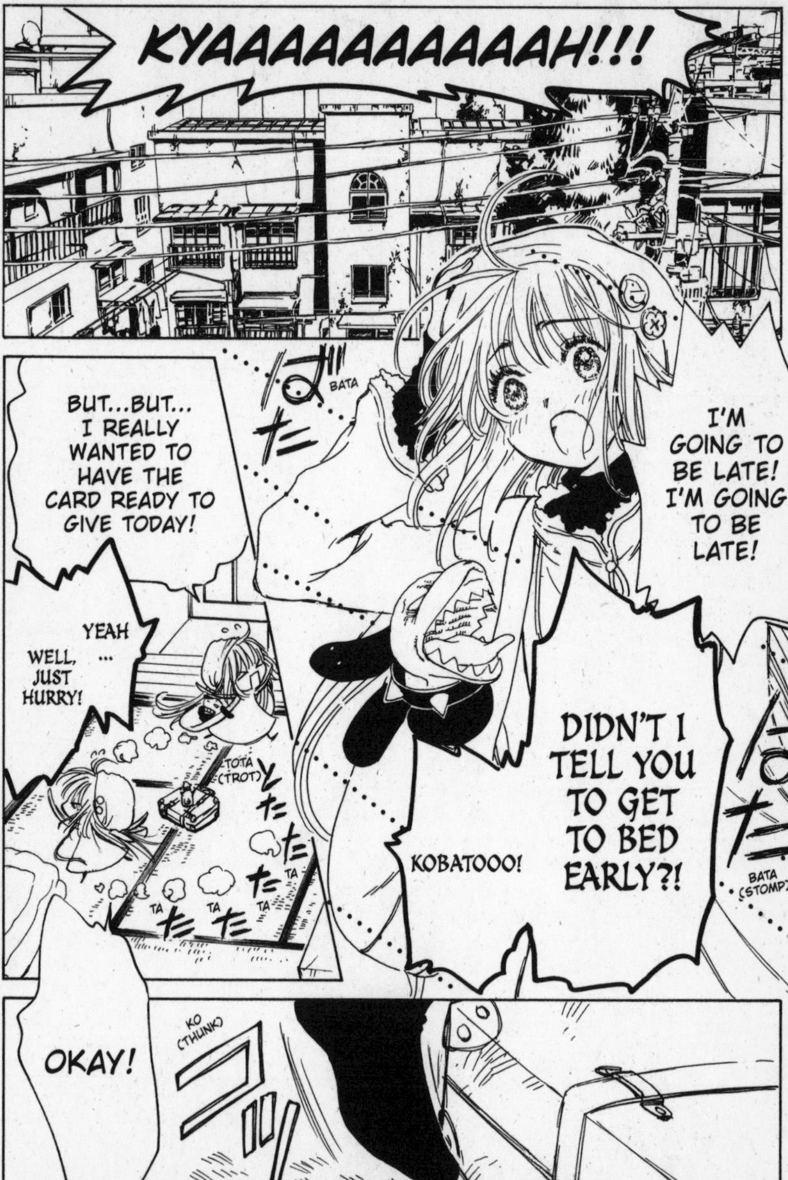
KYAAAAAAAAAAH!!!
I'M GOING TO BE LATE! I'M GOING TO BE LATE!
BATA
DIDN'T I TELL YOU TO GET TO BED EARLY?!
BATA (STOMP)
KOBATOOO!
BUT...BUT... I REALLY WANTED TO HAVE THE CARD READY TO GIVE TODAY!
YEAH...
WELL, JUST HURRY!
TOTA (TROT)
TA
TA
TA
TA
KO (THUNK)
OKAY!

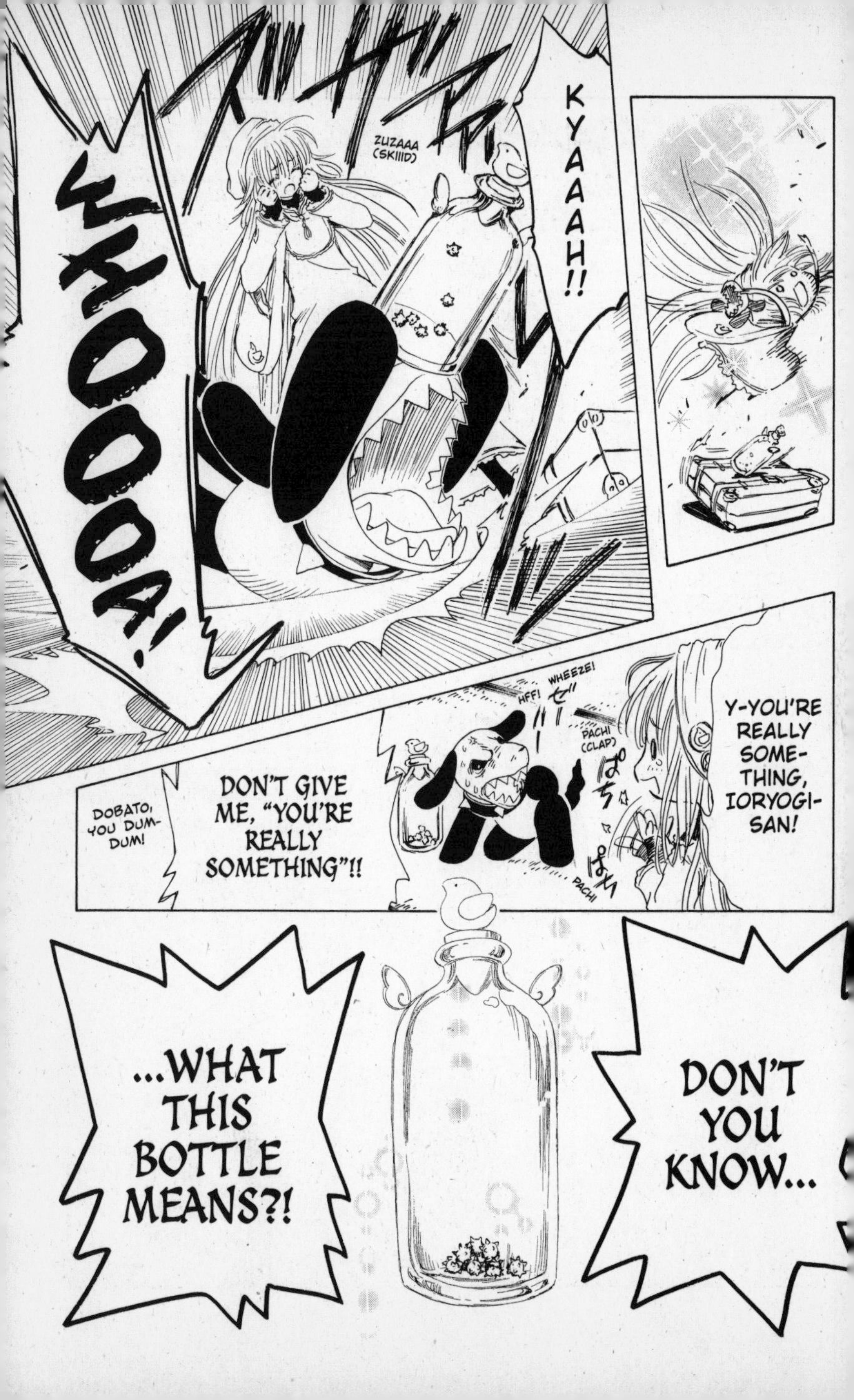
KYAAAAH!!
ZUZAAA (SKIIID)
WHOOOA!
Y-YOU'RE REALLY SOME-THING, IORYOGI-SAN!
PACHI (CLAP)
PACHI
WHEEZE!
HFF!
DON'T GIVE ME, "YOU'RE REALLY SOMETHING"!!
DOBATO, YOU DUM-DUM!
DON'T YOU KNOW...
...WHAT THIS BOTTLE MEANS?!

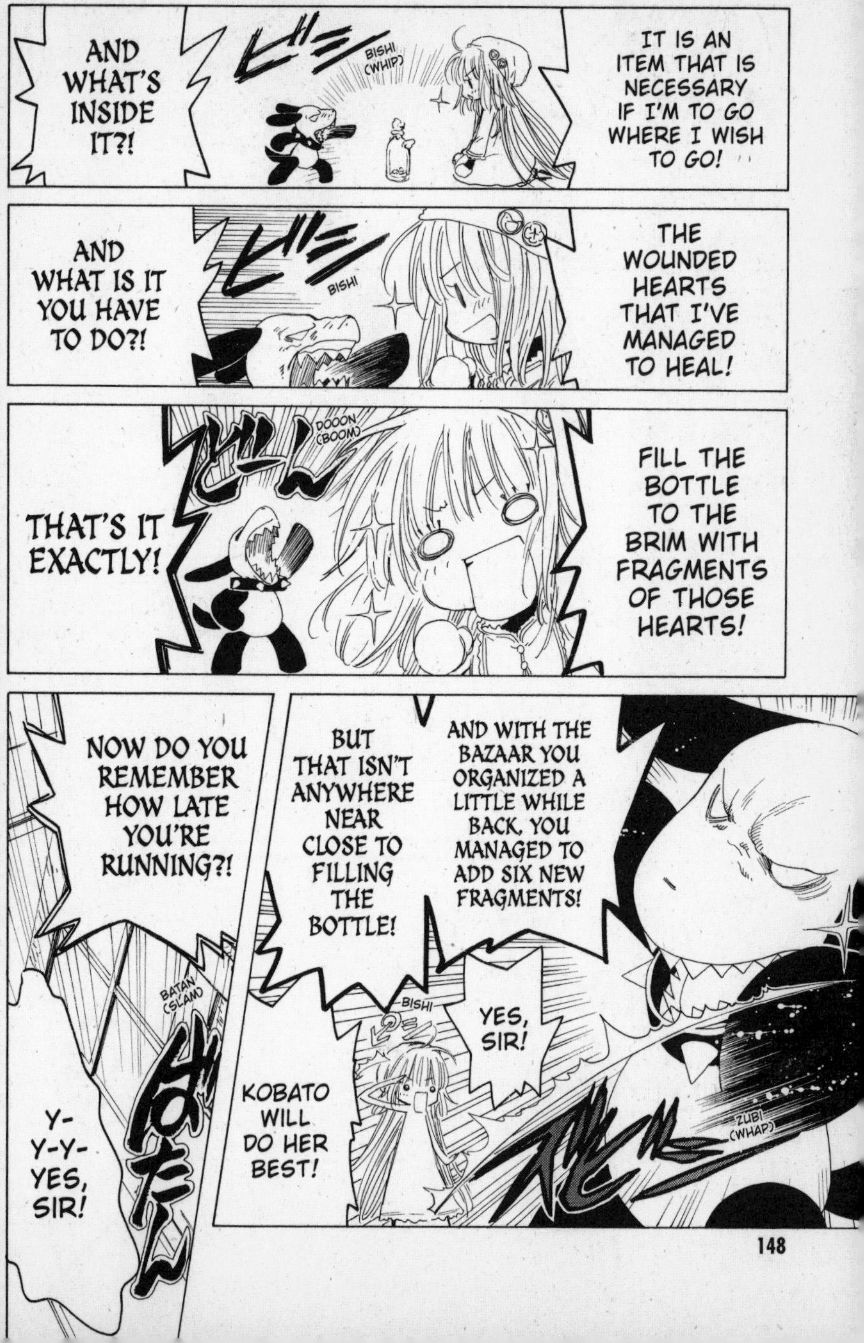
IT IS AN ITEM THAT IS NECESSARY IF I'M TO GO WHERE I WISH TO GO!
BISHI (WHIP)
AND WHAT'S INSIDE IT?!
THE WOUNDED HEARTS THAT I'VE MANAGED TO HEAL!
BISHI
AND WHAT IS IT YOU HAVE TO DO?!
FILL THE BOTTLE TO THE BRIM WITH FRAGMENTS OF THOSE HEARTS!
DOOON (BOOM)
THAT'S IT EXACTLY!
AND WITH THE BAZAAR YOU ORGANIZED A LITTLE WHILE BACK, YOU MANAGED TO ADD SIX NEW FRAGMENTS!
BUT THAT ISN'T ANYWHERE NEAR CLOSE TO FILLING THE BOTTLE!
ZUBI (WHAP)
BISHI
YES, SIR!
KOBATO WILL DO HER BEST!
NOW DO YOU REMEMBER HOW LATE YOU'RE RUNNING?!
BATAN (SLAM)
Y-Y-Y-YES, SIR!

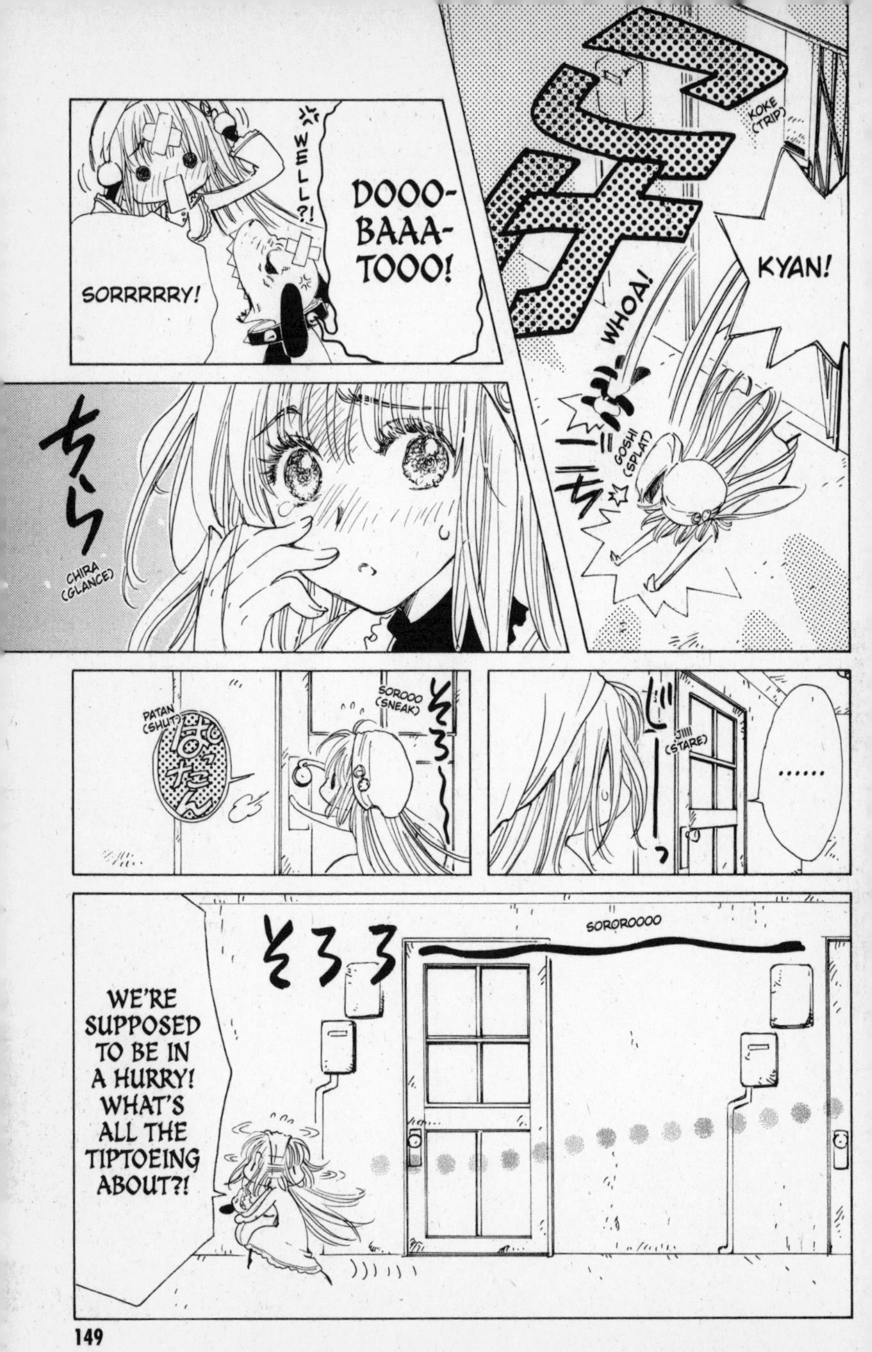

KOKE (TRIP)
KYAN!
WHOA!
GOSHI (SPLAT)
WELL?!
DOOO-BAAA-TOOO!
SORRRRRY!
CHIRA (GLANCE)
......
JIIII (STARE)
SOROOO (SNEAK)
PATAN (SHUT)
SOROROOOO
WE'RE SUPPOSED TO BE IN A HURRY! WHAT'S ALL THE TIPTOEING ABOUT?!

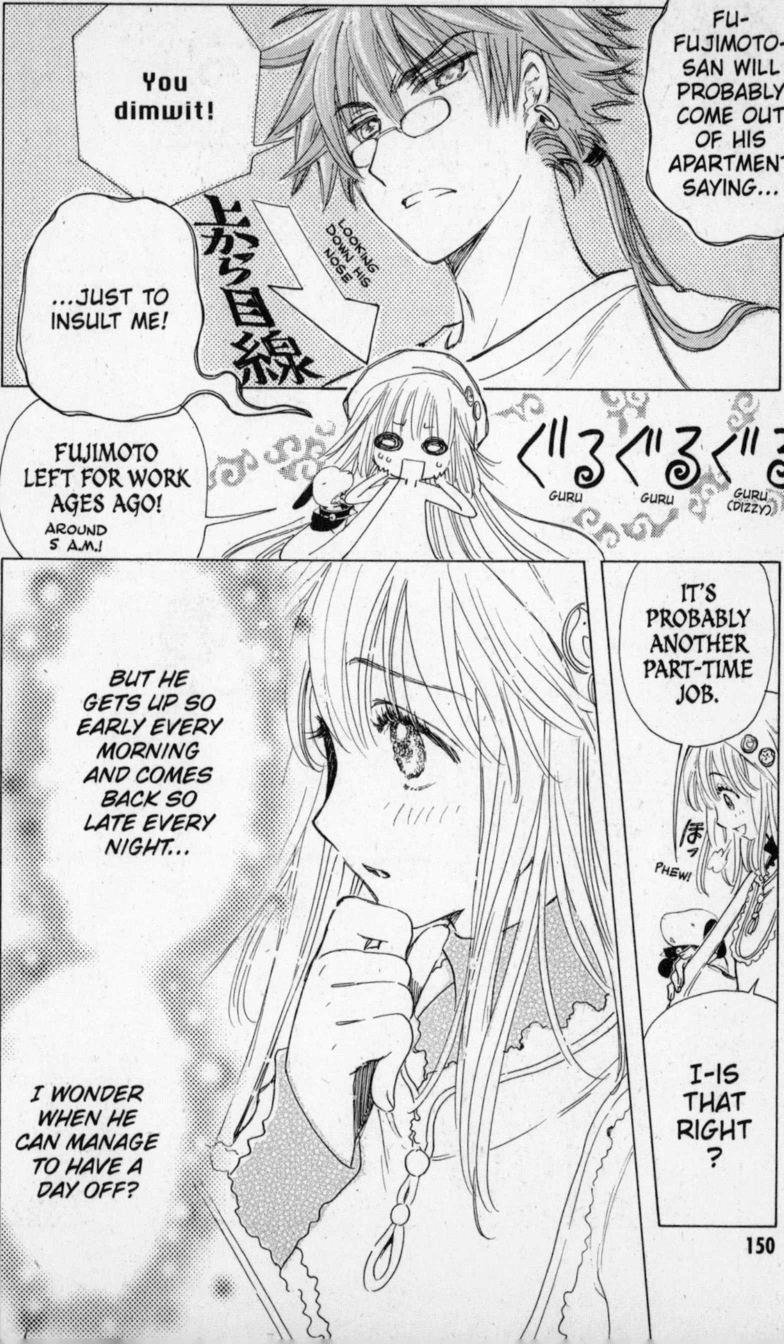
FU-FUJIMOTO-SAN WILL PROBABLY COME OUT OF HIS APARTMENT SAYING...
You dimwit!
上から目線
LOOKING DOWN HIS NOSE
...JUST TO INSULT ME!
ぐるぐるぐる
GURU GURU GURU (DIZZY)
FUJIMOTO LEFT FOR WORK AGES AGO!
AROUND 5 A.M.!
IT'S PROBABLY ANOTHER PART-TIME JOB.
ほっ
PHEW!
I-IS THAT RIGHT?
BUT HE GETS UP SO EARLY EVERY MORNING AND COMES BACK SO LATE EVERY NIGHT...
I WONDER WHEN HE CAN MANAGE TO HAVE A DAY OFF?

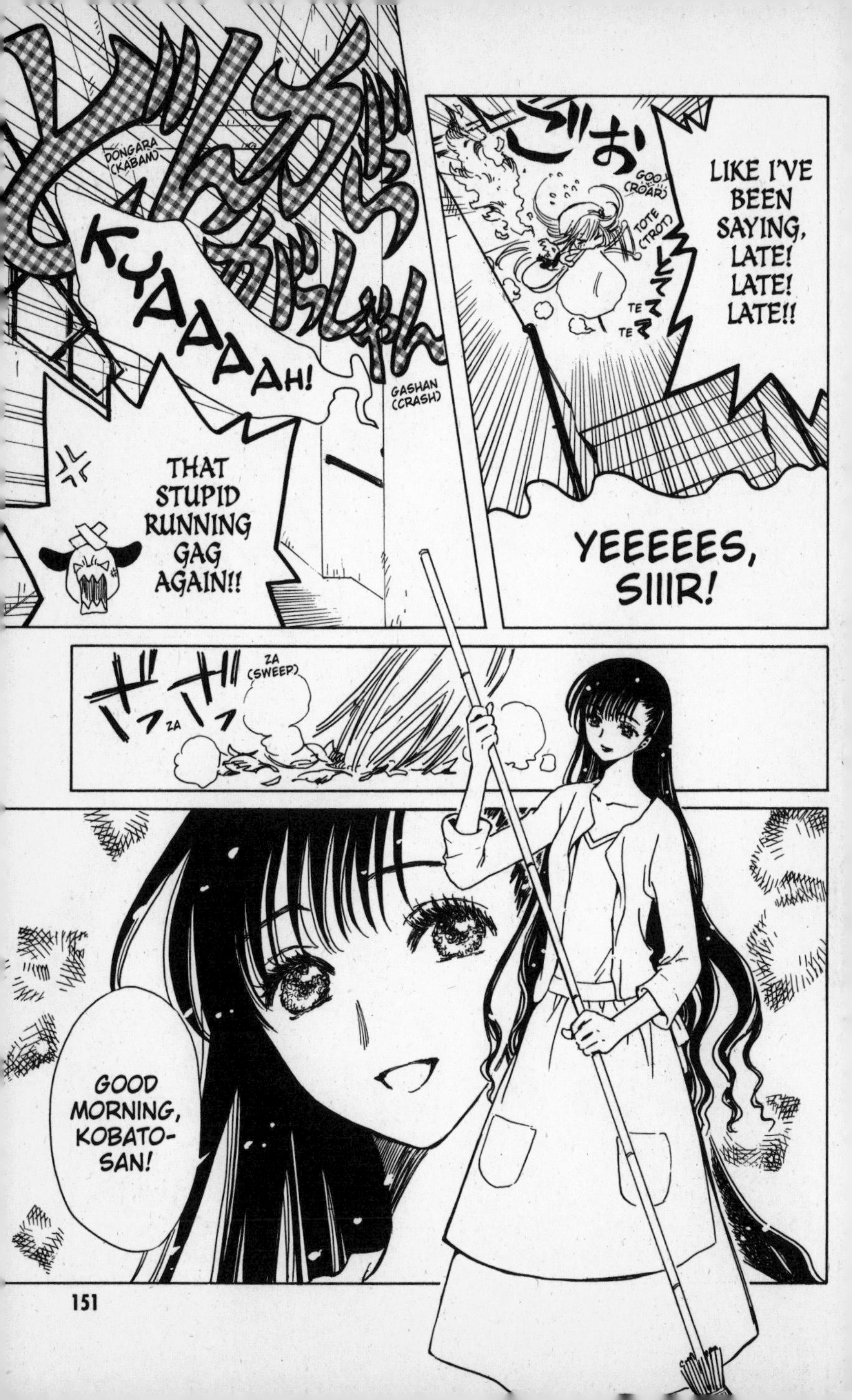

ごお
GOO (ROAR)
TOTE (TROT)
とてて
TE TE
LIKE I'VE BEEN SAYING, LATE! LATE! LATE!!
YEEEEES, SIIIR!
どんがら がしゃん
DONGARA (KABAN)
KYAAAAAH!
GASHAN (CRASH)
THAT STUPID RUNNING GAG AGAIN!!
ざっざっ
ZA (SWEEP)
ZA
GOOD MORNING, KOBATO-SAN!

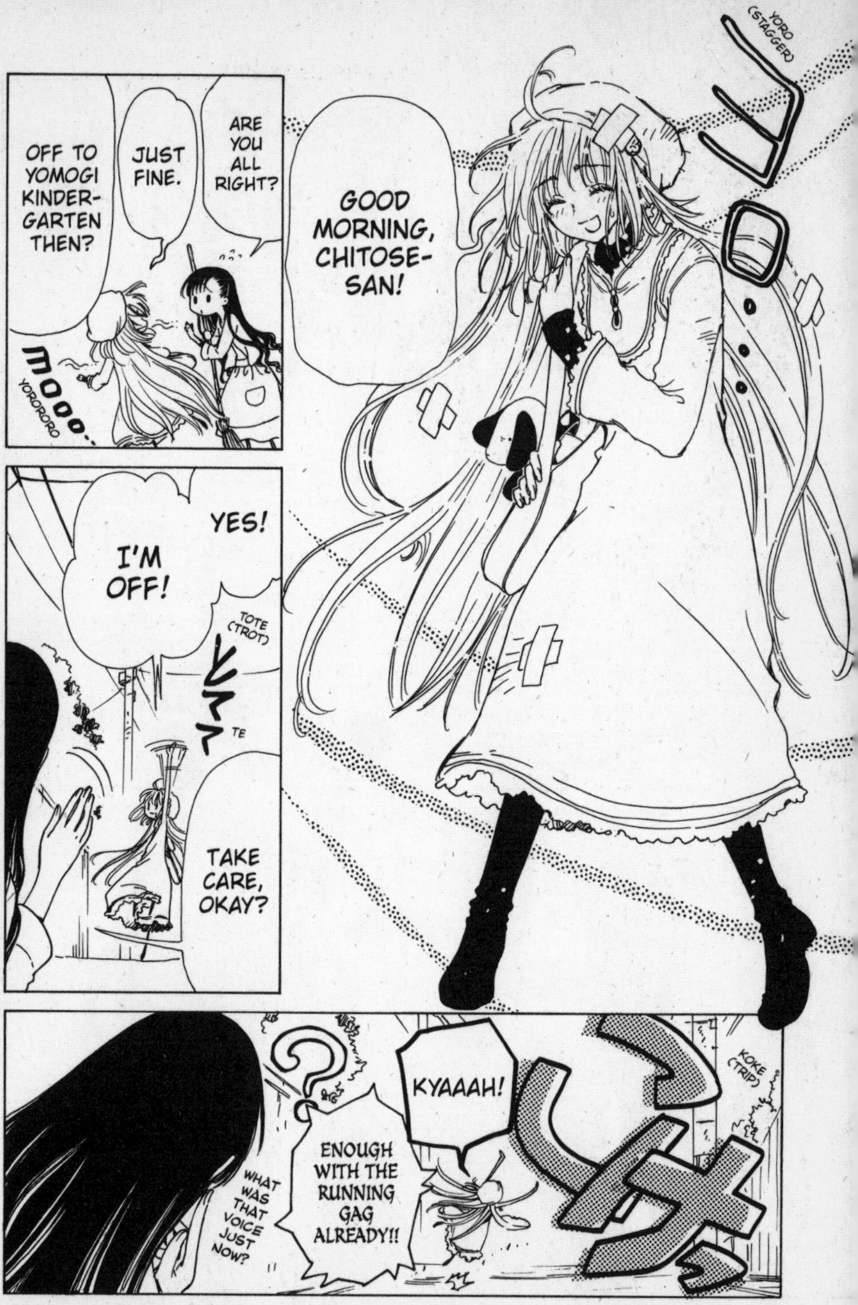
YORO (STAGGER)
GOOD MORNING, CHITOSE-SAN!
ARE YOU ALL RIGHT?
JUST FINE.
OFF TO YOMOGI KINDER-GARTEN THEN?
YORORORO
YES!
I'M OFF!
TOTE (TROT)
TE
TAKE CARE, OKAY?
KOKE (TRIP)
KYAAAH!
ENOUGH WITH THE RUNNING GAG ALREADY!!
WHAT WAS THAT VOICE JUST NOW?

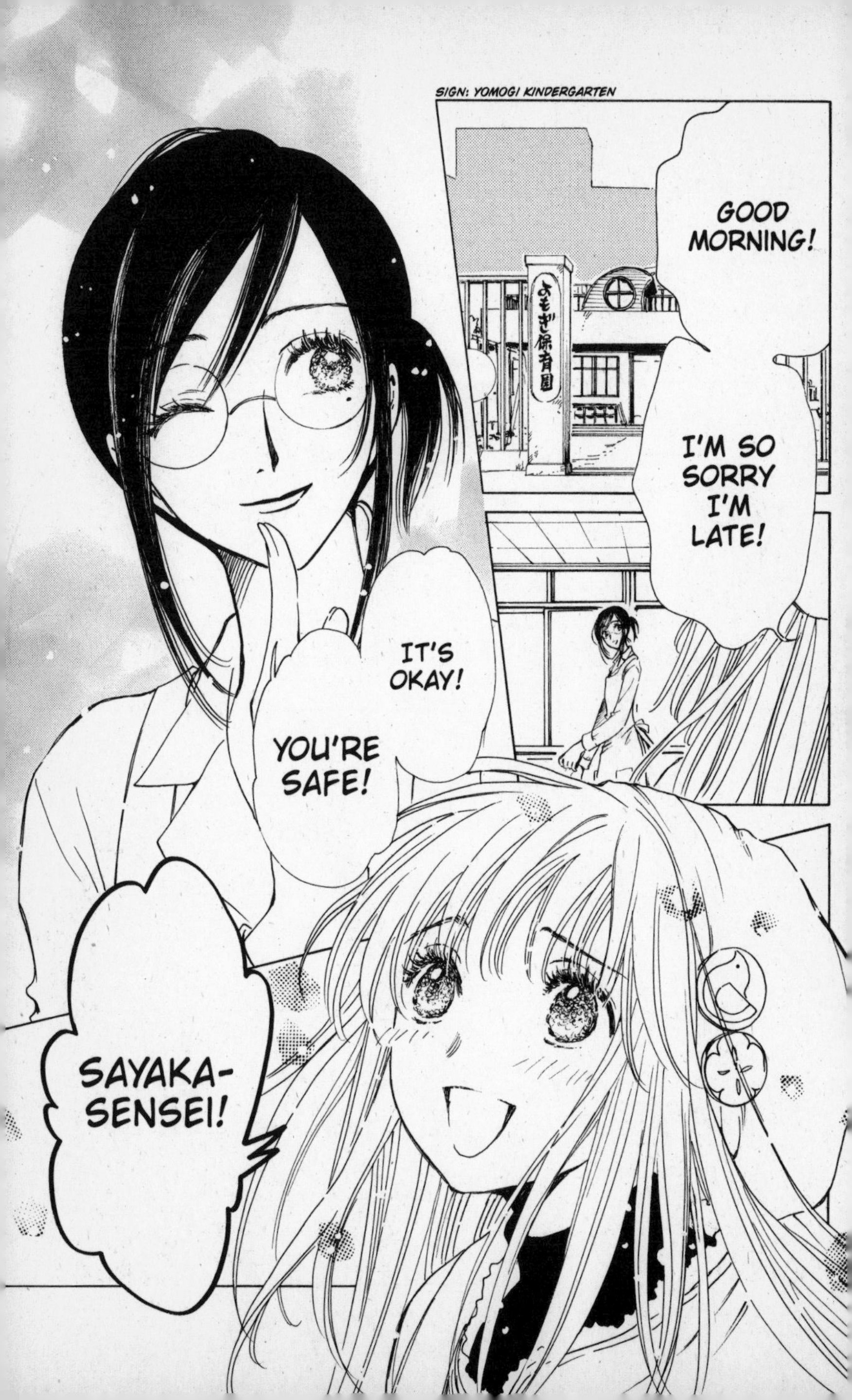
SIGN: YOMOGI KINDERGARTEN
よもぎ保育園
GOOD MORNING!
I'M SO SORRY I'M LATE!
IT'S OKAY!
YOU'RE SAFE!
SAYAKA-SENSEI!

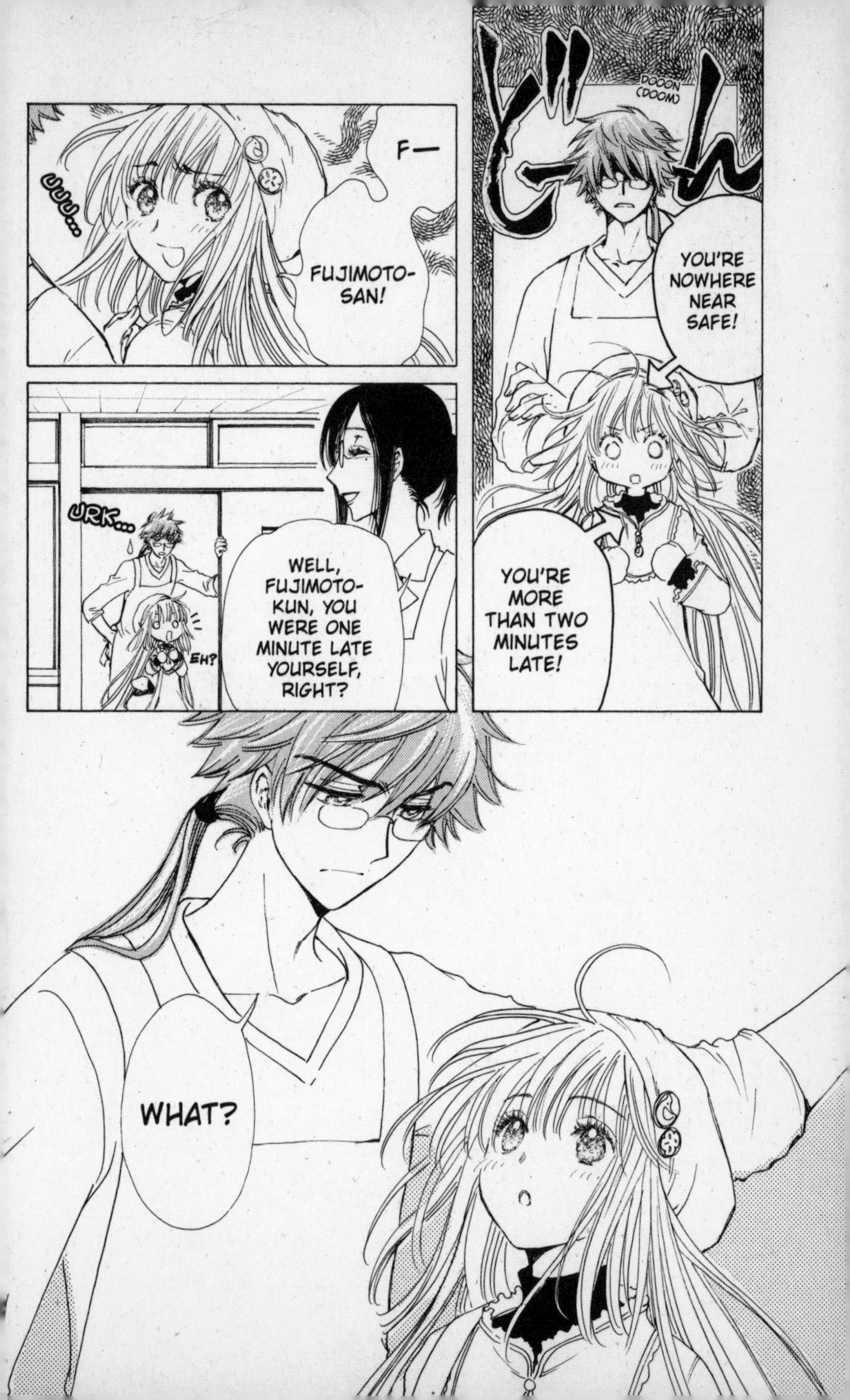
DOOON (DOOM)
YOU'RE NOWHERE NEAR SAFE!
YOU'RE MORE THAN TWO MINUTES LATE!
F—
FUJIMOTO-SAN!
UUU...
WELL, FUJIMOTO-KUN, YOU WERE ONE MINUTE LATE YOURSELF, RIGHT?
URK...
EH?
WHAT?

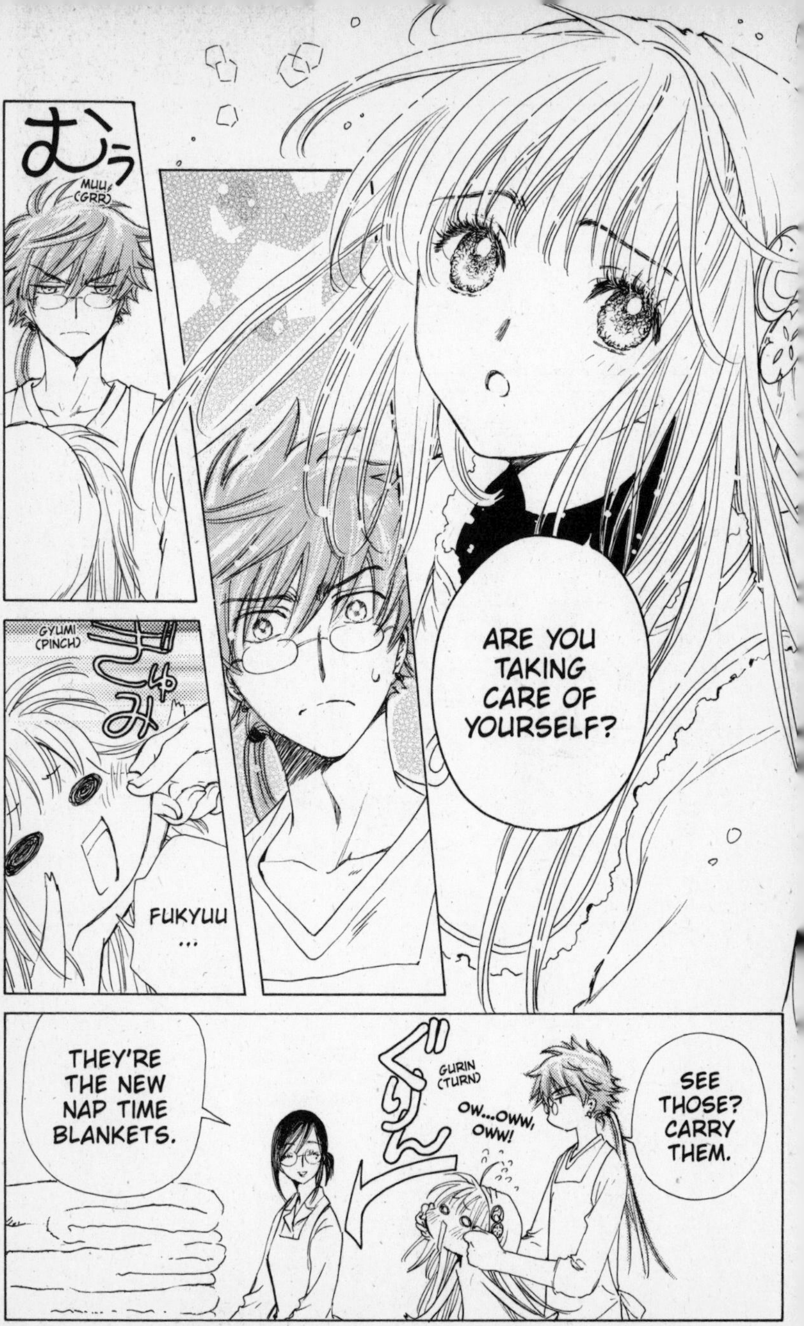
ARE YOU TAKING CARE OF YOURSELF?
むぅ
MUU (GRR)
ぎゅみ
GYUMI (PINCH)
FUKYUU ...
SEE THOSE? CARRY THEM.
OW...OWW, OWW!
ぐりん
GURIN (TURN)
THEY'RE THE NEW NAP TIME BLANKETS.

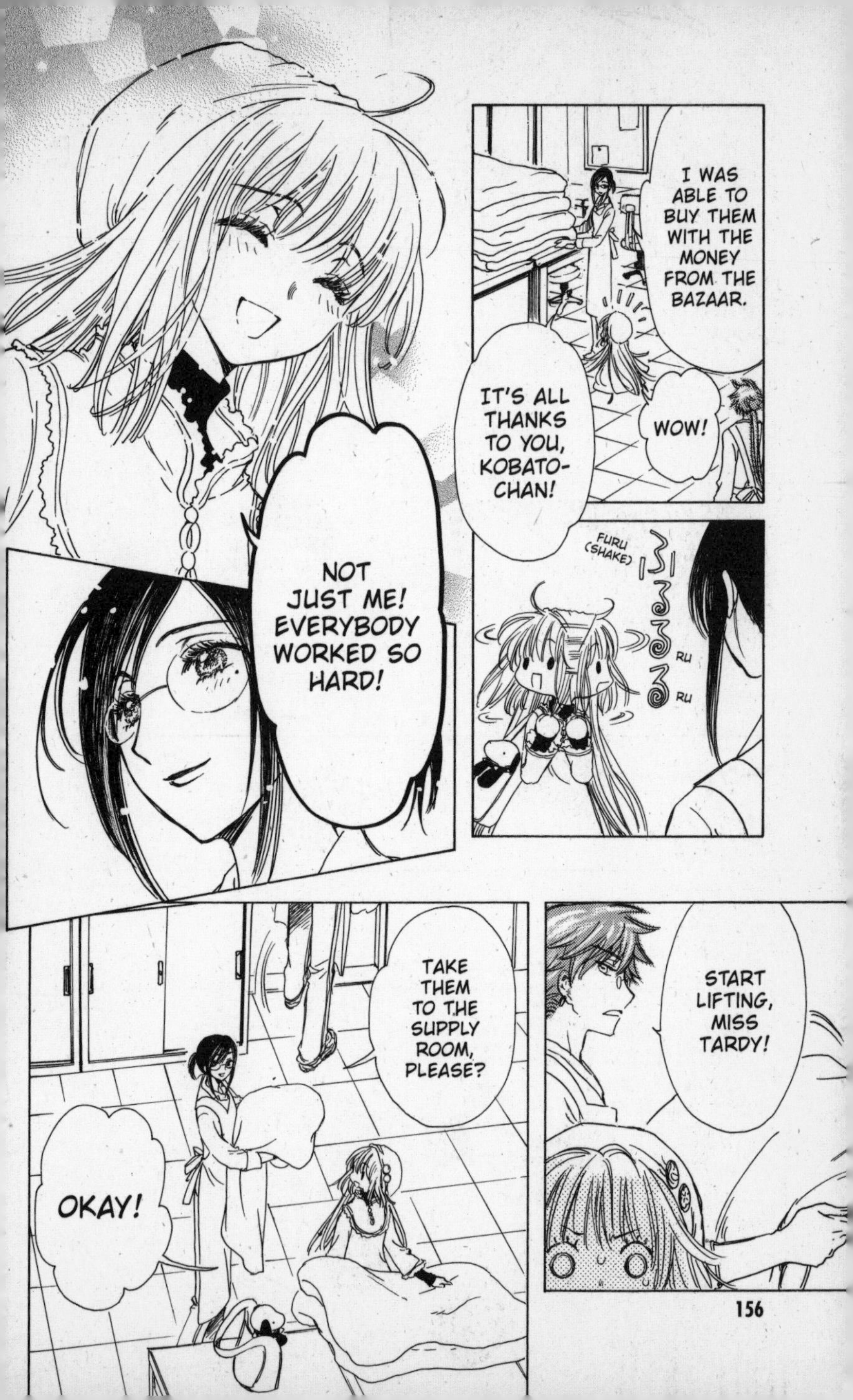
I WAS ABLE TO BUY THEM WITH THE MONEY FROM THE BAZAAR.
WOW!
IT'S ALL THANKS TO YOU, KOBATO-CHAN!
FURU (SHAKE)
RU
RU
NOT JUST ME! EVERYBODY WORKED SO HARD!
START LIFTING, MISS TARDY!
TAKE THEM TO THE SUPPLY ROOM, PLEASE?
OKAY!

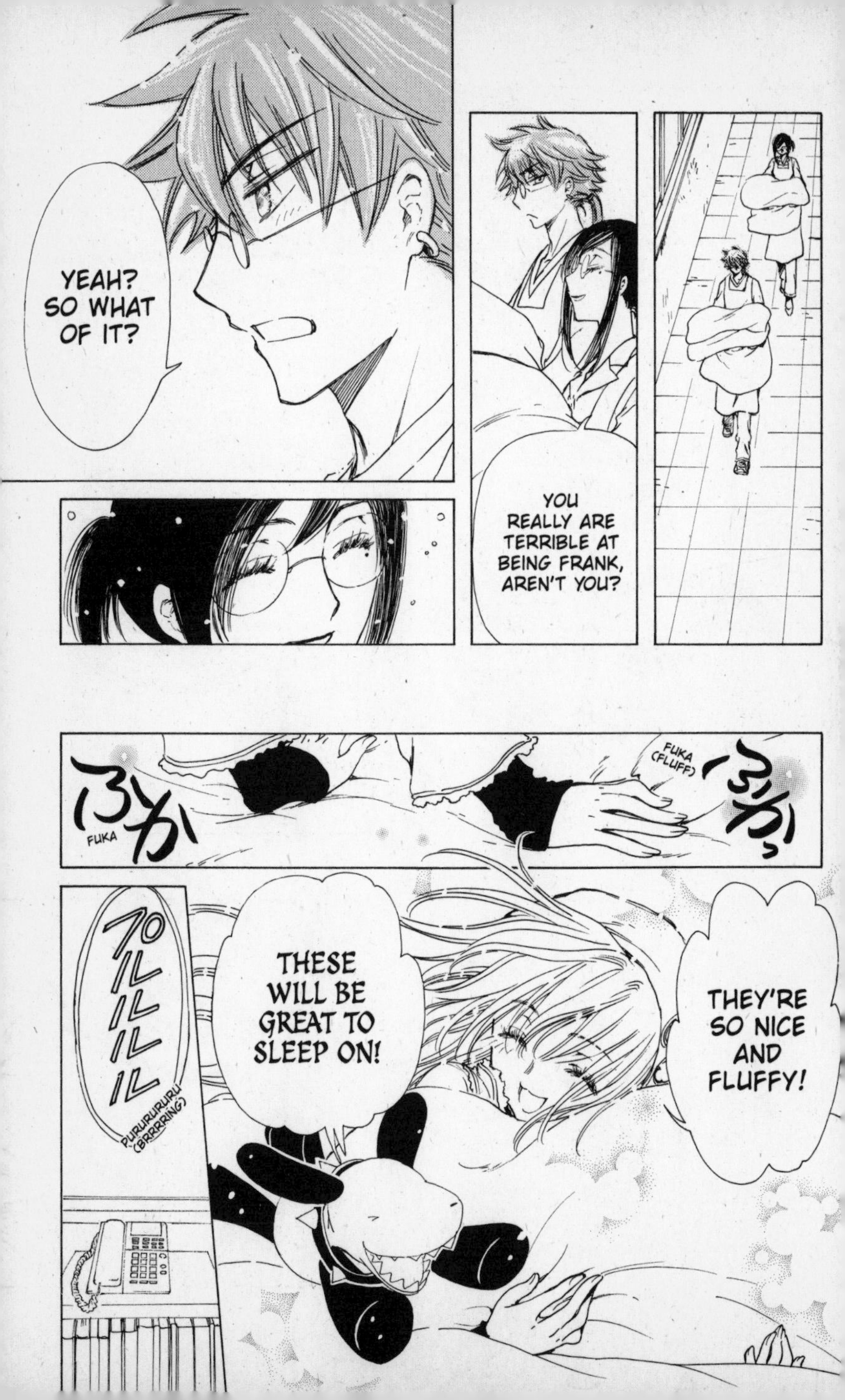

YOU REALLY ARE TERRIBLE AT BEING FRANK, AREN'T YOU?
YEAH? SO WHAT OF IT?
ふかっ
FUKA (FLUFF)
ふか
FUKA
THEY'RE SO NICE AND FLUFFY!
THESE WILL BE GREAT TO SLEEP ON!
プルルルル
PURURURURU (BRRRRING)

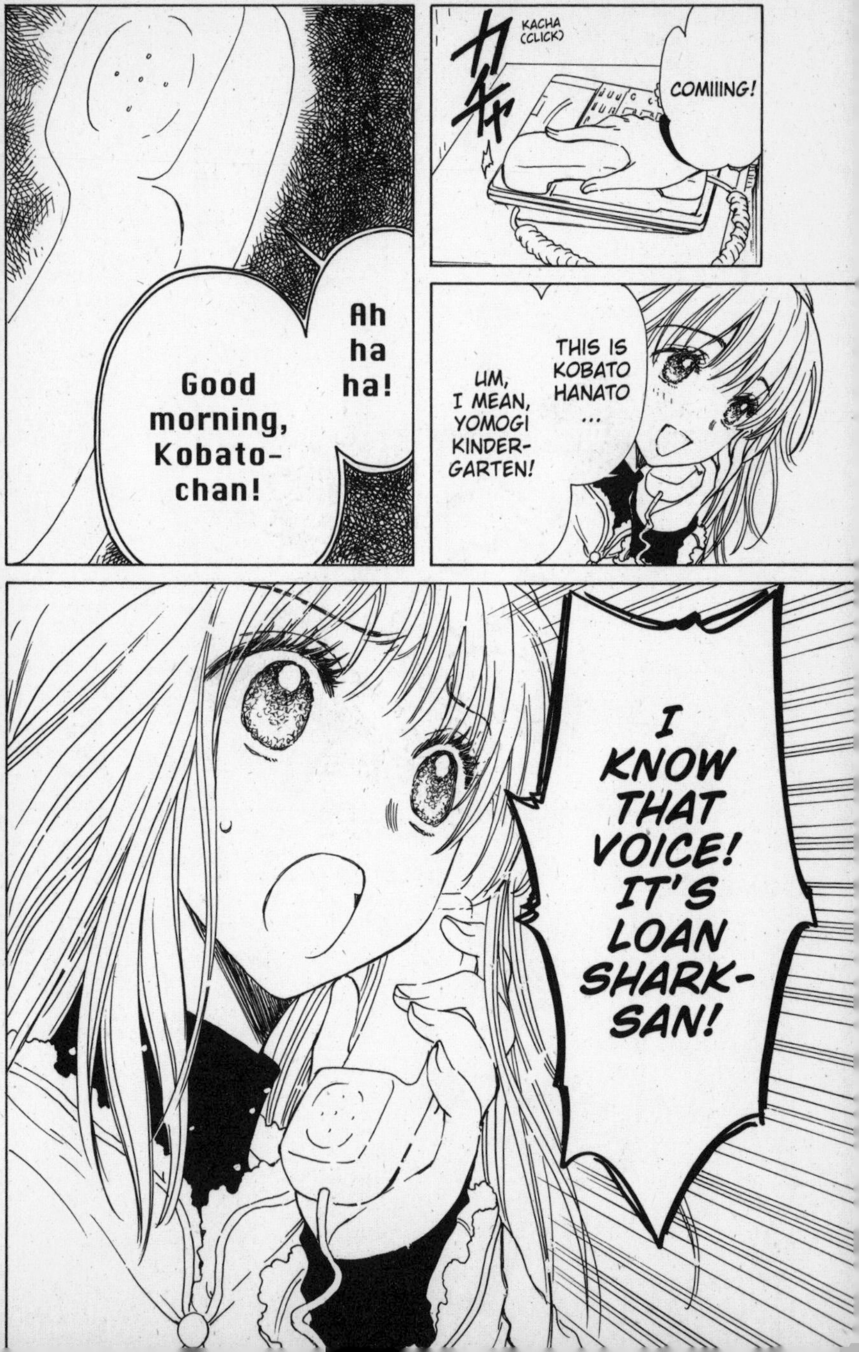
カチャ
KACHA (CLICK)
COMIIING!
THIS IS KOBATO HANATO ...
UM, I MEAN, YOMOGI KINDER-GARTEN!
Ah ha ha!
Good morning, Kobato-chan!
I KNOW THAT VOICE! IT'S LOAN SHARK-SAN!

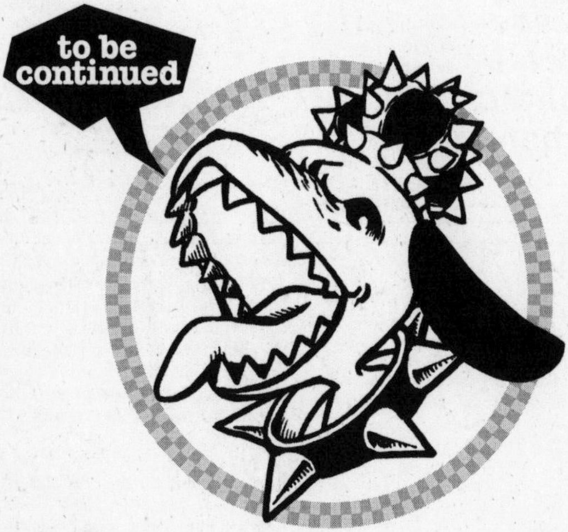
to be continued

TRANSLATION NOTES

COMMON HONORIFICS

no honorific: Indicates familiarity or closeness; if used without permission or reason, addressing someone in this manner would constitute an insult. This is how the loan shark addresses Sayaka-sensei, which prompts comment from Ioryogi-san (page 70).

***-san*:** The Japanese equivalent of Mr./Mrs./Miss. If a situation calls for politeness, this is the fail-safe honorific.

***-sama*:** Conveys great respect; may also indicate that the social status of the speaker is lower than that of the addressee.

***-kun*:** Used most often when referring to boys (though it can be applied to girls as well), this indicates affection or familiarity. Occasionally used by older men among their peers, but it may also be used by anyone referring to a person of lower standing.

***-chan*:** An affectionate honorific indicating familiarity used mostly in reference to girls; also used in reference to cute persons or animals of either gender.

Page 5 - **Tatami mat**
Most traditional Japanese rooms are floored with rush mats called tatami mats. They have a bit of "give" to them that allows one to spread out a thin Japanese futon mattress and sleep on it in relative comfort. But since Kobato doesn't have a futon, she sleeps directly on the mat. The mats have a distinctive weave, so anyone seeing the marks on Kobato's face would know that she slept with her face directly on top of the tatami mat rather than on a futon or pillow.

Page 5 - **I'll see you later/Take care**
In the Japanese edition, Kobato and Chitose use standard phrases for when one leaves the place one resides or "belongs to" (such as a work place). The person leaving says, "*Ittekimasu!*" which translates literally to, "I'm going, and I'll be back." The person left behind responds (or precedes) that phrase with, "*Itterasshai*," which literally means, "Go and come back."

Page 12 - **Airing out the futons**
In the West, we usually just leave our mattresses on our beds all the time, but Japanese futons are meant to be folded up and stored in closets during the day. They aren't exactly lightweight, but they're light enough to be carried without too much strain. About once every few days, one is expected to take the futon outside onto a balcony railing or clothes rod and air it out in the sun for a few hours. The practice is meant to dry out any moisture that has accumulated, help kill vermin like mites, et. al., and rid the futon of odors.

Page 73 - **Don't account yourself on my trouble.**
Here, Kobato is actually trying to say a standard phrase, "*Okamainaku*," which means "Don't trouble yourself on my account." Instead, she says the standard phrase one commonly says to old friends after not having seen them in a long time, "*Okawarinaku*," which means "You haven't changed."

Page 75 - **I'm home/Welcome home**
These may sound repetitive in English, but it is perfectly natural in Japanese. When one comes home or back to a place one regularly frequents, one says the phrase "*Tadaima*," which is short for "*Tadaima kaerimashita*" ("I have just now returned"). That phrase can be preceded by or followed by a phrase said by the person who is already there, "*Okaerinasai*," which translates to something like "Welcome back." Although Kobato isn't a family member, in certain cases, a guest might also welcome the person back.

Page 88 - **Parent advisory notes**
The parent advisory notes, or *renrakuchou*, is a notebook the child carries home with him/her in which the teacher informs the parent of the child's activities for the day and expectations (homework assignments, etc.) for the next day and for upcoming events. Some kindergartens include detailed information on food consumed and bowel movements, but most tend to include the child's attitude for the day and his/her accomplishments.

Page 127 - **Running gag**
This was a not-quite-exact translation. The word Ioryogi uses, "*yakusoku*," normally means "promise," but in this case, it is a word often used by Osakan comedians for a gag that a performer always performs. It is a gag that everyone knows is coming, and when the circumstances are right, like a promise, the gag happens. Still, western-style running gags are very similar to this, so it's a pretty close translation.

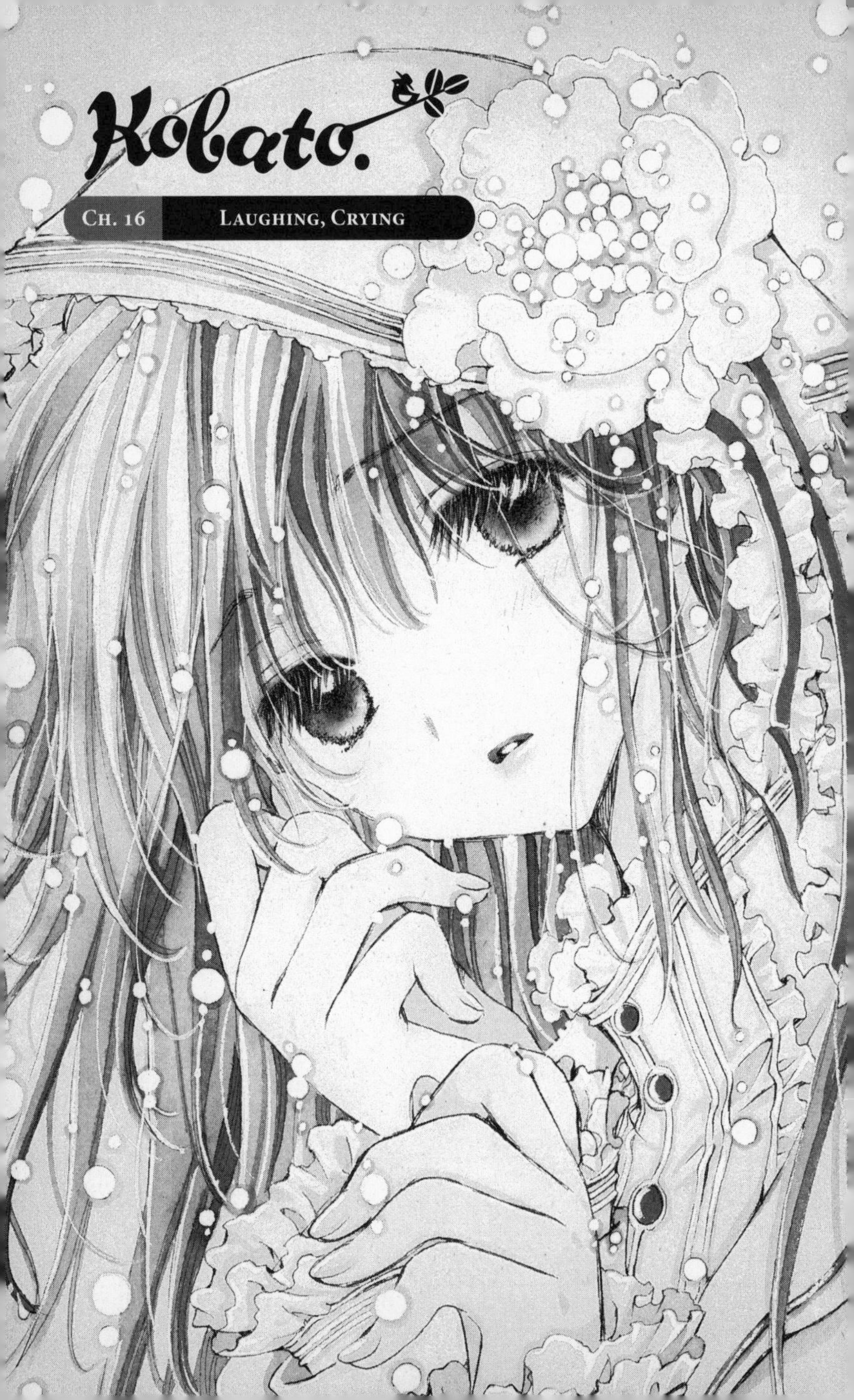
Kobato.
Ch. 16 Laughing, Crying

KOBATO.